*Shane's book is a brilliant rea___
worthwhile one too — everyt___
as an athlete. Her book is a n___
champion in the family.*

— Raelene Boyle

*This book was difficult to put down! Shane's problems are life's
problems, magnified by her early sporting fame and her chosen
lifestyle. She has led an exceptionally rich and varied life — it's
an inspiration to ride along with her on the bumpy but
exhilarating journey.*

— Ursula Carlile

*What an enthralling book. This is the best autobiography by a
sports champion I have ever read. Shane Gould was our greatest
swimmer and this tale of her problems in coming to terms with
fame at such a young age is compulsory reading for all associated
with sport and will be of great interest for those who are not.*

— Ron Clarke

*I couldn't put this book down. A very interesting story behind
a great Australian.*

— Susie O'Neill

MotHeRs Day 2005 from Alexi Catherine

B Nicholson

SHANE GOULD

tumble turns

HarperSports
An imprint of HarperCollins*Publishers*

Visit Shane Gould's website at:
www.shanegould.com.au

HarperSports
An imprint of HarperCollins*Publishers*, Australia

First published in Australia in 1999
This revised edition published in Australia in 2003
by HarperCollins*Publishers* Pty Limited
ABN 36 009 913 517
A member of the HarperCollins*Publishers* (Australia) Pty Limited Group
www.harpercollins.com.au

HarperCollins*Publishers*
25 Ryde Road, Pymble, Sydney NSW 2073, Australia
31 View Road, Glenfield, Auckland 10, New Zealand
77–85 Fulham Palace Road, London W6 8JB, United Kingdom
Hazelton Lanes, 55 Avenue Road, Suite 2900, Toronto, Ontario M5R 3L2
and 1995 Markham Road, Scarborough, Ontario M1B 5M8, Canada
10 East 53rd Street, New York NY 10022, USA

National Library Cataloguing-in-Publication data:

Gould, Shane (Shane Elizabeth), 1956– .
   Tumble turns: an autobiography.
   ISBN 0 7322 7767 1
   1. Gould Innes, Shane (Shane Elizabeth), 1956– .
   2. Swimmers – Australia – Biography. I. Title.
797.21092

Cover and spine image by Sport. The Library.
Cover design by Louise McGeachie
Internal design by Melanie Calabretta
Typeset in Berkeley Book by HarperCollins Design Studio
Printed and bound in Australia by Griffin Press on 79gsm Bulky Paperback

7 6 5 4 3 2 1   03 04 05 06

To Ron and Shirley Gould. Thank you.

All Things Green and Gould

The question quite simply deserves to be raised
On nights where we gather for stars to be praised
When one heart unites us in clapping our hands
From various backgrounds, from various lands
With dazzling glamour — so golden so glitzy
With legends like Dawny, Herb, Suzie and Spitzy
Take stock for a moment — forget the distractions
Closing your eyes, think of life's satisfactions
Drift back to your childhood — the days of your dreaming
The innocent passion that sent you out steaming
As wonderful images start to appear
Ask yourself honestly — why are we here …?

There she was, standing alone on the edge
She vowed she would make it — yes, that was her pledge
Her young eyes were focused — the other side beckoned
This was one race where she couldn't be second
She plunged to her challenge now measured in litres
Her arms going mad for that ten gruelling metres
I doubt, in her conquest, if one breath was taken
As powerful dreams were about to awaken
Ten measly metres — it doesn't sound much
But ominous joy was alive in her touch
That was the scene in a pool at Fiji
The girl in the swimming togs — not even three
But as young Shane Elizabeth splashed like a puppy
The world lay before this phenomenal guppy.

'Keep up your training Shane — who knows?' they'd say
'Maybe you'll make the Olympics one day?'
The words of a coach that the dreamer absorbs
And she kept up her training — she joined up with 'Forbes
Carlile the Mile Master' making the call
'Don't glide the finish Shane — push to the wall!!'
That's where the writing was — capital letters
Mornings at Pymble — aquatic vendettas
Stopwatches riding the waves she was making
Our girl was on fire and records were breaking
As awesome performances quickly unfurled
Her warning was obvious — 'BRING ON THE WORLD'.

As healthy a fish as we've ever exported
She came for her claim and the papers reported:
'Never before in the history of water
In one single Games, have we witnessed such slaughter
The aqua assassin is only fifteen
Though in '72 she'll be hailed as the queen
For a hat trick of triumphs that might have been five
If her arms, legs and lungs had a chance to revive
It's no wonder at Munich she had the world fooled
To believe that our colours were now green and Gould!'

From her bullet-like sprint to her honest persistence
She once held the record for every distance
The thrill of achieving was certainly nice
But she soon learned the concept of 'paying the price'
A talented child in an adult's domain
Along with the joy, she remembers the pain
She might not have done it if ever she'd known
Surrounded by millions but so much alone
Torn and confused by a limelight of strife
The kid went away and got on with her life
Away from the pressures — away from the stresses
Four kids of her own were her four best successes
With Joel, Tom and Kristen and don't forget Kim
The shine of those medals would certainly dim.

She was always so proud of her fun-loving fam
The way she was raised was the way that she swam
And now when she ponders, at home with her horses
At peace with herself and with nature's great forces
Dancing and singing with native galahs
I bet she remembers those Southern Cross stars
She learnt where to find them in cold morning skies
Waiting for training with gold in her eyes
To scatter the mist with that first early dive
To swim and enjoy it — to know you're alive
To fly for her country — to honour the cheer
That, in a nutshell, is why we are here
And that, in a nutshell, is why we will stay
As fish of the future enjoy the new day
But tonight there's a toast and we cannot be fooled —
To all things Australian — the green and the Gould.

Rupert McCall

Acknowledgements

The support of many good people in my life have made it possible to write this book. Shirley Gould, my 71-year-old mother, helped me with prose and writing. She would often encourage me, saying, 'That's a great story darling, but you have a quirky way of writing it'. Colleagues including Rob Woodhouse and Forbes Carlile; friends Peter Panegyres and New Year's Eve readers at Busselton encouraged me to keep writing the hard bits.

Congratulations Lynne for your illustrations, they give the book another dimension. Thanks also to Milt Nelms for his 'segment people' drawing on page 264 depicting an aquatic signature and an aquatic line.

Thanks to HarperCollins staff, particularly Alison Urquhart and editor Jacquie Brown who, with the invaluable input of freelance editor Robyn Flemming, pruned and structured where necessary. When I had doubts about continuing, they assured me that I had a fabulous story to tell. Thanks for the respect and freedom you've given me to make it my book.

Thanks to Michael Wenden for his foreword and historical corrections. Thanks to Ed Lacy, the Margaret River High School English master, for his excellent insights and suggestions for the integrity of the first and most difficult to write chapter.

Thanks to Tom and Kristin for their patience for the six months I was writing. They'd often ask 'You're always on the computer Mum, are you addicted?'

Thanks, too, to my swimming and sport friends who have given me a warm welcome back. Here is the story of why I left you and why I have returned.

Thank you to Rupert McCall for his kind permission to use *All Things Green and Gould*.

Foreword

PUSH, SHOVE, GO FASTER, poke, scratch, get out of the way . . . This was typical of the direct communication I once had with Shane Gould. I was an Olympic gold-medallist preparing for my second Olympic Games; Shane was a 15-year-old in a hurry as she swam into my feet during the 1972 pre-Olympic training camp at Scarborough, north of Brisbane. This communication was part of the universal language of swimmers, and the message was crystal clear: make room, get out of my way, I'm going places!

The Shane Gould I knew then was the same Shane almost everyone in Australia knew at that time — an athlete of immense talent who suddenly swept the swimming world before her and then disappeared just as quickly. Her swimming career was like a high-decibel concert that had such an impact it left your ears ringing. But it left you still humming the tunes long after it came to an end.

Shane's world revolved around family, school and swimming, because, to this young teenager, they were the essentials of life. She had an idyllic childhood, a loving family environment with doting, capable parents and the comfort of being a middle sister. She combined this with incredible achievements in a sport that was, and still is, significant in our national psyche.

I am sure that, for Shane, swimming itself brought simple joys, but there were other swimming pleasures too: the exhilaration of competition, the elation of winning, the satisfaction derived from meeting the challenge of developing the techniques, both physical and mental, needed for competitive swimming. Another challenge was to cope with the busy schedule of school, training, and competition. Success in this had a positive impact on her social development, but there were costs too. She was increasingly aware of being different from her school colleagues. Peer pressure is often lowest-common-denominator-based, and here was a teenager pursuing the highest of standards. Her simple world began to change. For Shane, the complexities of the world were budding.

Meanwhile serendipity reigned and significant elements began to align: the timing of the Munich Games relative to Shane's rate of development, the still unfolding East German juggernaut, and the 'coach' factor were all conspiring towards a certain type of experience for Shane at Munich. Her technical development was planned and implemented by the 'nutty professor' coach Forbes Carlile, the original scientific guru of the swimming world. It was Forbes who researched and found the ECG inverted 't' wave that indicated cardiac stress, and who had even tried hypnotism as a training technique in the 1950s. Forbes and his wife Ursula were a formidable team about to crest a wave of international success.

The coming together of all of these elements took place during the Munich Olympics, which came and went. Then, shortly afterwards, so did Shane Gould. Quit, retired, disappeared. We could not understand the suddenness of her departure, nor her motives. We speculated — an escape from the pressures of competition, from family, from coach? There was talk of disputes about commercialisation and the archaic amateur rules, there was a public spat between Forbes Carlile and Shane's father Ron, but we could only guess. Some of us conjectured that intertwined somewhere in the heart of it all was the conflict between the life of the very public 'Shane Gould, Swimmer' — 'property' as defined by the marketers — and the private life of a teenager going through the process of finding her place and role in the world.

As if in response to a maturity growth spurt, other worlds and experiences called to Shane. She was half of a courting couple, she was a commercial entity. She was also, in time, a married person, a parent, an adult, a homemaker, an income earner, an aware inhabitant of our fragile planet, a spiritual being and a friend. These roles held much more attraction than the role of swimmer in the black-lined, chlorinated environment from which she had emerged.

In the mid-1980s I found the opportunity to visit Shane and her family. It wasn't hard; I just had to get to Perth, hire a car, drive 300 kilometres south to Margaret River, and there I was. Shane had pride in showing off her family during the tour of the farm. Life was tough, but a 'happy tough'.

Over the years there was a slow re-emergence of Shane into the world of sport and public life, especially where it concerned the Women in Sport movement, and sports retirement — the processes for a smooth transition from super sportsperson to normal human person. With Shane's prodding, this process has now moved from obscure articles in psychology journals to everyday practices at institutes and academies of sport.

The early 1990s was a time of obvious stress for Shane — it was visible in her face. It was easy to assume the hard country life was taking its toll. After all, the bottom had fallen out of the sheep industry, and ongoing international economic forces and the dreaded 'economic rationalists' were slowly crushing the life out of rural Australia. But there seemed to be more to it than that. Her self-esteem seemed to be ebbing. It was an uneasy time.

Then came a new vitality, a blossoming and growth. Was it the re-creation of 'Shane Gould the Swimmer'? No, that person lived and thrived long ago. Now a new, strong, courageous person was working towards independence and a different life. And at last her story has emerged. But this is more than a simple story, for it not only covers the events surrounding her earlier public persona, it presents a picture of a brave woman capable of immense love and depth of feeling coming to grips with the problems, difficulties and challenges faced by many women today. The questioning, the uncertainty, the struggle, the resolve, the strength of character are all there for us to see.

Michael Wenden

CONTENTS

Preface

A TUMBLE TURN is a manoeuvre executed in a pool to change direction. It requires the swimmer to perform a somersault flip at a well-timed distance from the wall, then to use their feet to push off the wall before twisting the body in order to level out. My life has been full of just such turns, twists and changes of direction.

At age 15 I won five Olympic swimming medals for Australia at the 1972 Munich Olympic Games. Late the following year I retired from competitive swimming. It has taken nearly 30 years for me to understand not only what that achievement has given me in personal terms, but also what it has cost me and those close to me. This book tells the story of those years and of how my many tumble turns, both in the pool and in my life, have been a part of my growth towards acceptance both of that young swimming phenomenon called Shane Gould and of the woman I have become.

Writing my story has helped me to acknowledge my place in Olympic history. By revisiting the past, I gained a better understanding of myself during and after the 1972 Olympics, and recounting painful times has been personally therapeutic.

As I wrote, I discovered many aspects of my life that I had taken for granted. Some of these are my athletic gift, a childhood in Fiji, life in middle-class Sydney and Brisbane, participation in a radical Christian community and pioneer farming in Margaret River. I have known the richness of talent, the security of a loving home, the joy and exhaustion of parenthood, the stimulation of new ideas and the struggle of a low income.

The biggest aspect of my life I have taken for granted is the blessing of living in Australia. This is a story of an Australian woman doing tumble turns. I offer it to you.

PART ONE

the golden girl

CHAPTER 1

Goldfisch aus Australien

*It was in Munich that Shane Gould became
Our Shane. Her two names became one . . .
How did Shanegould go? She went real well,
actually. Three golds, a silver and a bronze.*

~

Mike Coleman, *Courier-Mail*, 1997

THE TWENTIETH OLYMPIAD HAD BEGUN. I was in the stands for
the opening ceremony, above the tunnel where the teams entered.
The dancers and the stirring music made me shiver with excitement.
My heart thumped in my chest. I felt like one of the doves set loose,
ready to soar to my own great heights. As I soaked up the colourful
spectacle, I knew I was ready to take on the best women swimmers in
the world. I was 15 years and 9 months old.

My family had farewelled me at Sydney airport with lots of hugs.
Chattering well-wishers and autograph-hunters moved among the
uniformed athletes. Each journalist asked the same question: 'How
many medals do you think you will win, Shane?' My polite, self-
controlled answer was, 'One will be great, more will be a bonus.' And
it would have been. Privately I thought differently. I knew I was going

for the ultimate possible goal: five golds in the five individual events I was entered in.

It was August 1972. I was a Year Ten schoolgirl and a member of the Australian Olympic swimming team. I was excited and scared at the prospect of going to the Olympics. I knew I was good, because during the year I had held all five freestyle world records from 100 metres to 1500 metres. But the Olympic Games presented a tough challenge. I was awed by the talent, confidence and team-spirit of the girls in the American swimming team.

In the build-up to the Games I had done hundreds of interviews and attended many public functions as Australia's 'Golden Girl' and Olympic medal hopeful. I felt an enormous responsibility to live up to these expectations. A lot of the time I was embarrassed and perplexed by the attention I was receiving.

I just liked to swim, and to compete. It was a private passion that had become a public spectacle. I liked the attention, but I also felt uncomfortable with the steady stream of congratulations and praise for my achievements and abilities.

My three sisters and parents had supported me (though sometimes they'd be irritable at the intrusion into their lives) to get to this point. It was good to have them at the airport to see me off.

We entered Germany at Frankfurt airport. Although I was used to international air travel, the security check was new to me. There was talk of 'terrorists' and 'hijackings'. I was puzzled. This was certainly outside my experience. Fear and distrust weren't part of the world I knew. But the strangeness was soon forgotten when we were cleared and were off on the last leg of our journey to Munich.

Outside the airport, we all piled into a bus to take us to the Olympic Village. At school in Sydney I was studying German, and I was pleased to find that I could understand many of the road signs and billboards. I thought, 'This will help me when I do my next German exam!' But my thoughts of future scholastic achievements were interrupted by Roger Pegram, the manager of the swimming team, who started to brief us on procedures at the Village. He stressed that no one was to talk to the media unless he was present.

The bus stopped outside one of the entrances to the Village, where a throng of reporters juggling cameras and microphones jostled for a position. We all tumbled out of the bus, eager for our first experience of being at the Olympic Games. One of the reporters called out, '*Willkommen!*' and I spontaneously replied, '*Danke schön. Wie geht es dir?*' (Thank you. How are you?) The silence was electric. Had I said something wrong? My heart started to beat faster and I blushed. That three seconds felt like an eternity! Suddenly I was bombarded with a torrent of questions in German. I quickly apologised: '*Ich spreche nur ein bisschen Deutsch.* (I speak only a little German.) Please ask your questions in English.' Roger then moved through the group of bright-eyed, blonde-haired Australian swimmers, wedged himself between us and the reporters, and took control.

But it was too late. I'd responded to a simple question in a mix of German and English, and that was it. As far as the media in Munich were concerned, I was '*Der Goldfisch*' and they singled me out and gave me very positive press coverage. The downside of this was that the special attention I received led to some ill-feeling among my team-mates.

I couldn't control how the media or sports fans responded to me. On the one hand, I wanted the other team members to have their fair share of acclaim for being good enough to be at the Olympics. On the other hand, I had to stay focused on my task in Munich, spurred by an inner drive for excellence. When I did that I had an entourage of reporters filming, photographing and questioning me.

Once we got away from the hustle and bustle of the reporters and sports fans and actually got into the Village, I just loved what I saw. The design of the buildings was so inviting and friendly. And the colour! Everywhere, the colours of the Munich Olympics — sky-blue, lime-green and white — were picked up on flags, posters and buildings.

The open spaces were so fresh and clean with yellow flowers in big tubs. Olympic helpers were all dressed in sky-blue and white uniforms. It was all so pretty. Overhead were big, brightly coloured pipes — I never found out what was in them, but I discovered that each colour led to a particular place, like the dining room, the recreation hall or the glass-walled information centre. I soon got the hang of finding my way around by following the pipes.

While the team managers were registering the team's arrival, I wandered over to the information centre. Outside, a huddled group of athletes of different nationalities were swapping pins. Inside were six or so large television screens, bigger than I'd ever seen. As I glanced through the information leaflets and studied the program of other sports, some I'd never heard of, I started to sense the size and importance of the Olympics. I came back to this central point of the Village later and swapped kangaroo pins with Olympians from other countries and watched some of the events on television.

The Village was still fairly quiet when we first arrived. The other early arrivals also looked a bit uncertain and awkward in the unfamiliar surroundings. Our team had arrived 14 days before the opening so that we could get over our jet lag and become acclimatised. The swimming events were on in the first week of the 16-day Olympic program. After a few days I knew my way around and was used to my bed and pillow, and the smorgasbord of different foods. As more athletes arrived, the atmosphere became more electric and expectant.

From the centre of the Village it was a good five-minute walk to our apartments where I shared a room with Bev Whitfield, a breast-stroker. Bev and I had shared rooms all through Europe the year before on a four-week swimming tour and she was a lot of fun. Our rooms were in the last block of double-storeyed apartments, near an open space fenced off with barbed wire. Beyond the fence and another open space were more grey cement buildings. Security in the Village was very tight, with compulsory accreditation cards, uniformed guards and underground access tunnels.

After a few days in the Village we got into a rhythm. As most of our rostered training sessions were at outlying pools, we got to see quite a bit of the city. The Olympic pool, where we also trained, was fantastic. The high roof looked like overlapping sails, and the vivid yellow of the non-slip pool deck contrasted with the dark blue of the water. The Munich Games were the first Olympics to be broadcast live in colour.

Bev and I sometimes became impatient with the bus schedules and walked the kilometre or so to the main pool for training. The number of spectators was increasing daily, and we were often stopped to sign autographs. A couple of days of doing this in the warm summer heat soon sapped our energy, and private minibuses were arranged for the team.

In training I didn't feel right. Doing so many sprints was taking the edge off my form. I felt like I needed another week of taper in order to sharpen up. The programs were set by Don Talbot, the head swimming coach, and supervised by Ursula Carlile, the assistant coach. One day Don had some business to attend to elsewhere and Ursula set my program. What a relief and pleasure it was to do familiar sets! During the remaining few days, what with the general chaos around the pool as reporters, photographers, coaches and managers all vied for the attention of the athletes, and with ten or so swimmers sharing each lane, I was able to ignore Don's program and follow my own. My body was telling me what it needed. Doing the familiar Carlile training routines steadied me. Instead of wasting energy by rebelling against Don's programs, I was able to focus on the enormity of the task ahead. I made a conscious effort to push the media attention aside as an unnecessary distraction. I took more responsibility for my own preparations. Part of this was to go 'inside myself' to prepare mentally, to enter the 'zone'.

I managed to spend some time with my personal coach, Forbes Carlile, who was in Munich as a radio commentator for the ABC, and with my parents, who had contrived to get through the security red tape that kept family members and other supporters at a distance from the athletes.

'How do you feel?' Dad asked.

'OK, Dad.'

'Is your diet alright?'

'If you mean, am I eating enough — yes!'

'Sleeping enough?'

'Dad, I can never get enough of that!'

Although I needed this contact, my main coping strategy as the pressure built was to withdraw into myself. This necessary aloofness isolated me from my team-mates. Judy Hudson, at 13 the youngest swimming-team member, told me recently that she remembered me replying to fan mail late into the night instead of going out partying. I remember using the fan mail as a convenient excuse to conserve my energy and to keep focused on my private goal. No longer was I just swimming for myself; I was swimming for Australia, with the world watching. I felt the weight of everyone's expectations that I would give the best performance of my life. But I was worried that I wasn't at my physical best. My usual heart rate of 38–42 bpm (beats per minute) was up around 52–56 bpm, a rate that usually indicated I was sick.

As the days passed, my excitement and the pressure mounted. It was hard to believe that I had made it this far, that I was actually at the Olympics. I was one of 7173 competitors, one of 1058 women, one of 173 Australians and representing one of 122 countries. I was number 16 in the Australian Munich Team Handbook, which recorded that I was entered in the 100, 200, 400 and 800 metres freestyle, the 200 metres individual medley, and the two women's relays — the 4 x 100 metres freestyle and the 4 x 100 metres medley. That was 13 possible races in six days. I hadn't entered in the 100 metres butterfly event, for which I held the Australian and Commonwealth records of 65.1. I also held those records for the 200 metres individual medley (2.24.4) and the killer event, the 400 metres individual medley (5.07.4). Earlier in the year, I held all five freestyle world records, and I went into the Games holding world records for the 100, 400 and 1500 metres (my 200 and 800 metres freestyle world records were taken from me by Shirley Babashoff and Jo Harshbarger at the US Trials about a month before).

My first event was the 200 metres individual medley. I was an outsider, so it was a good opportunity to have a practice swim, a warm-up for my main events. My heat time qualified me for lane seven, the second-slowest qualifying time. But I broke the usual pattern where the centre lanes lead the race and, to everyone's surprise, won the event in world-record time. I was surprised, too, because I was a body-length behind at the last lap turning out of breast stroke into freestyle! Suddenly I was no longer in the wings but on centre stage. I was no longer a child, but a new adult. As I walked out to the winners' dais, Dawn Fraser thrust a toy kangaroo into my hands, saying she had had it when she was presented with one of her Olympic medals. I was honoured to hold her old balding-tailed toy as the medals were presented. Mine had 'Gould Shane' and the event, '200m Lagen Damen', engraved on it.

As I stood on the dais and a German brass band played the Australian national anthem (at that time, 'God Save the Queen'), I wept. I was overcome by joy at my achievement, and by the uncertainty of what lay ahead. My success had already alienated me from others in the team. I was aware of a coolness towards me. Had I somehow offended them by winning? That 200 metres win was fantastic. But in being the winner, I felt very alone. My parents, watching from the stands, experienced similar emotions and wept with me. With the wisdom of adulthood they comprehended the enormity of the event: I had gained an Olympic gold medal, and lost my childhood in the process.

Afterwards, Michael Wenden came up to me as I was drying off. 'Welcome to the Club,' he said, with a big grin. 'Which club?' I asked, puzzled. 'The Gold Medal Club, Shane.' Then he said: 'Take time to savour the moment. It's a rare one.' I did savour the moment. I was now the one to chase. The tables had turned.

My next event, the 100 metres freestyle, threw me one of life's tougher lessons, though. As an 'L-plate adult', I was to learn that things don't always go the way I planned or hoped. As the current world-record holder, I had high hopes of winning the blue-ribbon event. I felt I had a claim on the sprint title. But as soon as I surfaced after the dive start, I didn't feel right. I felt flat and lethargic. When I sheepishly looked up at the scoreboard at the end of the race and heard the Americans cheering their first and second place-getters, I thought: 'Let's do that again.' As I gulped for air and floated in the comfort of the warm water, I slowly became aware that something in me had changed. Underneath my huge disappointment at placing third, I felt calm resignation. 'People can see that I'm human after all,' I thought. I can lose too. As the cheers died down and the congratulatory handshakes were given, I underwent what I now would call an initiation. I believe that my bronze medal race was a test of character. As such, it was my greatest win.

After the 100 metres race, I returned to my room where Bev had strung up pink and white toilet paper. She squealed with delight at my surprised reaction, then hugged and congratulated me. This was the best congratulations I've ever received from another athlete.

I was debriefed on my initiation by my team captain Michael Wenden. Michael had been unable to defend his title in the 200 metres freestyle final, won in Mexico City at the 1968 Olympics. We shared our feelings. Meanwhile, the media conference went on without me (it was two hours before I could produce a urine sample for drug testing). Australian reporters thought I was sulking. 'Shane Fails' was one headline. They were right in one sense, but wrong in another. I had learned how to lose, and then get on with the next challenge, the 400 metres freestyle.

Olympic runner Raelene Boyle, a wise woman refined by other initiation fires, said of her silver medal in the 200 metres at Munich: 'If you make it into an Olympic team, you're good; if you make it into an Olympic final, you're great; and if you win an Olympic medal, you're a freak.' No athlete who wins a silver or bronze medal in an Olympic final can ever be considered a loser. In coming to understand that I had not 'failed', I retained my self-respect.

Next up were the middle-distance 200- and 400-metre events, for which my training had prepared me perfectly. With my adrenalin pumping, I stood on the blocks for the 400 metres final. I felt strong and confident. I couldn't see anyone close to me after 200 metres. Racing against myself and the clock, my focus and determination came together for a very satisfying win by three seconds. A world record, too. It was an affirmation swim — a YES! swim — the result of good race planning and controlled stroking. It boosted my confidence in my form, fitness and my feel for the water.

I rested the next day, sleeping a lot and gathering my inner resources. And I marvelled, along with the rest of the world, at Mark Spitz's fifth and sixth gold medals (for a final tally of seven). For about half an hour I contentedly played pool in the recreation centre with a lone, tracksuited athlete who beckoned me to join him in a game. Neither of us spoke each other's language; he was black, I was white. It represented to me what the Olympic Games can be all about: a peaceful harmony among people of different sexes, races and creeds. But that harmony was soon to be shattered.

Of all my Olympic races, I am most satisfied with the 200 metres freestyle final. I had seen the American swimmers in T-shirts bearing the words 'All That Glitters is Not Gould'. It was an attempt to psych me out, but it backfired because I knew they were worried. As the finalists waited in the marshalling area of the women's locker room under the stands, I psyched myself up and attempted to psych out my opponents by slowly and noisily filing my fingernails. The American girls were also playing mental games, joking and talking loudly among themselves, and appearing to be bold and confident. It distracted me, as it was meant to do, and it took all my mental energy to stay focused.

Finally the waiting was over, which was fortunate as I was fast running out of fingernails to file! The noisy, electric atmosphere of the crowd blurred the time it took for the long march from the marshalling area to the back of the blocks. This was a perfect way to get that extra, necessary charge of energy. I felt I was ready for this race!

Part of the ritual of a swimming race is the courtesy introduction of the competitors to the spectators. This is the hardest part for me, as it's the time when I really need to concentrate, to be inside myself, to gather all my resources for a peak performance. It's when prior and proper preparation come together. If the preparation hasn't been adequate, it's too late to do any more when you are on the blocks.

Positive thinking, focus and 'getting in the zone' were the final preparation for me. I couldn't allow myself to listen to the achievements of the other competitors, the most formidable of whom was Shirley Babashoff who had taken the world record from me. When my name was called, I stood up and waved to the crowd. Apart from that, I just heard noise; I was getting into the 'zone'. I stripped off and neatly folded my tracksuit and T-shirt. I did my usual long exhales, wiggled my arms to release any tension and looked to the end of the pool. Mentally, I felt confident. Emotionally, I felt calm. Physically, I felt like I was about to burst out of my skin.

My Munich 200 metres freestyle final was an athlete's dream race. There was great competition, with Shirley Babashoff and Keena Rothhammer hugging my hip and heels the whole way. I had a moment of panic about 15 metres from the end when Shirley started to gain on me, but the adrenalin rush urged me on. I finished well ahead, with good split times and a world record by two seconds. I was completely satisfied with my performance. All the factors in the race had come together for me. It felt great to be a winner!

There was a time lag between the end of the race and the presentation, to allow for the medals to be engraved. A caravan fitted out with engraving tools was stationed under the stadium for this purpose. While we waited, the winners' national flags and national anthems were readied.

Away from the pool deck I was bombarded with congratulations and received hearty hugs from team officials and my team-mates. I felt shy and a little awkward about all the fuss. I eased away and got dressed, all the while savouring the heady moment.

I love brass band music, and the band that played for the medal presentation ceremonies at the swimming stadium was the best I've ever heard. Tears welled in my eyes as the band music resonated through me.

As the winners were introduced, my swimming life flashed before my eyes. The miles of training, the early mornings, the aching muscles, the disciplined daily routine, the travelling for competition experience, all affirmed my position as the gold medal winner on the podium at the Olympic Games.

With this success, I felt that more responsibility was coming my way. Now I'd be seen even more as a role model for others. Those moments on the dais were like another initiation — an initiation into leadership.

In that impossible-to-describe moment, I felt immense satisfaction. I felt privileged to have the skills, the talent and the opportunity to be there. I felt humbled by all the praise. I felt that too much fuss was being made about the fact that I had swum fast in a race. I felt for the other place-getters who had also hoped to win. I felt irritated that I couldn't share the moment with my parents. I felt embarrassed about weeping. I wondered if I could handle the huge responsibility that had been placed on me. I felt alone. I felt proud of the Australian flag and anthem. And I felt happy for the fans who had wanted me to win.

I was very glad when I finally managed to get to bed.

The next morning I awoke feeling like death warmed up. It wasn't a good way to start an endurance event, the 800 metres freestyle, and I was disappointed after feeling so good the night before. During the morning heats I thought I was going to die. I felt like I was dragging lead weights. It was hard to get air. My lungs burned, and every muscle in my body screamed. I had a respiratory infection, and I was deathly tired. My body was saying, 'Give me a break!'

I gave myself a stiff talking-to. 'You've overcome pain and tiredness before in training, Shane. Push through this, too! A sleep will help.' The team doctor, Ken Fitch, propped me up with more encouragement and some sort of legal cold-relieving medicine. I then slept for three hours.

At the final that evening I felt much better, though not energetic. Again, it was a great race, but Keena Rothhammer was too good. She won by nearly three seconds, breaking the world record. I was pleased with my time, two seconds faster than my previous best, though I was never so glad to see the end of 16 laps. It was a silver medal for me. Michael Wenden again took a positive view: 'Now you've got one of each colour!' That put a smile on my face.

My coach, Forbes Carlile, in an article for News Limited, wrote:

> . . . *Shane came out of the encounter [with Keena Rothhammer]*
> *with honour and, once again, made friends of the hordes of*
> *pressmen who probed her 'failure'. She made no excuses, although*
> *. . . having to swim an 800 metres was about the last thing she felt*

ready to do. Had she been home in Australia she would not have swum the race . . . Later she told me that this race 'hurt' her more than any she can remember . . . I believe we have not seen the best of Shane Gould yet. Australia can be proud of this young girl who has [shown] so much mental and physical courage here in Munich . . .

I had a short but sound sleep that night. My races were over. I felt a bit flat, still coughing and headachey. The flatness was emotional. The Olympic Games were over for me. I spent some of the day reading the fan letters that had accumulated, but I had no energy left to appreciate them. I decided to send my thank-you notes later. I did a few interviews and saw Mum and Dad.

Up until now I hadn't seen much of the Games as a spectator. I had tickets to see some of the athletics and gymnastics events, and I decided to immerse myself in the atmosphere away from the swimming events. Bev had arranged for a few of the Australian girls to visit the American girls in their quarters for a party that evening to celebrate the end of our swimming events, and I was more than ready to let off steam.

We arrived at Keena Rothhammer's room at about 11 pm. Seven or so girls were lolling about on cushions and mattresses, laughing and joking, eating junk food and drink, and telling ghost stories. Keena was a bubbly, cheerful person, and now that the serious stuff of racing was over, it was fun getting to know this other side of her. At about 2 am, she and I went exploring in the underground tunnels that were used for service and supply. Keena and I played together like little kids. We skipped and ran. We hid in dark corners, and jumped out and spooked each other. We coo-eed, and our voices echoed in the eerie emptiness of the tunnels. Eventually, we got back to her room, where I found a spare soft place on the floor next to Bev. I fell asleep, exhausted and satisfied.

Unbeknown to us, not far from where we had been playing, eight Palestinian terrorists, members of the Black September Movement, were getting into position. The events that followed would result in the deaths of 11 Israeli athletes, a policeman, and five of the terrorists. They would also threaten the remainder of the Olympic Games.

After about three hours' sleep, Bev and I left Keena's room. Although somewhat sleepy, we were still in good spirits. We were scheduled to join some Australian and American swimmers who were going to the nearby town of Regensburg that day to do some demonstration swimming races and attend a civic reception. But first we headed to the dining room for breakfast.

Immediately we noticed that something was wrong. There were few athletes around the Village square and none in the dining room, and there was an atmosphere of suspense. We asked the waitresses where everyone was. How I wished my German was more fluent! All I could gather from the frightened and confused staff was that something was very wrong in the Village. We gulped down some orange juice and toast and raced outside, rather confused ourselves, and anxious not to miss the bus to Regensburg. To get to our room we had to go through a security checkpoint at a barbed-wire-topped mesh fence. We were greeted at the checkpoint by several soldiers with machine guns. We explained our business, and one of the armed guards escorted us to our room. At each corner, he would indicate for us to hang back until he was sure the way was clear. It all seemed unreal, and Bev and I made some weak jokes about James Bond. We had no idea what was going on.

The soldier stood guard outside our room while we packed our bags for the day. As we came out of the room I caught a glimpse of a man on a balcony in the building that faced ours across the patch of vacant land. He, too, appeared to have a machine gun. I wondered what machine guns had to do with the Olympics. We later learned that the building housed the Israeli team and that the terrorists had already killed one Israeli, mortally wounded another and were holding nine athletes hostage.

After our out-of-town excursion, I tried unsuccessfully to find out what had happened by reading German newspapers and watching German TV news. I couldn't understand all the words, but I certainly caught the feeling of shock, outrage and grief that was being expressed. The Games were suspended for one day, and a memorial service was held for the murdered Israeli athletes. For some reason, the Australian women weren't allowed to attend the memorial service. Perhaps there was the threat of further terrorist acts. We watched it on television while the men attended.

I recall feeling left out and uninformed. I still wasn't sure what had happened and what the service was about. I really felt like the 15-year-old I was. My parents were staying in a house on the outskirts of Munich and, on the advice of team officials and my father, I left the Village to stay with them. My father was concerned that, as a successful athlete at the Games, I might be a further target. I heard that Mark Spitz, who was of Jewish background, was whisked out of the Village to Hamburg. Years later, at the 1998 World Swimming Championships in Perth, Mark explained to me that he had just left the Village as planned to return to the United States.

Leaving the Village was an anticlimax. I had my swag of medals, but there was a bag of unopened mail left behind. I felt bad about not acknowledging the letters, cards and telegrams from well-wishers. My plan to see other Olympic events from the spectator stands was dashed. And my hopes of making connections with other Australian athletes didn't eventuate. It was about 20 years before I got to meet them.

However, the time spent at Trudering gave me another kind of experience. I went with my parents to the Bavarian Alps, where I saw snow for the first time. I walked on grassy hillsides, patting tame cattle wearing cowbells. It was a delight to walk in the peacefulness of the Black Forest. I thought over the meaning and significance of my Olympic achievements, while wishing I was back in the Village.

As the days passed, the tensions and emotions surrounding the massacre diminished and the Games continued. I was advised not to attend the closing ceremony, another likely target of further terrorist attacks, but I was determined to march with my team-mates. I begged and pleaded with my parents and the Australian team officials. 'EVERYONE is going, Dad!' (I've heard that argument from my teenagers since.) Then, finally, 'I just HAVE to go!' My persistence and determination wore them down and it was agreed that I could participate if I remained inconspicuous. I respect the decision I made then to 'finish' my Games experience. I was picked up by an official car and returned to the Olympic Village. And I marched in the closing ceremony, where I was happy just to blend in.

There was disorder and delight at the close of the Games. I felt like a child at an adults' party. Teams mixed together, milling around like a mustered and yarded mob of sheep. There was music, fireworks, speeches, exchanges of hats, badges and addresses, and abundant hugs. It was a great release from the intensity we had all experienced, yet it was also tinged with grief for the murdered athletes. I realised that participating at the Olympic Games was more than a celebration of youth, sport and culture; it also gave me the experience of being a global citizen.

On the plane to New York, I read an article in *Time* magazine about what had happened the day of the terrorist attack in the Olympic Village. When Avery Brundage, president of the International Olympic Committee, made his 'The Games must go on' speech, it revived some of the spirit and mystery of the Olympic Games. Many athletes thought the Games would be cancelled. Raelene Boyle had her bags packed before her 200 metres finals. The spirit of the Olympics was strengthened by that speech. It was a wise and bold decision for the IOC to continue the Games after due respect had been given the dead Israelis. It motivated Raelene to unpack her bags and run hard and fast in the 100 metres and 200 metres and win two silver medals.

We went to New York for the launch of my mother's book, *Swimming the Shane Gould Way*, which was being published by Oak Tree Press. The book was part of a series of sports 'how to' books. I had been warned by the Australian team officials that my amateur status would be threatened if I promoted the book. It was another ten years before such archaic and hypocritical rulings were to change. Mum's book was launched after the Olympics, even though it was ready beforehand. We were worried that if it was promoted any earlier, I might have been excluded from swimming at Munich or that, if I did compete, any medals I won would be stripped from me. There was such a lot of anxiety at the time about avoiding the taint of professionalism.

On the way home to Australia we stopped off in Hawaii for a couple of days. My father worked for an airline and was able to get cheap airfares and accommodation. In the hotel pool it was a treat to be anonymous and just to swim and play in the water like anyone else. The tourists lolling about poolside were relaxed, and no one paid me any attention. Dad hired me a long surfboard from the legendary Duke Kahanamoku's surf shop and I had a fantastic surf on the long waves at Waikiki. An American hamburger topped it off.

It was a very relaxing few days, and I felt ready to go back to school and family life again. In 1972 I missed about 14 weeks of school, nine of them in August and September. I had a bit of catching up to do! I also missed my three sisters, Lynette, who was 17, Debbie, who was 11, and Jenny, the youngest at 8. At Sydney airport, we were met by my grandparents, my Uncle Barry and Aunt Cynthia, and my sisters. There was a short interview with the press and a few photographs were taken.

The Australian Olympic Team had won eight gold, seven silver and two bronze medals. They were ranked sixth on the national scorecard. As far as I know, there was no acknowledgement of this outstanding result by the prime minister of the day, nor did I hear of any welcome home ceremony. The massacre of the Israeli athletes was so shocking, so overwhelmingly appalling, that it must have dampened any attempt at celebrating the positive aspects of the Games.

Turramurra High School's teachers and students took it into their own hands to celebrate our achievements by organising a 'Welcome Home' ceremony for their two gold-medallists. Gail Neall had won the 400 metres individual medley in world-record time. She and I were clapped and cheered by about a thousand students lining the entry walkway into the school. A large banner bore the words, 'Thank heavens for little girls with big hearts'. We were presented with flowers, and the cry 'Three cheers for Gail and Shane' rang out across the schoolyard.

After we made a short speech of thanks, we joined staff and prefects for morning tea. Gail and I really appreciated the thoughtfulness of our headmaster, Harry McDowell, in arranging such a great welcome for us. It seemed a little odd, though, to be getting the 'red carpet' treatment from my teachers when I knew everything would soon be back to the normal teacher–student relationship.

I was home again, but I felt I was a different person after the amazing experience of my one and only Olympics. I had swum in five heats, one semi-final and five finals for individual events, and the final of the women's 4 x 100 metres relay. These 12 swims are forever etched in my memory. I had swum my way into sporting history with five individual Olympic medals: three gold, one silver and one bronze.

I was thrilled to own these achievements. At the same time, I felt worn out. I wondered what the next challenge would be. Looking back now, I have to concede that the young Shane Gould was an athletic phenomenon. Her swimming achievements were to shape my whole life, bringing in their wake some welcome developments, and some not so welcome. If I'd had any idea that success at the Munich Olympic Games would turn my life topsy-turvy, scarring me and hurting my family, I may well have stayed at home. At 15, I could know none of that, because I loved swimming. I loved racing and improving my times. I also liked winning.

~

In September 1972, back at home, I agreed with Dad. He advised me to 'put my head down and my tail up' and get ready for my School Certificate examination in two months' time.

CHAPTER 2

Out of my Depth

*. . . it is right for a gull to fly, that freedom is the
very nature of his being, that whatever stands
against that freedom must be set aside. The only law
is that which leads to freedom . . . There is no other.*

~

Richard Bach, *Jonathon Livingstone Seagull*

A WEEK OR SO AFTER OUR RETURN HOME, the whole family
travelled to Melbourne for a reception to mark the VFL Australian
Rules football final at the Melbourne Cricket Ground. In Sydney we
were more familiar with Rugby League, but my older sister Lyn
preferred Australian Rules football and helped me to understand what
was going on.

Lyn was a nonconformist, for which I have always admired her. She
was an adopted child and not only looked different from my other
sisters and me but was also more academically inclined.
Unfortunately, the media is not especially interested in an A score in
an ancient history examination, and my achievements tended to
overshadow hers. The year following the Munich Olympics, Lyn
attended the Aquarius Festival in Nimbin, in northern New South

Wales, and later did a practice teaching stint at the Nimbin community school. During her radical student days in Sydney she lived in squats and proclaimed herself an anarchist. Yet, despite the imbalance in our relationship as teenagers, Lyn always defended me when I was described as 'a machine' or as having 'a waterlogged brain'. In one instance, when she was 18, she wrote in response to criticisms of me, 'Shane is a difficult person to get to know because her range of experience is so far outside most people's. Shane is the most worthwhile person I know, and when she has time to look around and do a bit more growing up, she will be an even more worthwhile person.'

Lyn was really important to me. She was my buddy and my playmate. She was the brave one, the first to go into deeper water (both figuratively and literally), and she urged me to climb ever higher and to be more daring. Lyn has experienced a lot of heartache in her life, and I feel some responsibility for that. If I had ever thought that my sporting fame would impact negatively on my sisters, my parents and, later, my husband, I'm sure I would never have pursued it. But pursue it I did, and it has taken many years for some of the effects of that public attention I experienced as a young girl to become apparent.

After Munich, I tried to keep my feet on the ground, my head out of the clouds and the continuing accolades in perspective. Fame is fleeting and fans are fickle. My parents had drummed into me the danger of resting on one's laurels, so I had guidance in differentiating what was good for me from what was not.

In Melbourne at the VFL final, my sisters and I were driven around the oval while 100 000 people applauded us. It felt strange to sit in a car and wave to people, and I soon became uncomfortable. I felt sure the spectators wanted us to leave so that the game could start. The nicest part of the day for me was petting a mounted policeman's horse that had taken a liking to my flowers. I was like any other 15-year-old.

At Mum's suggestion, I gave thanks to God for my success at the Gordon Methodist Church in Sydney. Mum had read that the winners at the ancient Olympic Games would place their laurel wreaths on the altar in their home town as a way of giving thanks to their gods. Mum thought it would be a good way to keep me from getting a swelled head. She arranged everything with the minister and helped me to write a simple prayer that I would recite. We all went along to the church, and during the service I was given a few minutes to place my medals on the altar, say my prayer and give thanks. It was a simple thing to do, but it had a profound and comforting effect on me. I could now see my achievements as something outside of myself, as a gift to be appreciated and a responsibility to be honoured, not as an ability to be owned and controlled. That awareness has stayed with me, particularly during those times when I almost wished I had never won the medals.

My parents have often been asked what effect my swimming had on the family. The short answer was that it was hard being under the spotlight. No one likes to have their privacy invaded. The more complex answer was that the effect was catastrophic. It was as if the family was caught up in a tornado that buffeted it on all sides and from which there was no escape. My parents did their best to give me opportunities while shielding me from the media. They were also trying to give time and attention to my sisters. In the eyes of the outside world, though, I was the most significant member of the family; in fact, my swimming training schedule and the media demands on me became the pivot around which our family revolved.

Many Australian families are caring for an 'exceptional child', such as a child diagnosed with Down's syndrome or who has some other physical or intellectual disability. These families know that the disability becomes a dictator that rules their lives. Swimming was the dictator in our family, and I was the 'exceptional child'. My parents had always given equal recognition to each of their daughters' achievements, but the influences that pressed in on the family from outside skewed the balance we had formerly maintained. There was too much focus on me, which shifted power from my parents to me and weakened their position as head of the family.

Mum and Dad no longer felt they could give me strong directives, such as: 'Just get back into school and swimming, and forget about the Olympics.' It was impossible to forget the Olympics. Then the fan mail started. Letters arrived from all over the world, some addressed just to 'Shane Gould Australia' or 'The Shane Gould Australian Goldfish'. One morning our postman delivered over 60 letters from Turkey after an Istanbul newspaper printed our address.

Nearly all the fan letters requested a signed photograph. A few people sent postal vouchers to cover the cost. We soon ran out of the photos Uncle Barry had printed for us, but the letters kept coming. How could our family service this demand? Eventually, the Australian Office of Information printed 1000 photographs, and the Australian Swimming Association paid for the postage. It was a family effort to address the envelopes. When my hand got too tired from signing, Lyn put my signature on a few photos.

At school, my good friends Leah Housman and Debbie Bollom helped me catch up on the work I'd missed. My practical life experience also came in handy, particularly in German and geography.

In the pool, I trained half-heartedly. My coach, Forbes Carlile, and the assistant coach, Tom Green, helped me to set an immediate goal: the Australian Nationals in Adelaide in February.

Meanwhile, Dad had a long holiday due to him, which he took over December and January. My parents felt they needed to spend time as a family after a very disruptive year, and to get away from Sydney and the media attention for a while. Lyn had finished her final school exams in November, so she, Dad and I headed up to Port Macquarie with the caravan and settled into a caravan park near the mouth of the Hastings River. Mum, Debbie and Jenny came later in December when primary school finished for the year.

Lyn and I went horse-riding soon after we arrived in Port Macquarie, though neither of us could ride very well. The horses were fresh and fast, and Lyn fell off and broke her wrist. She was most unimpressed when her arm was put in a plaster cast for the whole of our six-week holiday! A keen bodysurfer, she was miserable about not being able to go surfing and tried wrapping her cast in plastic bags when the waves were too good to resist.

I trained each morning and night, played cards, Monopoly and Scrabble, got thrashed by Lyn at chess and checkers, read and surfed. I was on a diet of low-carbohydrate (no more than 60 grams a day) and high-protein foods and lost a lot of weight. At 60 kilograms, I was 4.5 kilograms lighter than at Munich and felt fantastic. In retrospect, I suspect this diet may have starved me of essential B-group vitamins, which are vital for dealing with stress.

I did training sessions with a friend from Sydney, Warren Plummer. While we often did good set times in training, I couldn't do 'effort' swims and felt noticeably different from my pre-Olympic training. It was as if my mind was saying, 'You don't have to subject yourself to this. Take it easy!' It was during this time that I began to seriously entertain the idea of quitting competitive swimming.

The holiday in Port Macquarie was a good opportunity to reflect on and get a perspective on my life. All the things I had done and that had happened to me in the last two years were extreme. I felt out of balance and I didn't know how to correct it. During the holiday an offer came from a business acquaintance and friend of Dad's, Paul Mariani, for me to spend some time in California. I jumped at the prospect. My parents saw it as a way of giving me a reward for doing well at the Olympics. There were no financial rewards for my Olympic successes — amateurism was still going strong — so their permission was their part of the reward.

In January 1973 I returned to Sydney by myself to compete in the NSW State Championships and taper for the Nationals in Adelaide in

February. Tom Green, who coached the morning sessions at Pymble, offered to have me stay with his family. Having been on a strict diet while on holiday, I started to crave chocolate; and when I found some chocolate-coated peanuts in the pantry, I ate them all. I then lied about having eaten them. Although I felt terrible about betraying my hosts' hospitality, I couldn't bring myself to own up.

I swam in the State Championships, winning five titles but swimming mediocre times. During January I received numerous accolades, including, for the second time, the ABC-TV Sportsman of the Year award (there was no gender distinction then). Then, on 14 January, I received my exam results (six As), along with the news that the Australia Day Council had declared me Australian of the Year. When Mum explained what this meant, I felt both stunned and humbled.

'It's great that Shane should be Aussie of the Year,' Lynette declared at dinner on the day of the announcement. 'She's the one who's been in the news all year.'

'Will you get a beautiful new dress and have a crown and a sash, like Miss Australia?' asked Jenny.

'Will we all have to go and listen to the speeches?' sighed Debbie. 'I hate speeches.'

The invitation was for 'Shane and her parents'. The venue was the Melbourne Town Hall, and the date, 26 January — Australia Day. Two of my idols, Dawn Fraser and tennis player Evonne Goolagong, had held the honour before me. It seemed that sportspeople represented the Australian identity.

The luncheon was a grand affair and included all the Melbourne Establishment. There were speeches, including one by me, which Mum and Dad had helped me to write. During my speech I announced that I had decided to take up an offer to live and train in the United States for some months. I said, 'I hope that this experience will broaden my outlook and generally improve my education, so that my efforts to promote Australia in the future will be more professional.'

In truth I was feeling very restless. I had seen and done so much. It was becoming harder to relate to my sisters and my peers. I felt comfortable with other high-achievers, but even those friendships were one-dimensional. Even at the award ceremony I felt like an outsider placed on a pedestal. I felt separate and isolated from everyone around me.

I was glad to get home after the long day in Melbourne. The award was probably the best recognition that my country could give me, but I wasn't sure what responsibilities went along with it. I felt uneasy and uncertain about my worthiness to live up to it. I decided not to think about it for the time being, and to concentrate on my swimming and my upcoming trip.

I missed both of my training sessions that Australia Day, but I was back in the water the next morning to complete a week of 72 kilometres swum over ten sessions. My heart rate was the lowest it had ever been, 36 bpm, and I was at my best racing weight.

When school resumed in early February, we were still finalising my living, swimming and schooling arrangements for California. Just before I left for the United States, I competed in the Nationals in Adelaide and won seven titles: the 100 metres butterfly, the 200 and 400 metres individual medley, and the 100, 200, 400 and 1500 metres freestyle. My 1500 metres freestyle time was a world-record 16.56.9. It was an easy swim, despite my beetroot-red face at the end; I felt I was really 'in the zone'!

An unusual thing happened just before the race. A boy gave me a tiny silver St Christopher medal. He said, 'Keep this medal with you and St Christopher will always help you.' This was definitely something out of the ordinary. This boy, whom I had at first thought was an autograph-hunter, turned out to be an angel in disguise. It was as if he saw that I knew there were deeper things in life than winning races. His gift came with thoughtful intentions. It touched my spirit and may well have triggered the start of a spiritual awakening for me.

~

Back in Sydney I said my farewells to my family and friends. It was to be the last time that I would live permanently with my family. I was 16 and very confused about whether or not I wanted to continue swimming, and about what future I was aiming for. Going to America was a kind of escape, in the sense that it got me away from the attention that came with fame. The whole family was disrupted by the changes my swimming successes had brought about in our lives over the last couple of years, and I was the most unsettled of all. In one sense I was a normal teenager growing up; while at the same time I had another tag and identity to act out — that of Australia's Golden Girl and Australian of the Year.

I felt unsure about these identities and didn't know what the protocol (if any) involved. Even my family found it bewildering when friends and new acquaintances gushed over them and asked often probing and intrusive questions about me. My sisters were individuals with their own interests, achievements and needs, but they were also sisters of a world-famous swimmer whose needs and achievements often overrode theirs. They gradually resented the fame I had attracted. Jenny, the youngest, felt left out of things. She later explained to Mum that because there was such an age gap between us, she didn't feel close to me. She felt that I didn't have time for her, in any case.

~

While my trip to California was one way to restore balance within the family, it was also a great adventure. My first port of call was Los

Angeles, where four Australian girls — Debbie Palmer, Gail Neall, Bev Whitfield and myself — competed in an International Invitation meet in a short-course 25-yard pool. I raced against Shirley Babashoff and Keena Rothhammer again. The depth of American swimming was noticeable when an unknown swimmer tied with me in winning the 100 yards freestyle. Shirley and Keena took the other places. The Americans trounced us in the relays, too. Afterwards we were taken to Disneyland as a treat.

During this time I read Richard Bach's book, *Jonathon Livingstone Seagull*. I realised for the first time that it's OK to be good; it's OK to be different. Like the special and gifted seagull, I longed for the freedom that I knew was at the very nature of my being, and that would come from understanding who I really was and *practising* it. And I understood that by creating myself as a 'creature of excellence and intelligence and skill', I would at times be an outcast.

I had already experienced this isolation while at school in Turramurra. Since the Olympics, I hadn't felt like 'one of the mob'. Some of the boys in my class made remarks about my shoulder muscles making me look 'like a Baltic wrestler'. And while they basked in some of the reflected glory that came from 'knowing Shane Gould', my peers and I couldn't get on a mutual social footing. We were on different wavelengths. The standard Australian way is to 'pull down' the exceptional person. Americans, on the other hand, accepted excellence. I thought by attending an American school, I wouldn't stand out in the same way, and could just be one of a peer group.

I settled into the home of the Mariani family in Los Altos, California, and attended St Francis High School at Sunnyvale, a nearby suburb. The Marianis were related to the Ciabattari family, with whom I had been billeted during a short visit to the United States in 1971. Paul Mariani and my father had since become acquainted through business and developed a friendship.

The youngest member of the family — there were five boys and two girls in all — was two years my junior and an outstanding diver.

I was away from my family, my school and my regular coach. Everything was new and fresh, and my enthusiasm for swimming soared in the exciting environment. I enjoyed school, where I studied unfamiliar subjects such as Christian ethics, American history, speech, and driver education. I even drove the family Pontiac to school after I obtained an American driver's licence, which is available to 16-year-olds in California.

I had an allowance with which to buy my breakfast and lunch and I soon developed a taste for fatty, sugary fast foods, which at that time weren't as prevalent in Australia as they now are. I complained that my clothes were shrinking in the dryer and asked for them to be hung on the line to dry. Before long I realised that it wasn't the clothes that were shrinking, but me expanding. In five months I gained nearly 13 kilograms in weight! I didn't feel very good about myself at all.

At school the students were friendly and open. The emphasis in class was on verbal rather than written work. I found this approach quite difficult, but I could appreciate how it made Americans more articulate than Australians. My speech class soon gave me considerable confidence with verbal expression and organising my ideas. I even came second in a poetry-reading competition with a recital of Banjo Paterson's poem, 'A Bush Christening'.

The Marianis lived in a big villa on a large area of land. I counted 13 bedrooms and six bathrooms in the house. With ten or 11 people living there, and friends coming and going, it was almost a miniature village. Mrs Mariani was a devout Catholic who was interested in the charismatic movement of the Catholic Church. She surprised me with her descriptions of 'flying' down the stairs and speaking to angels. The patriarch, Paul Mariani, was big in every way. He was physically big, with a big family and a big business; his big commitment to Catholicism brought him a papal knighthood. I found myself quite naturally calling him 'Big D'. I once overheard him telling my date for a school dance to look after me, and 'There's to be no screwing,' he said. Big D was big on straight talk, too.

I soon fell in love with this big-hearted American family. They showed me around San Francisco — we went to Fisherman's Wharf, listened to jazz in Golden Gate Park, and ate breakfast at their country club. They seemed interested in getting to know me as a person. I even developed a brief crush on one of their handsome sons.

~

There was some uncertainty about where I would train, even after I arrived. I wanted to go to the Santa Clara Club, where I knew Keena Rothhammer trained, but the club didn't want me taking up coaching time and skills if it would give me the edge on some of their top-swimming members. Instead, I had to rely on the Marianis to find a coach and a pool for training. It was extremely unsettling. I felt so independent, that I *should* be able to cope well, that I didn't say anything about how I felt, and most of the time I could put a brave face on it. I turned to the cookie jar of chocolate-chip cookies for solace.

I began training with Nort Thornton at Foothills College. Nort had been coaching swimming for 20 years or so and had produced some top American swimmers. Although I hadn't heard of him, I was prepared to trust him with my swimming life.

Nort's training programs were very mild compared to what I was used to. I was doing half to two-thirds of my usual mileage, and it wasn't enough for me. What I *did* enjoy were the different sets and the emphasis on stroke drills, which has now become a major part of swimming training internationally.

While my technique improved, I lost fitness very quickly because I wasn't putting in enough hours in the water. I was still fit enough, though, to compete in two competitions: the Crystal Palace Coca-Cola meet in London at Easter (I flew to the UK on my own); and the National Short-Course Championships in Cincinnati, Ohio, in April. In Cincinnati, I broke some US records and won the high point score trophy, which included a medal inset with a small diamond. (It is now in the NSW Sports Museum at Homebush, in Sydney, along with most of my other medals.) That was the last competition in which I swam well. From there, it was all downhill. My strength and fitness were gone, and I had sabotaged myself by putting on too much weight.

Nort was a great person, but when he had to reprimand me severely for dancing on a restaurant table, I knew my behaviour greatly disappointed him. It took a while to regain his respect. I was breaking out from the good-girl mould and exploring my boundaries. It's a normal teenage thing to fool around, but it was out of character for me. Around this time I also had my one and only puff of marijuana.

I spent hours talking with Nort on the pool deck. Often, he would be late in getting back to his family, and I would be late for school. I really loved that man! He was a special person, a mentor and an 'uncle'. Nort is one of a handful of people in my life with whom I've made a strong connection. Our totally innocent relationship was seen by some as unhealthy, however — such as when he once massaged my tight shoulders in a hotel room before a race. Sadly, some coaches lack Nort's moral character and *do* sexually abuse their athletes. Nort went on in the mid-1970s and 1980s to become a truly great coach of international swimmers. In 1974 he became head coach at the University of California, specialising in coaching sprinters including several world-record holders and Olympians such as the great Matt Biondi.

Another big influence on me at this time was the religious atmosphere both in the Mariani home and at school. My conversations with Nort, who was a Catholic, often included theological subjects. This met a deep need in me, as I was feeling emotionally empty and uncertain about whether I wanted to continue swimming. One day at home I sat down with Big D to discuss my options. At the top of a sheet of paper, we wrote 'Retirement from further competition?', with two columns beneath headed 'Pros' and 'Cons'. We compiled a long list of arguments both for and against my retiring, each of which had merit. I felt no closer to being able to make up my mind.

In the course of talks I had with Big D, I was able to confide in him about how the inordinate amount of attention I got bothered me a great deal and made me feel very guilty, particularly about my sisters. He asked me a number of questions that helped me to clarify my thinking. Did I demean myself in order to elevate others? Did I want to get out of competitive swimming because it was easier to direct attention away from myself than to direct it towards others? What could I do to help my sisters experience the thrill of accomplishment themselves, in an area that interested them or in which they were talented? How could I inspire them and be an example to them? I felt guilty about and had no control over the BAD THING (attention) that was a by-product of a GOOD THING (winning). During this period of soul-searching, I became aware that I had a need to even the score — to give to others, because I had received so much.

In May, Mum, Dad, Jenny and Debbie flew over to visit me. My parents were distressed to see how heavy I had become. They seemed like strangers, but I pretended that nothing was wrong. They were worried that I was transferring my allegiance to the Mariani family and that they were losing their child. 'We want you to come home,' they said. 'America isn't good for you.' I argued that I wanted to stay and finish school, and then go to college, but my parents won the argument.

I felt resentful. I was 16 and thought I knew everything. My parents were upset. After everything they had done for me, it seemed to them that it was all for nothing. The family was falling apart. It was a terrible time for all of us — particularly for my father, who was tormented by the thought that perhaps he shouldn't have encouraged my swimming ambitions to the extent he had.

Before returning to Sydney, I swam my last races at the Santa Clara International swim meet and did very poor times. I came sixth in the 100 metres freestyle with a time of 62-plus seconds, a time I used to do in training and my winning time when I was 12! I felt disappointed, embarrassed and ashamed. I certainly wasn't living up to all the accolades I had received in the last two years. 'See,' I said to myself. 'I'm not as good as people think I am!' My future was uncertain; just a blurry fog. I had so many expectations to live up to, and others' hopes and dreams to fulfil. I felt weighed down by the whole catastrophe; bewildered and lost in the whole experience. I needed Jonathon Livingstone Seagull to teach me to fly.

> *We can find ourselves as creatures of excellence and intelligence and skill. We can be free. We can learn to fly!*
>
> *Who is more responsible than a gull who finds and follows a meaning, a higher purpose for life? . . . to learn to discover, to be free.*

CHAPTER 3

Divided Loyalties

You're too young and too good to quit.

~

Ursula Carlile

The world's your oyster, Shaney!

~

Ron Gould

BACK IN THE POOL IN SYDNEY IN JULY 1973, I had no heart for training and did only about three sessions a week. I was very out of condition. I spent long hours just hanging around, talking. Forbes Carlile was intensely annoyed and impatient with me. I felt out of place at school, too. The only activity I enjoyed was coaching a junior girls' netball team after class.

I was supposed to be training for the First World Swimming Championships in Belgrade, but Dad pulled me off the team, saying: 'Shane, you can't go. You're not fit enough. It would be an embarrassment.' The Australian selectors agreed with him. The end of my competitive swimming career was an unspectacular fizzle, coloured by shame, guilt and confusion.

Behind the scenes a raging storm was brewing between Dad and Forbes, with me in the centre. Dad bombarded me with inspirational pep talks about putting everything in perspective — 'The world's your oyster, Shaney!'; while Forbes fired passionate letters at me, full of convictions about my responsibilities to my talent. My loyalties were excruciatingly torn. I wanted to please both of the men in my life. I tried hard to look into the future, but I lacked the platform built from experience from which to get a view. I was ill-equipped to make the huge life decisions I was being called to make.

Dad's propositions were laterally expanding, while Forbes tried to stretch me in a linear way by appealing to my love of physical challenges. Forbes was intent on building my character through endurance — through keeping on keeping on. The counter-arguments I used with Forbes expressed the anguish and confusion I felt. Forbes argued that as the best, or potentially the best, at my sport in the world, I should exploit my talent to the full. I replied, 'I'm the best in the world already. What is better than best? Wasn't that good enough? If I'm even better, it's going to alienate me even more from other people.' I argued that I needed to have some fun, that I needed to concentrate on my studies (although this was more for the benefit of the press), that I needed to know what was the right thing to do. Should I continue to live at home, where I felt my parents were too involved in my life? Too many people wanted a piece of me.

Dad tried to treat me as a whole person. He had seen the gamut of competitive swimming — the sacrifices, the stress, the glory and the fame, the public ownership of his daughter. No way did he ever want me to go through another Olympics! He felt that Forbes wanted to use me as an experimental athlete and a promotional tool for his swimming business. He thought the media would continue to use me to pad out their columns. He saw it all as using. 'What's in it for you, Shane?' he kept asking me. 'There's certainly no financial gain. It's time for the using to stop.' Even this argument sat badly with me.

I hadn't gone into swimming with the expectation of financial rewards; I just liked doing it.

Dad was full of ideas about what I might do. Promote Australia. Tread new ground in sports psychology. Work in public relations. Try other sports. He used words like 'maturity', 'quality of life' and 'prioritise'. Dad worked in travel marketing and was an ideas man. He constantly suggested ways in which I might stretch my abilities and grow as a person. Sometimes his ideas weren't realistic, but they helped me to understand that I had choices and to think big.

Forbes thought that Dad was putting ideas into my head, and that he was an ambitious father. I think that everything both of them were saying had an element of truth. Yes, I was too young and too good to quit, but I didn't want to keep doing it. Yes, Dad was ambitious for me, in a fatherly way, but his ideas were too grown-up for me to grasp.

Whatever decision I made could please only one of them. So I had to be sure that whatever I decided was the best for me. My life experience at the time was lacking, especially when it came to making such a choice. At the time I didn't feel confident about making any decisions.

~

Dad believed that Forbes's aims for me would further disrupt our family life. Lynette, Debbie and Jenny hated all the public attention I was given, the invasion of the family by outsiders, the time given to endless talk about me — time that was stolen from them. Dad discussed the conflict with Channel 10 and they arranged a public debate between him and Forbes. When Forbes turned up at the studio, he was unaware of what it was all about. Dad couldn't communicate to Forbes his concerns and distress and concerns about me any other way than this confrontation. We don't think the program was put to air, but newspapers reported the conflict. In 1999, Forbes says he doesn't know why why Ron and Shirley didn't come to him and explain how they felt.

The strain on Dad as the parent of a successful child was terrible. One night he broke down and sobbed uncontrollably. Mum had never seen him cry before and became alarmed. She felt unable to come up with a solution, and yet she had to keep the family stable. Somehow during this family trauma, she managed to deal with the diverse needs of five other people. More than anything else, Mum wanted me to have educational opportunities. If swimming could have given me those opportunities, then she would have encouraged me to stick with swimming as a means to that end. She felt that I'd reached the top of amateur sport and there was no point in doing it all over again. She saw how half-hearted I was about training, so she supported Dad's view that my competition days should end.

My self-doubt grew as the war waged on. Forbes called me immature, mixed-up, undisciplined, lacking in willpower, a loser who wanted to give up without a struggle. Ursula Carlile wrote to me: 'You're too young and too good to quit.'

It was the mid-1970s, and neither my mother nor Ursula was forceful enough to take the argument away from the men and work at it using a more feminine approach. The men saw the problem as raw and urgent, and wanted a quick resolution. Each wanted to win — Forbes for the sake of swimming, and Dad for the sake of his family.

There was no doubt that the family was feeling the tension. Swimming had taken over our lives and the media wasn't letting up. As a result, my family made a carefully considered decision to move from Sydney to Armidale, a rural town in the northern tablelands of New South Wales. We needed to take back control over our lives.

We were pretty experienced at moving — this would be our eighth family home. There would be sad farewells to friends, the packing and then the settling-in period. Dad was our leader again and Mum the executive officer.

Armidale is inland, and has light snow in winter. It isn't known for its water sports, but for its excellent educational institutions — a university and some fine schools. My parents hoped that all their daughters would attend the University of New England.

Mum, Debbie and Jenny went to Armidale in the August school holidays. On their return, they were enthusiastic about the prospect of country life. Lynette would transfer from Macquarie University in Sydney to UNE. I could finish high school before going to university, too.

While Mum and my two younger sisters were away, Dad, Lynette and I stayed on in Sydney. Dad went to work each day, Lynette studied, and I was supposed to be training. Everyone else was busy and I felt left out. After my school experience in California, I felt like a stranger at Turramurra High School. And swimming training had lost its zing for me.

I didn't fit anywhere now — at home, at school, at the pool. I was in limbo. Achieving the adult goals of world records and Olympic gold medals created the illusion that I was an adult. Heaven knows how hard I tried to be one. And at times I fooled everyone — journalists, parents, and even myself. There was no way I would ever admit that I felt too young, too inexperienced, or too lacking in judgment to make wise decisions.

While the arguments between Dad and Forbes continued, I felt like a prize they were fighting over. I was at a crossroads in my life. I felt it was terribly unfair that Dad and Forbes were arguing publicly about my future. I was 'between a rock and a hard place'. In a surge of independence, I decided to take responsibility for my own life. Not Dad's or Forbes's way, but a third way — *mine*.

It was all too much. Forbes had a plan for me. Dad had several. The public (via the media) wanted continued performance. I owed it to them somehow. If I went with Forbes, I challenged Dad. If I went with Dad, I would have to bear criticism from Forbes. If I went with public expectation, I wasn't being true to myself. How could I resolve all this? I couldn't. So, another strategy was needed. I consulted my bank book. Life savings, $30. Enough. I left a note for Dad on the kitchen table.

I was running away from it all. Carrying a few clothes and my toothbrush in a Pan Am airline bag, I set off for Pymble railway station, about five kilometres away.

Escape was the only thought in my head. As I walked through the leafy streets, I made a plan. I would take a train to northern New South Wales and live on a beach. I imagined the warm sand, and watching the gulls. I could float in the sea far away from everything I couldn't deal with. I would be at peace. Everything would be different. All the problems would disappear.

I got off the train at a small railway station outside Newcastle, 100 kilometres north of Sydney, and started walking in a direction that I hoped would take me to a beach. It was getting dark and I realised I hadn't brought a blanket with me. Suddenly I realised the stupidity of what I was doing, and how concerned my father would be. I decided to head for Armidale instead. A young man picked me up and then drove to a quarry outside the town, where he leaned over and tried to kiss me. Alarm bells went off in my head and I pushed him away. I was very lucky that he was halfhearted in his attempts and agreed to drive me to a railway station. I don't know if he recognised me; I think he saw me as just another 'chick', which was quite refreshing in a way, despite the dangerous situation I had just been in.

I boarded a train for the overnight journey to Armidale, and next morning I asked directions to the property where Mum was staying. I walked the four or five kilometres there and arrived in the midst of a rural drama. My sister Debbie had just escaped being decapitated when the horse she was riding rode under the wire clothes line. She was thrown off and had a burn mark on her neck. My sisters never seemed to have much luck with horses.

After a quick hug, Mum just asked me: 'Are you all right?' I said, 'Yes, I'm fine. I've made a few decisions.' Mum said, 'That's great. We'll back you in whatever you want to do.' Then she took Debbie, whose needs were more pressing than mine, to the hospital. It was a relief to be put second and to know that there would be no pressure on me to change my mind.

Meanwhile, Dad had been searching everywhere for me. The first place he thought of going was the morgue! He feared some crank might try to do me harm, as I was easily recognised. It was a tense, nightmarish time for him as he checked with the missing person's bureau.

In trying to come to a decision, I had looked pragmatically at my situation. It was undeniable: I had lost my fitness, and I knew it would take hard work and focused effort to regain it. When I was totally honest with myself, I saw that my heart wasn't in the competitive swimming scene anymore.

Beneath the push of the media, the pull of my coach, the distress of my parents and the confusion of a 16-year-old who was bluffing her way and pretending she knew it all, was something else: the essential purity — the harmony — of the swimming experience itself. It had been my child's play, then a source of triumphs, awards and accolades as my personal delight became public entertainment. It ended in confusion, unease and guilt. It was time to retire from competitive swimming. But having known that special feeling, I knew that I would search for it again.

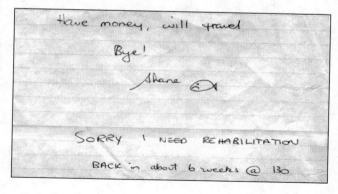

Have money, will travel

Bye!

Shane

SORRY I NEED REHABILITATION

BACK in about 6 weeks @ 130

PART TWO
childhood

CHAPTER 4

The Little Girl

There was such freedom and space to play [in Fiji].
It was like being in a natural adventure playground.

~

Shane Gould

AFTER THEIR MARRIAGE IN 1951, my parents, Shirley and Ron Gould, lived for a time in an apartment in Vaucluse, Sydney. The postwar housing shortage was still a real problem and they felt fortunate to have a place of their own. They were ready to start a family, but months went by without Shirley getting pregnant. She was distressed about it and eventually became ill. Ron was very concerned about her and suggested that they adopt a baby. After an 18-month wait, they were told their baby would be available in a month.

Lynette was brought home on 23 November 1954. She was ten weeks old and was instantly the centre of attention of her adoring parents and doting grandparents. Shirley was often overawed by the enormity of what she had undertaken. She knew nothing of her baby's genetic or temperamental inheritance, and felt totally responsible for every aspect of her growth and nurture. 'I was somewhat of an over-anxious and over-involved parent, always struggling to do the 'right' or 'best' thing and not trusting my intuition.' Ron, on the other hand, seemed to take to fatherhood easily and naturally.

When Lynette was about a year old, Shirley and Ron sought further medical advice and Shirley had a minor physical problem attended to. They then started to keep a temperature chart to ascertain when she was ovulating. Maybe now she would be able to become pregnant.

Late in the summer of 1956, the young family joined friends, Lynne and Bruce Leabeater and their toddler, Paul, at Sussex Inlet, on the south coast of New South Wales, for a short holiday. They all shared a rather primitive cottage, which had a wood stove, no laundry and an outside toilet. The two men spent their days fishing, while the women cared for the two young children.

Every day, Shirley checked her temperature. One day, it went up and they all cheered. Bruce and Lynne then got bossy. 'OK, you two. Off you go. We'll wash up. Have fun getting your baby!'

Shirley knew, that night, that she had conceived a child. And when her pregnancy was confirmed, she was ecstatic. She didn't mind the morning sickness and the tenderness of her breasts — they confirmed that this was the real thing. She craved cabbage cooked in butter for breakfast. She was proud of her swelling figure and wore maternity clothes long before they were necessary. 'I wanted everyone to know I was a lady-in-waiting,' she says.

Each day after lunch, she lay down with Lynette on their sunny verandah and read her books. One of their favourites was *Scuppers the Sailor Dog*. Shirley describes those nine months as the most joyful of her then 28 years.

On 23 November 1956, I was born at Crown Street Women's Hospital in Sydney. The umbilical cord was wrapped around my neck, but prompt action by the obstetrician, Dr Robert McBeth, averted any complications. I was covered in a white, powdery substance called vernix. 'It's great for the skin,' one of the nurses told

Mum, as she helped herself to some from the crease in my tiny arm and applied it to her own.

'I had a strange feeling, bordering on regret, when I saw you wrapped so neatly, lying on your side in the little hospital crib — the peach-bloom on your cheeks and that unforgettable sweet, clean baby smell,' Mum later told me. 'You were now separate from me; no longer one with me. I was in awe at this perfect new creation.'

Mum's musings soon gave way to the practicalities of feeding and changing me. The worshipper became the servant, attempting to translate the language of the baby-master.

Lynette had been looking forward to having a playmate sister and was disappointed by my tiny size and inability to walk. However, she soon adapted to my shortcomings.

When I was born, Mum and Dad still hadn't decided on a name for me. They talked it over with their neighbours in the apartment building, the tennis player Lew Hoad and his wife, Jenny. Dad's father had been Welsh and he wanted to choose a Welsh name for me, but 'Bronwyn', 'Caitlin' or 'Rhonda' didn't seem right. Lew suggested a Welsh name he had heard recently while playing at Wimbledon — Sian. He was told it was a variation of Joan (Mum's middle name), but he was unsure about how it was pronounced. He thought the correct pronunciation might be 'Shane'. (It's actually pronounced as 'Sharne'.) Mum and Dad like the sound of 'Shane', but discarded the Welsh spelling. A few months later, the American movie *Shane*, starring the popular actor Alan Ladd, came to Australia. Many people mistakenly thought I was named after the movie hero. I was given 'Elizabeth' as my second name, after Dad's mother, Elizabeth Ann Gould (nee Coles).

As a natural child born following an adoption, I was what health professionals refer to as 'the miracle child'. The adopted child is referred to as 'the chosen child'. Mum says, 'I have always had immense gratitude to Lynette, our chosen child, for inviting three miracle children — Shane, Debbie and Jenny — to join our family.'

Recently, Mum and Lynette made contact with Lynette's first mother. 'It was a very heart-warming event,' Mum said.

After I was born, we all lived at the apartment in Vaucluse. It was close to the harbour beaches of Nielsen Park, Vaucluse Bay, Parsley Bay, Watsons Bay and Camp Cove, and we seemed to spend half our time in the water. Before I could walk I would crawl down the beach and into the little waves at the shoreline. I could control my breathing so that I never got water up my nose when I was tumbled around by the waves. Mum says I just used to come up laughing. Mum and Dad saw that I had a special relationship with water and gave me a rubber tyre to float on in a neighbour's pool. I loved it!

Dad worked as Airport Traffic Manager with the American airline, Pan Am. When I was about 18 months old, we all went to Fiji, where Dad had a brief assignment at Nadi airport. Lynette's smallpox vaccination came up in the usual blister, but mine didn't 'take' and I was vaccinated again. Soon after we arrived at the Lautoka Methodist minister's house where we would be staying while Reverend Peter Davis and his wife, Betty (a schoolfriend of Mum's), were away on leave, I was badly scalded by pulling a jug of near-boiling water over myself. Mum says my screams of pain and terror caused her gut-wrenching anguish as they hurriedly drove me to the nearby Lautoka Hospital. She berated herself for not having been quick enough to avert the accident and says my screams echoed in her head for weeks afterwards.

Mum, Lynette and I returned to Sydney just as my smallpox blister came up and took hold in the burn tissue. The double dose of the vaccine then created a rare side effect: a form of brain inflammation that for several days kept me awake all night and asleep all day. It was a near miss for full-blown encephalitis. I recovered quickly, but it took my parents and grandparents longer to get over the scare.

From the time I was able to sit up, I would watch Lynette's every move. By the time I could walk, I was attempting to copy her actions. In this way, I learned to ride a tricycle and to use my feet as brakes before I was two. Mum was very impressed by my coordination and thought I had a fine understanding of what I could ask my body to do. I rarely fell. My gross motor function such as walking and climbing was excellent, though it took longer to develop finer manual dexterity, so I could be counted on to spill my milk at every meal. Lynette's name for me was 'Spiller Diller'.

In September 1959, two months before I turned three, Dad accepted a work transfer to Nadi airport in Fiji. Mum was thrilled at the prospect of living on a Pacific island, which she had longed to do since reading the book *A Pattern of Islands* by Arthur Grimble as a teenager. She hoped that, by living in Fiji, she would get to understand at first hand some of the indigenous culture. Instead, she became a company wife, living in a company house, and was expected to be a hostess to Dad's business customers. Her attempts to learn the local dialect were frustrated by the lack of grammar books; they were all in the 'high' Fijian of the eastern part of Viti Levu. Despite Mum's personal frustrations, she found the lifestyle delightful; it was perfect for a family with young children.

We lived in the residential area near Nadi airport, in the location known as the Pan Am Compound. The house faced the main airstrip, and we saw the planes landing and taking off each day. We weren't bothered by the noise, which only lasted for a brief time; in any case, there weren't many planes. The house was built on a concrete slab: some of the floors were painted green, while the rest were covered with lino tiles. Lynette and I liked to lie on the cool floor when the weather was hot; we didn't mind that it was hard.

The walls of the house were constructed of a double thickness of woven bamboo, with insect screens instead of glass windows. The roof was a thick thatch of reeds. The house was sturdy enough to withstand three hurricanes during our time there. As it was made of Fijian materials and in the manner of Fijian houses, it was always referred to as 'Goulds' Bure'.

We lived about a kilometre from the Nadi Airport Club, which had a swimming pool. I wasn't yet three when I was able to swim the width of the pool (about ten metres) and jump off the one-metre springboard and swim to the edge. By the time I was six, Mum felt confident about letting Lynette and me swim unsupervised with the other airport children. I was a competent swimmer by that age. It was also perfectly safe to ride bicycles around the compound. The Fijian, Indian and European workers walking or driving on the roads were always friendly and helpful to us kids. Mum felt it was a blessing to live in such a safe environment.

I remember those days in Fiji with feelings of positive enjoyment. There was such freedom and space to play. It was like being in a natural adventure playground. A hedge of red hibiscus acted as a fence around the garden in which there were several old mango trees, mature coconut palms, paw-paws and a kapok tree. Flowering vines of yellow Allamanda and Hawaiian wood roses crept over the thatch with blue petrea. There was a row of frangipani trees, one of my favourite flowers, at one end of the garden. Whenever Lynette and I were restless, Dad would tell us to run five times around the frangipani trees and he would pretend to time us on his wristwatch.

There was one ancient mango tree with a broad trunk and strong climbing branches that conveniently grew horizontally, so that swings and ropes could be hung from them. This tree was a gymnasium for Lynette and me. We used it every day. My upper-body strength, needed for swimming, developed quickly. The more I did it, the more fun it was, and I was soon able to climb hand over hand up a knotted rope. Eventually, I could pull myself a little way up a coconut palm. If getting coconuts had depended on me pulling them down, then I would have found a way to get to the top. As it was, there was usually an obliging Fijian ready to shin up a palm or to sell us coconuts he had already harvested in the village. I liked to squat in the shade of a tree and slurp down the cool, coconut water and eat the slippery, green coconut flesh. The coconuts were hard to open, so when we were playing away from the house we relied on a passing Fijian worker to open them for us with a cane knife.

When the mango trees had fruit on them, I ate them green — crisp and sour like an unripe Granny Smith apple. I carried a little packet of salt to dip the flesh in. Of course, the mangoes were best when sweet and ripe. The overripe ones that had been nibbled by flying foxes were great missiles for throwing at each other or at the school wall on weekends.

We had weekly visits from a local Indian gardener, Pandit, who grew peanuts, and either salted them or spiced them with chilli. He would announce his arrival with 'PEANUTS! You want to eat the peanut, Memsahib?' Yes, we did! They were often still warm through the brown paper bag. The peanut man smelled of curry, herbs and sweat.

My other mother in Fiji was Tima, Mum's 'housegirl' help. Tima — whose full name was Timaima Uluibua Caqi-ni-toba — came from Nawaka Koro (village) near Nadi township. Sometimes there were other housegirls: Luisa and Marieta were also from Nawaka. Flo and Pushba were Indian. With their help, my mother was able to give time to a slightly more gracious style of family life. We had three meals a day together as a family, and the table would always be set with placemats and table napkins. Each of us had our own place at the table. There was sociable conversation interspersed with sibling arguments. One day Lynette challenged Dad to pour a cup of milk over her, and — much to her horror — he did! We both gained new respect for our father. After lunch we would play board games, listen to Shari Lewis or Captain Green Jeans records, or have stories read to us.

From about the age of five, I had a close friend, Michelle Trotter, whose father worked for Qantas. We got up to lots of mischief together, climbing on to roofs, smoking straw and cigarette ends, throwing wads of wet toilet paper at the ceiling, pinching beer and drinking it in a tree. The things other girls did were a bit boring compared to the adventures we had! I got into trouble at school, too. One time I climbed a wall dividing the boys' from the girls' change rooms. I didn't have any brothers and I was curious about boys' 'bits'. My excuse when I was caught was that I was practising my climbing.

Keeping cool in Fiji was a major priority. Water was the best way, so we often went to the pool or played under the sprinkler. When I went to play with Michelle, we spent a lot of time in the Trotters' bathroom, which was tiled. It was fun to push off the wall and skid along the floor after soaping ourselves well. Many years later, my kids used to like to do the same and I encouraged them, only emphasising safety.

There was a sugarcane field at the back of Michelle's house and, beyond that, the Sky Lodge Motel. We would chew on sugarcane as we walked through the field to the hotel to use the pool. We used the excuse that we were looking for our parents. Many times we 'accidentally' fell in. One day I rescued a kitten from the pool, even though it was doing a creditable cat-paddle towards the safety of the edge. I thought that cats couldn't swim, but this valiant little one certainly could. So far as I remember, I hadn't put it in the pool so that I could get in, too — though it would have been a likely antic!

Lynette and her older friends discovered there was a tunnel beneath the airstrip, and we would go into it, goading and daring each other to stay there while a plane landed above us. We felt fantastic fear and excitement if we stuck it out.

When a large refrigerator was delivered to our house, I asked Dad if we could use the plywood crate it came in as a cubbyhouse. We spent a lot of time playing in it, and occasionally slept the night there. It was under a great climbing tree. (For many years I judged a tree by its suitability for climbing.) Pan Am employed a Sikh nightwatchman called Poona Singh, who often undid his turban and used it to flap away mosquitoes. One night when we were in the cubbyhouse, Poona Singh came to investigate the muffled sounds coming from the crate. We got a fright when he suddenly opened the lid, and ran screaming back to the house. He was even more surprised and swore profusely at us in Punjabi.

Once I stayed with Marieta in Nawaka. Only a few houses in the village had electricity, and the paths between the houses were shrouded in darkness. People sat around the cooking fires, chatting, singing and rocking babies. It was a strange, new and beautiful experience, tinged with anxiety. I held Marieta's hand tightly. I dipped my buttered white bread in their cups of sweet tea and joined in when they talked and joked in English. I liked the villagers' food, too. They served *dalo* (taro), *kumala* (sweet potato), rice, boiled fish and *rou rou* — *dalo* leaves cooked in *lolo* (coconut cream). Eventually, while Marieta gossiped with yet another group of friends, I fell asleep on a bed of Fijian mats made of woven *voi voi* (like pandanus).

In the morning, I went to the river with the village children for a bath. We mainly swam, splashed about and laughed, as we lost the soap. I was shown how to gather *kai*, the freshwater shellfish (called pipis in Australia). It involved feeling for the shellfish with our feet, then retrieving it with our toes, if possible, or by duck-diving. It was enormous fun.

When my father got a boat, we were able to go out into Nadi Bay and have picnics on one of the small islands in the bay. Occasionally, as we headed towards an island, we would notice that another boat was already there and we would change course for a different island that would be the Gould family's own island for the day. These islands were unsuitable for permanent habitation, as most of them lacked fresh water. We wore sneakers to avoid cutting our feet on the broken-coral sand. With its coconut palms and clear, clean water, it was the epitome of a tropical paradise.

Lynette and I snorkelled over the reefs, keeping close contact with Dad. With every armstroke, we would touch his back, and this gave us the confidence to swim around in the deep water, watching the beautifully coloured fish darting in among the coral. On one trip,

Mum was in the boat with the new baby, Debbie; Lynette, Dad and I were having a peaceful snorkel nearby. Suddenly we saw a shark moving alongside us, swimming in the same direction. In a panic we struck out frantically for the boat and, while Mum grabbed our hands, Dad pushed our legs over the side. He then hauled himself in and landed with such a heavy thud that the boat nearly overturned. The locals said later that the sharks were well fed and would only 'go for you' if you had speared a fish and tied it to your waist.

Our everyday fun was mostly at the Nadi Airport Club swimming pool, where we swam year-round. During the winter, or dry season, of each year a swimming coach, Paul Krause, arrived in Nadi from New Zealand. Mr Krause conducted a training squad for children over the age of eight, and he selected me to be in the squad even though at six I was officially too young. I was pleased to be able to join in with Lynette, and for the next three winters Mr Krause helped me with my strokes and fitness. We would stand on the grassy bank next to the pool, swinging our arms around doing stroke drills, and then race down the bank and into the water to practise them. I loved the lessons and soon started to win age-group races in school swimming carnivals, including the 1962 Nadi Airport School Junior Swimming Championship.

The Nadi Airport Club had a small restaurant run by a Chinese family. I loved the fried rice, which would come in a bowl to which I would add soy sauce. (When I later got into top competition, fried rice minus the pork fat and salty soy sauce became my favourite pre-race meal.) The icy poles we bought at the club were great to lick and bite into on the way home, their sticky sweetness melting on to our clothes and hands.

Tima, our housegirl, had a daughter called Uca (pronounced Ootha) who often spent school holidays playing with us. She and Lynette were good friends, and Mum would often find them asleep in the same bed. Uca was shy with my parents, but fun to play with. She was strong, could climb trees well, and could husk, crack and grate a coconut with admirable speed and efficiency.

I can now really appreciate Tima's kindness, though at the time I took it for granted, as children do. She never got angry with us, and always told our parents we had been good girls even when we hadn't. She lovingly and expertly massaged our legs if they ached after a day of bike-riding, and covered us in her coconut oil if we had the slightest sunburn. We then smelled just like Tima! I still love the smell of coconut oil because of the memories it evokes.

When Mum and Dad went out to dinner parties at night, Tima and Luisa were our babysitters. Their failsafe way to get us into bed, and to stay there, was to threaten us with a visit from Sairusi na Bogi Bogi, who was said to be an escaped murderer with a fearsome reputation for terrorising people. He was the local version of our bogeyman. It only took Tima or Luisa to mention his name and then look out the window to check whether he was hiding there, to stop us from bouncing on the beds and throwing pillows. We would dive into our beds, where we would pull the sheet up to our chins and lie very still.

We children sat with Tima and Luisa while they grated coconut and laughed and joked in Fijian. We couldn't understand their jokes, but their laughter was infectious. They were so expressive, talking with their whole bodies and using their arms to emphasise points. I'm aware that I use my hands and arms a lot to express myself when I talk, and I'm sure I learned this from my Fijian other-mothers.

In around 1962, US Air Force personnel began doing scientific testing of upper-air samples, in connection with American nuclear testing in the Pacific. The U2 planes used for this purpose needed to land in Nadi to refuel. They were small, could take off almost vertically, and could glide slowly over long distances in the stratosphere. They needed a parachute at the tail end to slow them down on landing. When they were parked, one wing was secured to the ground, which made them look lopsided. We soon found that the resting wing of a parked U2 made a great slippery-slide! The guards didn't seem to mind our playing in this way with the top-secret aircraft.

Dad frequently went back to his office after hours to check the telex messages. We children loved to go with him. While he worked, we found fun for ourselves. We spun on the swivel chairs, rode on the baggage trolleys and conveyor belts, and played 'secretaries' on old manual typewriters using thin coloured paper.

Our family spent nearly seven years living in Fiji, and it was a wrench when it came time to leave in December 1965. We had seen other families depart for their homelands — New Zealand, Canada, Australia and America — before it was our turn. The biggest loss for me was my cat, Tiki Tiki Timbo, who couldn't return to Sydney with us. My cuddly little orange-and-white friend, named for a little Chinese boy in one of Shari Lewis's songs, was handed on to new owners.

The years on Viti Levu had been perfect for me — now nine, my life had been full of fun, physical activity and a happy family life. My sisters Debbie (aged five) and Jenny (two) had been born (in Sydney for the better hospital facilities) while we lived in Fiji. Mum and Dad decided it was time to return to Australia, because Lynette, at 11, was nearing high school age. Had we remained in Fiji, Lynette — and then later I — would have had to attend either Suva Grammar School or Ravenswood Ladies College in Sydney as a boarder. Another option discussed was for Dad to take up a posting in Lagos, Nigeria, which would have meant that Lynette and I would go to school in Rome! By returning to Sydney, we would reclaim our Aussie-ness and be able to stay together as a family.

CHAPTER 5

Energy to Spare

Goulds can do anything they want to do.

~

Ron Gould

MUM MADE A TRIP TO SYDNEY to find us a new home. She chose a newly built timber house at 1 Culburra Street, Miranda, in Sydney's south, which was within easy commuting distance from Sydney airport where Dad expected to be working. The house was at the enclosed end of a cul-de-sac, which Mum and Dad thought would be a safer option than a through road, as we girls weren't used to traffic. It was chosen with one eye on the family's budget. In Fiji, expatriates' salaries were generous and included housing. Back in Sydney, our living expenses would be much higher.

Within a month of our return to Sydney, three of us got measles and two, including Dad, got the mumps. Sydney seemed grey and overly restrictive compared to Fiji.

Our next-door neighbours were an extended Italian family who had not long been in Australia. They all shared a large double-storeyed red-brick house and the garden was laid out to grow vegetables. Their tomatoes were huge, red, healthy and perfectly staked. We were invited by this happy group of people to watch how they made their tomato sauce. In the backyard, the women pushed very ripe tomatoes through funnels into large beer bottles. The bottles were then placed in a 44-gallon drum, which was heated over an open fire to sterilise and cook the contents. The resulting mixture, with added herbs, was great on spaghetti.

After our house and garden in Fiji, the house-block in Miranda seemed very small and the yard very bare. The rooms were also small, and Lynette and I slept in bunk-beds in the bedroom we shared. Mum had her work cut out for her turning the yard into a garden with grass, trees and shrubs. It took a while for the place to start to feel like home.

After sorting out the house, Mum and Dad's thoughts turned to how they would deal with the exuberant energy of four little girls. During our visits from Fiji to Sydney, we had usually stayed with Mum's parents, Clive and Amy Reid, in Willoughby. Our grandparents were very tolerant and loving, but they found it difficult to restrain me from doing acrobatics on the furniture and swinging from the door lintels. Poppa Reid called me 'the Mexican jumping bean'. It seemed that I was simply a kid with lots of physical energy, and I was adept at finding places to use it. I saw my environment as a potential gymnasium and I tried out every pole, every cross-bar, every fixture that looked like a climbing opportunity.

Given the amount of energy I had and the small size of our house, Mum and Dad decided they would have to find ways to tire me out. Lynette was energetic too, but she would easily settle down and get lost in a good book. Debbie preferred imaginative, more sedate games; while Jenny was happy to fit in with whatever was going on. A good way to tire me out, it was decided, was to enrol me in the nearest swimming club, which was about five kilometres away at Sans Souci. Lynette and I were soon invited by the Sans Souci swim coach, Ken Wyles, to join his squad.

I was rather shocked when I learned what was involved: two hours of organised swimming of specific lengths, during which I would have to keep up with the others in freestyle, breast stroke, butterfly and backstroke. I hadn't done much butterfly and I found it very tiring. The water temperature was much colder that what I had been used to in Fiji, and swimming hard seemed to be the best way to warm up. I was able to have a 'rest' in the breast stroke lengths, as I found this an easy stroke. The biggest difference, though, was the size of the pool — 50 metres. (The pool in Nadi had been 30 metres.) It seemed a long way between ends.

When Lynette and I got home after our first coaching session, we were exhausted and ravenously hungry. We had something to eat and then slept for two hours. Mum thought it would be our first and last session, so she was astonished when I announced that I would go back the next day and planned to keep going for the rest of the school holidays. Lynette wasn't so certain and gradually backed out.

After about three weeks I was hooked on training. I couldn't wait to get to the pool each day. The system of club racing with officially accredited timekeepers provided a perfect form of feedback for young swimmers. I eagerly sought out my timekeeper to find out my times, which I was bettering each week. Winning a race was now less important than the time, which became a personal challenge to beat. I could feel my breast stroke was becoming more efficient, and in backstroke I was managing to swim in the centre of the lane, rather than on the ropes. I was getting more pull under the water in freestyle, and butterfly was becoming a little easier. I no longer needed a two-hour sleep after each training session.

At one inter-club meet in those early days at Sans Souci, I won a breast-stroke event, only to be disqualified for 'dropping a leg'. I was shocked, and Mum and Dad were dismayed at the harshness of such a ruling against a nine-year-old. But it was a lesson that strokes had to be mastered correctly. I got the message.

After a month of training, Ken Wyles suggested I enter the NSW State Swimming Championships in the 50 metres breast stroke.

In those days, age was determined as at 1 October, the beginning of the summer swimming season when pools (all unheated) reopened after the winter. With my birthday at the end of November, I would be able to swim as an under-ten competitor for two years. (Currently, age-group swimmers must all be the same age in the calendar year.) I was surprised to come second, which further kindled my enthusiasm for swimming, as I now wanted to measure my efforts against state swimmers. I just had to get faster.

At the start of the 1966 school year, the three eldest Gould girls enrolled at the Miranda Primary School. Lynette was in Sixth Class. Lynette, 'the brain', could have gone into first year at high school, having skipped Fourth Class in Fiji. Instead, she went into this last year of primary school to catch up with the NSW education system. I was in Fourth Class, and Debbie, who was going to school for the first time, was in Kindergarten in the Infants' section of the school. We set off with our new school uniforms, new shoes and shiny new bags. Jenny now had Mum all to herself.

My teacher was Mr Calderbank. He had told his class that the three Goulds would be coming from Fiji, so there was an expectation that we would be racially Fijian — golden-brown Melanesians with curly, black hair. After some initial disappointment over our unexceptional blonde hair, we were soon drawn into the life of the school. My successes at the State Championships and the school swimming carnival drew attention to me and I found myself elected class captain before I had really got to know any of my new classmates.

It wasn't easy to move into the NSW school system. The Nadi Airport School had been geared to the New Zealand system and curriculum. Before becoming independent in 1970, the colony of Fiji's international airport at Nadi had been serviced mainly by New Zealanders (air traffic controllers, the fire service, meteorologists, customs officers, and so on). The children of these employees were therefore provided with a New Zealand Department of Education school.

I had studied New Zealand history and geography and knew a little about New Zealand agriculture and South Island sheep. There was a smattering of Maori culture, too. While my Australian contemporaries were learning 'Click Go the Shears', I was learning about the Land of the Long White Cloud and singing 'Po Kauri Kauri Ana'. (We sang the corrupted version, too: *Po Kauri Kauri Ana, I had a squashed banana. I threw it at the teacher. The teacher said, 'Come here'. I said, 'No fear. I'll see you next year and punch you on the ear.'*) I had also been taught the New Zealand style of running writing, but now I had to change to a cursive script without loops. One of the first things I learned was how to use the new decimal currency, introduced on 14 February 1966. Counting in multiples of ten rather than 12 was so much easier.

At school I had a sense of being different from the other children, because I didn't know what they knew and took for granted. I wasn't familiar with the local ways, and at first I had to bluff my way and pretend I understood them. I became alert to subtleties of accent and idiom and modified my own accordingly. I watched and learned the rules of the informal playground games, so that I could join in. It took me several months to adapt to the new systems, both academic and social, and to look as if I fitted in. It was just as well that I learned how to fit into a new primary school, as I would have to adapt to a new school seven more times before I was through!

My inner sense of separateness remained, however. I had lived in an exotic place, in a multicultural society. I had American, Fijian, New Zealand, Tongan, Indian and Canadian friends. My experiences made me different. I was actually a *global* child, whereas my classmates were more children of a *locality*. In Fiji I had learned to get on with people of different races, and to relate to and value older people. Racism was never an issue.

The swimming season ended each year with the closure of the public pool around Easter. Winter brought two new discoveries in sport. The first of these was netball. Lynette and I joined the Miranda

Magpies netball team. Our uniform was a white, triple box-pleated tunic trimmed with black, with a silky, black-tasselled cord worn around the waist. To complete the outfit, we wore black knickers, white socks and tennis shoes. It was the first time we had had a proper sports uniform. Every Saturday morning we would sit very carefully in the car on the way to the netball courts to avoid spoiling the pleats. The rest of the family came along as our cheer squad. Each team had a manager who, in addition to dealing with membership matters and club draws, made sure we had quartered oranges to suck on during the games' intervals. There was also a coach for each team. We had a weekly training session where we ran, learned how to throw the ball and shoot goals, and were taught the rules of the game.

That first winter back in Australia, I also discovered that there was a small heated pool owned by a man called Harry Gibbons in the neighbouring suburb of Cronulla. Mr Gibbons was like an uncle to the swimmers who trained at his pool. His son John, who was keen on gymnastics, used to take us to a YMCA gymnasium for extra strengthening and flexibility. My parents were pleased that I had found this additional means to discharge my energy in a positive way. Gymnastics was fun for me. I loved doing handstands and somersaults, though my favourite was dive forward rolls over the 'horse'. Swimming indoors in warm water was a new experience for me, too. My sister Debbie, who had been reluctant to swim in the cold water of the Sans Souci pool, was now willing to have swimming lessons. Little sister Jenny, looking very cute in her tiny nylon Speedo costume, also came along.

The following year, our family moved from Miranda to Watford Close in North Epping, a suburb in Sydney's north-west. Our new red-brick house, one of 12 in the street, gave us five bedrooms by the simple means of using the dining room as a bedroom and eating our meals in the very big kitchen. We four girls appreciated having rooms of our own, and we found ready-made friends among our new neighbours, who included 36 children! We played soccer in the street, rode our bikes, threw frisbees, played skipping-rope games, and caught tadpoles in the creek. Jenny was happy to have some small companions of her own age, and they took turns playing in each other's houses. Debbie and I had an easy walk to the North Epping Primary School, while Lynette had to travel by bus and train to Cheltenham High School.

We joined the Dence Park (Epping) Swimming Club and I got a new coach, Bruce McDonald. He was a big, jovial man who used to train racehorses and sometimes used horseracing terms in his swimming coaching. 'You beat him by a head (or a nose),' he would say. Some of the teenaged boys in the club were good competitive swimmers, including John Cottee, Roger Wyndham and Gary Debus. Gary had suffered from asthma as a child and swam to keep it under control; he became a champion backstroker.

There were trampolines for hire at the Dence Park pool, and the swimming squad earned free turns for picking up chocolate wrappers and other rubbish left lying around. The big boys sometimes helped to clean the pool. In those days it was unheated, and it could get very cold as the sun didn't get to it until late in the morning and shadows fell over it again early in the afternoon. I was a skinny 11-year-old and felt the cold terribly. Some mornings when I dived into the pool it would be so cold it would take my breath away, and I would have to get out after just one lap. I would then spend the rest of the session warming myself up on the trampoline. I got quite good at it, and I can still do a trampoline somersault!

Trampolining to keep warm proved to be a positive, if accidental, addition to my swimming training. It was an early form of what is now called cross training. It is now well recognised that one physical activity benefits another. In becoming a skilled athlete, the brain becomes adept at improving muscle reaction and control. For instance, my ball-handling and catching ability means that I have a good knowledge of my arm's length, which comes in useful in the pool. Bruce McDonald observed that, in addition to keeping me warm, trampolining strengthened my leg muscles and made me generally fitter.

Bruce soon saw that my backstroke was weak. My hips would sink, and I couldn't synchronise my arm-pull. With great patience on his part, and considerable frustration on mine, I finally learned the technique by using a bench and pulleys in the warm pump room.

I started experimenting at this time with vitamin supplements, such as vitamins C and E, and B Complex. Bruce used to say that if they worked for his swimmers, he would use them for his horses!

We trained in the McDonalds' private backyard pool a couple of times a week in the winter. (The pool had been built from racehorse winnings and was kept going with learn-to-swim classes.) Bruce wanted me to do more sessions, but that would have interfered with netball. Lynette and I had joined the local netball club and were again playing on Saturday mornings.

I was chosen to play for a Sydney metropolitan team in the State Netball Championships, which were held in Inverell, a country town about 600 kilometres from Sydney in northern New South Wales. It was a new experience to travel so far by train, and fun to be with girls of my own age in the charge of a teacher. We were billeted with local families, and I was lucky to be staying on a farm. I loved the early-morning mist, the crisp air and the animal smells. The standard of play of the netballers in the competition was very high. I felt I was a middling to good player, but I was pushed to a higher standard by the other girls' skill and competitiveness. It was both scary and exhilarating!

On Sunday mornings, my sisters and I went to Sunday School at the Uniting Church, near Epping railway station. We would wear our best dresses and carry a coin wrapped in a hanky for the collection plate. It was tempting to spend it on cobbers and other sweets at the milk bar near the church instead. We all enjoyed the stories and hymns, though neither Lynette nor I sang very well. One of our Sunday School teachers was Mrs Bonynge, mother of the orchestra conductor, Richard Bonynge, and mother-in-law of the famous opera singer, Dame Joan Sutherland.

At North Epping Primary School, we had a wonderfully helpful librarian who always seemed to know what books would appeal to different children. When she learned that I was especially drawn to books by the Australian authors Colin Thiele, Ivan Southall and Mavis Thorpe Clarke, she made sure they were available for me to borrow. I particularly enjoyed stories about children growing up in unusual places and books about Aboriginal culture. *The Min Min* and *Hill End* were favourites. I would lose myself in the characters and stories.

In 1967 and 1968, my name started to appear in *International Swimmer*, a magazine put out by Speedo, the Australian manufacturer of swimsuits and other sporting goods. Each month the magazine compiled lists of the top ten swimmers, men and women, age-group and open. I could see from these lists which girls were doing similar times to mine. Often I knew these girls from inter-club meets. I couldn't help noticing that many of the top ten girl swimmers belonged to the Ryde Swimming Club and were coached by Forbes Carlile. At the time, I saw swimming as my summer sport and netball as my winter activity. I had no real commitment to either one, other than the fact that I enjoyed them both. And when the rollerskating craze started in the neighbourhood, I got into that, too! We didn't have knee and elbow guards then, so skinned knees patched with bandaids were a frequent fact of life.

I was elected school captain at North Epping Primary School in 1968, my last year there. Sometimes I was called upon to make little speeches to welcome guests or to thank some official person. This seemed an ordinary thing to do and I took it in my stride. I think my physical competence (and receiving ribbons and medals for it) gave me a confidence that translated into social maturity. I was more at ease with adults than with my own age group, whose jokes I often couldn't understand! Lynette has since told me that she felt awkward in dealing with adults, and she used to push me forward in her place when she had to talk to them. I just did what she told me to do, because she was my big sister.

The responsibility that went with being school captain felt natural. I didn't get a buzz from it, because I didn't have to work at my leadership skills. It was the same with my sporting achievements. They came easily. I only got a buzz when I had to work hard at something, like doing well in spelling.

During that final year of primary school, our family exchanged houses for a month with one of Dad's work colleagues in French-speaking Noumea. I was introduced to some new tastes and aspects of the adult world, and I loved it. A friend of Dad's visited regularly and brought us delicious Toblerone chocolate flecked with little pieces of nougat. We played checkers and listened to records by the comedian Bill Cosby, while munching on Toblerone. If this was what being an adult was like, I thought, I can't wait to grow up!

Each day, Lynette and I went to the shop to buy *un pain*, a loaf of French bread. Lyn had studied French at school, so she would do the talking. On one occasion, we visited the Isle of Pines, a former penal colony, for a business dinner with one of Dad's colleagues and ate raw fish under the clear, starry night sky.

As always, we were drawn to the water in Noumea. At one beautiful beach lined with coconut palms, Lynette and I bodysurfed the beach break. She showed me how to catch a wave like a dolphin, by pushing off the bottom in front of the wave so that I could be picked up by its energy and flung out of the face of the wave as it broke. The white water then pushed me along until I was washed up in a tumble with fallen coconuts and cowrie shells on to the sandy beach.

My father had always encouraged his daughters to be physically active and to extend ourselves. He knew how far I could extend myself to the next degree of difficulty without experiencing failure, and he never put me in a situation where I would be harmed or feel disappointed because a goal was too hard to reach. My father's support and encouragement, and his belief that I could do whatever I set myself to do, were essential in developing in me a love of physical activity and a fascination with improving my skills through competition. I even enjoyed exams at school because the results told me objectively what my abilities were. I always looked for external evaluation, that could only come from testing.

There was no boy-child in our family to make a coalition with our father. We were never told that 'only boys can do that'. Gender was absent in Dad's attitude to us. He would often pronounce, 'Goulds can do anything they want to do' and 'Goulds can be the best in the world if they want to be'. He didn't say 'girls', he said 'Goulds'. Dad had always played with us kids a lot, teaching us ball-handling skills and sharpening our reflexes with indoor games. But water sports were his real love, and he was delighted that his children shared his enjoyment.

Ours was a healthily functioning family. We children felt secure in the knowledge that our parents were responsible for us. We always felt able to talk about anything, to be spontaneous and uninhibited. We were encouraged to express all our emotions — anger, frustration, sadness and jealousy, as well as joy, admiration and compassion. We were taught how to solve problems for ourselves and to take on responsibilities. And, as we grew, we were encouraged, especially by Mum, to become more independent. And independent I did become, perhaps more so than other girls of my age.

CHAPTER 6

Training and Competing

Keep up your training, Shane. Who knows?
Maybe you'll make the Olympics one day!

~

Denise Spencer, 1948 Olympian and swim instructor

IN EARLY 1969, Dad got a transfer with Pan Am and our family moved from Sydney to Brisbane. This time, Mum insisted on building a house. All our previous houses were ready-built or too small. Our big, two-storey, five-bedroom house, with a large playroom downstairs, was in the new suburb of Jindalee, situated on a bend in the meandering Brisbane River.

I started high school, with Lynette, at Indooroopilly High School, but neither of us really settled in and after one term we switched to St Peter's Lutheran College, across the road. It was a smaller school, more personal, and we were very happy there.

There was a 50-metre pool at Jindalee and the Gould girls naturally gravitated to it. Denise Henderson (formerly Spencer), who taught the junior swimmers, knew about me and the times I was doing through *International Swimmer*, as well as through the Brisbane paper, the *Courier-Mail*. She was very encouraging: 'Keep up your training, Shane. Who knows? Maybe you'll make the Olympics one day!'

Before she was married, as Denise Spencer, she had swum for Australia at the London Olympics in 1948. 'The Olympics are an incredible experience,' she told me. 'One that you never forget. But remember, you can't eat medals.'

At Denise's suggestion, I joined the Fortitude Valley Swim Club, where the coach, Gordon Peterson, had a squad of advanced swimmers doing good times. The Valley was in Brisbane's city area, so I would take a train after school, then walk a kilometre to the pool. After the session, Dad would pick me up.

I was 12, and was growing quickly and getting stronger. The older, more advanced swimmers in Gordon's squad made the level of swimming harder, and I did my best to keep up with them. One of the squad was Brad Cooper, who went on to win a gold medal at Munich in the 400 metres freestyle. During the 18 months I was in the squad, my times improved and I won many age-group events, swimming in the maroon colours of Queensland. My best effort was to lower my 100 metres freestyle time to 1.01.9 in March 1970, when I was 13.

I was also growing up. I got my first period, and I started going to school dances and kissing boys behind the classrooms. In July 1969 we all sat in the science room for three hours and watched the first man land on the moon. Life was pretty good in Brisbane — the water was warm, we lived in a big, cool house, and I was enjoying school.

Then, disaster! Dad changed jobs and moved to the Australian carrier East West Airlines. It meant a return to Sydney! I was dismayed by the loss of friends, school, squad and coach. I had become aware of how important swimming was to me and how very much I wanted to do well at it. I put on a bit of an act with Dad, and then struck a bargain with him. 'If I have to go back to Sydney, I want to swim with Forbes Carlile at the Ryde Club.'

Dad warned me that this would mean harder training, and giving up my social life and netball. But I was sure. I wanted to train with outstanding swimmers like Karen Moras, Jane Comerford, Diana Rickard, Gail Neall, Buddy Portier and Paul Jarvie. They were all from Forbes's squad, and all six were selected for the 1970 Commonwealth Games team in Edinburgh.

Some of the Queensland officials had hinted that I might have a good chance of being selected in the team also. I went to Sydney for the trials in the North Sydney Olympic Pool. It was all so important and exciting, and I tried too hard. I was thinking of the result, rather than the process, and was expecting to do well on pure talent alone. I came fourth or fifth, with my rough, thrashing stroke and limited top-level competition experience, and wasn't chosen for the team. But I now had an idea of what top-level swimming was about. I realised that success required better skills, more race practice and better mental preparation. I was still a novice. What none of us could have predicted, though, was that I was in such a rush to improve, I bettered their times in meets at home while the Commonwealth Games team was away.

We bought a house in North Ryde after determining that its location was equidistant from the outdoor 50-metre pool at Ryde and the 25-metre indoor pool at Pymble, both of which were used by the Carlile swimmers. I had got my way with Dad: I could join the Ryde Swimming Club and be coached by Forbes. Dad worked in the city, so the location suited him, too.

My parents checked out the background of my chosen coach. He had been in the Australian Olympic team at Helsinki in 1952, competing in the modern pentathlon. He had lectured in human physiology at Sydney University, working with that great researcher, Professor Frank Cotton, before he became a professional coach in 1955. He had trained several world-record holders and was recognised for using scientific methods to back up his theoretical approach to swimming. His wife, Ursula, was a physical education teacher and a partner in coaching.

I began at North Ryde High School, but after a few months we moved house again — this time to West Pymble. We didn't fit into the neighbourhood in North Ryde. I made one good friend, though — an English girl, a new migrant, who was having a hard time adapting to the climate and ways of Australia. Her parents were also struggling with new jobs and living in a crowded apartment with other migrants while trying to find their way in this new and very different country. My friend was often sad. I suppose she was homesick.

Lynette and I switched to Turramurra High School, where Gail Neall was a year ahead of me. The school was surrounded by natural bushland, which we used for cross-country running in phys ed. On hot summer days, the cicadas would be shrilling noisily outside, while in the unairconditioned classroom our sweaty legs stuck to the chairs and our sweaty hands left smudges on our books.

Swimming for the Ryde Club and being coached by Forbes Carlile was exactly what I had wanted. I fitted in with the routines of the training programs, and Forbes, or his assistants Tom Green and Henry Wagner, explained the purpose of the particular routines. Forbes also put out a newsletter every week and we thoroughly got the message that swimming fast only happened through strength and endurance — that is, miles and miles of training. Forbes had a number of motivational signs up around the walls of the Pymble pool. One of them was: 'Miles swum regularly makes champions.' Another one, a big green sign with yellow writing, said: 'We don't make champions but create an atmosphere where champions are inevitable.' When the Pymble pool was demolished in 1983, the sign was souvenired by Mark Morgan, a Commonwealth Games champion and now head coach of the Carlile club. He offered it for auction at a testimonial dinner for Forbes and Ursula on the Queensland Gold Coast in 1996. The sign was bought by Laurie Lawrence, extrovert coach of Olympic swimmers, for $2000.

I liked having a logbook to complete each day and to hand in each week. It was terrific to get weekly written feedback in addition to the daily verbal evaluations and encouragement. Forbes was collecting scientific data through our subjective evaluation of our experiences. We learned to take our resting heart rate each morning — about 38–42 bpm for me — and to time our recovery heart rate after effort, by placing two fingers on the carotid artery in the neck. Sometimes I could get my heart rate up to 210 bpm. After a minute, it would drop to 90 bpm. The quick recovery was a good sign of fitness. The most looked-at piece of equipment was the pace clock, an invention Forbes created in the 1950s when he was developing interval training with Professor Frank Cotton. Using Forbes's clock taught me about pacing and timing in competition — in training we did sets of short rest repeats, for instance, 16 x 50-metre laps with a ten-second rest between each lap.

I thrived on the training methods, the logbook gave me feedback on training, the squad was eager and competitive, and the coaches motivated me with their encouragement. The whole environment enabled me to focus on what was now becoming clear to me. I wanted to be an Olympic swimmer. The next Games were at Munich — only two years away.

My training program was aimed at doing 40 miles (64 kilometres) a week. This distance was considered a hefty task for a teenager in the 1970s. Forbes was known for his 'miles miles miles' philosophy, with which many people disagreed. But the program had already been modified from the one he had used with his swimmers in the late 1960s. A number of Forbes's older male swimmers training for water polo and surf-lifesaving competitions felt that they were overtraining. The young girls, however, seemed to thrive on Forbes's scientifically calculated programs of speed through endurance.

In a note in my logbook for 6 February 1972, Forbes, with his distinctive use of capitals for important words, wrote of my mileage in the pool:

. . . there are few top swimmers in the world doing as much . . .
The key is COOLNESS and a good ROUTINE. We can never say
for certain when your GREAT times will come. When you are FIT
(& this should be all the time) IT IS IN YOUR MIND! Keep the
right muscles strong with dynastatics.

Forbes was always telling me to do more resistance training with my dynastatic machine at home, but I had trouble doing it for even five minutes. I just didn't like doing it. And I was often tired and sore. My training sessions lasted for two hours (4.45 to 7 am and 4 to 6 pm). Another hour was taken up by travelling and getting changed. Seven hours of the day (8.30 am to 3.30 pm) were allocated to going to school. I had eight or nine hours of sleep at night. This left me with four hours for eating, doing homework and chores, and watching TV.

The very tight structure of those days helped me to value time. Every minute of the day was important. Every day I made my bed, put my dirty clothes in the laundry, did my homework and packed my school bag ready for the next day; at weekends, I vacuumed and dusted my room. The routine and the fine organisation of time seemed to suit me.

Occasionally there would be a break in the routine, for a night out or having visitors. And sometimes, when they could see I was very tired from a heavy training schedule, Mum or Dad would turn off my alarm clock and let me sleep in. They would ring Forbes and let him know I would be having a morning off.

My usual routine was to set the alarm for 4.27 am. After taking my early-morning heart rate, I would get up, make my bed, put on my swimsuit and tracksuit, and try to leave the house without waking anyone. Libby, our Beagle, would start barking when I came out, but I could quieten her by slipping her a dog biscuit. By the time she had munched it, I was walking down the drive and getting into Forbes's big V8 station wagon. He would pick me up most mornings, as it meant making only a small detour on his way to the pool. Some mornings, if I was early or Forbes was late, I enjoyed the silence and anticipation of the new day. The sky glowed with stars and I learned to recognise the Southern Cross. The city lights glowed on the horizon. On chilly mornings, I would blow steam rings into the crisp morning air. I love that time of the day.

The pool at Pymble was only 25 metres in length and had six lanes. When we arrived in the early morning, there was often a mist floating above the glassy surface. I liked diving in first, breaking the stillness. After half an hour the surface would be a boiling cauldron, with arms and legs flailing in the thick, steamy air. One morning, I took part in an international television program done for the United Nations Children's Fund. It was called 'Children of the World', and its purpose was to show what children all around the world were doing at a particular time. Danny Kaye, the American entertainer, hosted the program, and I talked to him via satellite from the edge of the pool. It was remarkable, later, to see what children elsewhere had been doing. Some were at school, others were going to bed, or playing games in the street or helping to collect food. It captured my imagination and expanded my world by giving me a window into other children's lives.

In training, we had to keep to the left of the lane and swim one behind the other. The fastest swimmer went first, and the rest dragged behind in the bubbles, leaving at five-second intervals. The program for each session was written in chalk on a blackboard at the end of the pool. The morning program had more long distances, such as 8 x 400 metres doing one every six minutes or 4 x 800 metres every 12 minutes. Swimming 8 x 400 means 400 metres, eight times, starting the next lap six minutes after the start of the previous one, and having maybe one to one-and-a-half minutes' rest. The faster you swam, the more rest you had. One aim in doing these repeats was to try to maintain a constant speed for each one. Another variation was to 'negative split': swim the second half faster than the first half. Yet another variation was to do each one just a little faster than the previous one, building speed, to learn to judge pace. The coach might write on the board this abbreviation: 8 x 200 freestyle (4), build. Swimmers are good at mental maths; counting laps, doing subtraction to calculate times, converting metres to miles — all distances then were measured in miles — and multiplying to get heart rate per minute. Swimming training is much more than the boring same pace for lap after lap. There is lots of room for creativity in designing interesting training programs.

The afternoon sessions had more people, often ten to a lane, so we did shorter repeats like 16 x 100 metres, one every two minutes, or 30 x 50 metres every minute. Otherwise the last, slowest swimmer would be overtaken. I would often swallow chlorinated water from the chop, or get bruised arms from hitting another swimmer. On one occasion, I got a split lip from a paddle (used to build arm muscles) when I lifted my head to assess an opportunity to overtake. Amazingly, this was the only injury I sustained in swimming — I never suffered from any joint or muscle strain problems.

At the weekends there were club races, held at Pymble in the winter. They always started with the under eight-year-olds, so the open swimmers had to sit around, waiting their turn. We talked, gossiped, played cards, flirted and told jokes. Then I discovered crochet. I think Jane Comerford taught me. One winter season, we all made woollen caps and scarves. I taught my sister Debbie how to crochet, and she then taught our youngest sister, Jenny.

Nineteen seventy-one was an amazing year for me in the pool. It started off with the NSW Swimming Championships, when I won the four freestyle events and the 200 metres individual medley. Then, in February, at the Australian National Championships held in Hobart, I won the 100, 200 and 400 metres freestyle events and the individual medley. In March, at the Girls Secondary School Swimming Carnival, I went under the minute for the 100 metres freestyle, the second woman in Australia to do so — 59.7. I was thrilled! Dawn Fraser's world record of 58.9 was now in view!

Many of the times I swam — I've forgotten which — were Australian records. As a result of doing so well, I was selected for a four-week European tour in April — a tour designed to give Australian swimmers a taste of international competition. Those on the team were considered as Olympic hopefuls for Munich in August 1972.

The first meet was at the Crystal Palace, London. I hoped to swim against Gabriele Wetzco of East Germany; she was then the fastest sprinter in the world. This was a prestigious meet, the stadium was packed to capacity, and there was world television coverage. I was swimming for Australia for the first time, and the significance and responsibility of doing this was very much on my mind.

My 100 metres freestyle win in 58.9 surprised everyone. This was Dawn Fraser's world record, set in 1964. I had equalled it, and joined her on the pedestal I had put her on in my imagination. My surprise was tinged with awe. I felt I had somehow gone beyond my limits. The evidence was there, checked by three timekeepers. I *had* to believe it.

Later I found that I wasn't the only one who was surprised. Forbes had estimated that I might be able to achieve Dawn Fraser's time when I was 16. Coaching experts believed that young swimmers were capable of distance swimming, but sprinting? That was another story. A good sprinter needed physical and mental maturity! So much for the theory.

The next day offered competition with Debbie Myer, the American holder of the world record in the 200 metres freestyle event. Karen Moras had broken the 400 metres freestyle record on the same day I had equalled Dawn Fraser's record. I didn't know that Debbie was out of form, so I put all I could into the race and beat her convincingly. The time proved to be a new world record — 2.06.5. This felt for me like my own record.

I tried to take it all in, as people came up to congratulate me. I had done something that had never been done before; I had joined an elite group. My record might go the next day, but for now it was mine alone. Excitement ran high around me. There was a lot of noise, with people clapping and cheering. I was bewildered. I didn't know what to do in the situation, and I didn't know how to express my happiness. Tears came to my eyes, and I wiped my face with my towel. An observant photographer captured the moment.

The media were in attendance, having been alerted by the events of the previous day. A film made that day was shown around the world several times in the following weeks. The newspapers pictured me as a shy, tearful girl, hiding her face in her towel. I had just come for a good swim, and I had had it.

After the race came the interviews, with questions that were difficult to answer. I had no idea what times I might swim when I was grown up, or what events I would swim in at the Olympics, if I got there. Dad had told me always to be polite to the people of the media. And Mum had told me that fame was fleeting and not to let it go to my head. I was still on a high, and don't recall what I said on that occasion. The interviews went on for so long that the manager had to get the rest of the team back to the hotel, and I was left behind to make my own way there.

When I got back to the hotel, everyone had gone to a dance. After the cheering of the crowds, the intensity of the media interviews and the huge sense of achievement I'd experienced, I suddenly felt let down and very alone. I had never known loneliness before. I lay on my bed and cried buckets of tears. It was both a necessary emotional release and a taste of how isolating an extraordinary experience can be.

After a while, Brad Cooper came back to the hotel and persuaded me to join the others at the dance. I was glad to go with him. Mischief was in the air at the dance, and someone poured alcoholic

Left: At four years of age in Willoughby, Sydney, 1960. My grandfather, Clive Reid, often used to call me a Mexican jumping bean. It was only swimming that used up my abundant energy.

Below: The Gould family outside 'Goulds' Bure', Nadi Airport, 1962. Lynette is aged seven, me five and Debbie 20 months. I used to hide my shoes under the bushes to the left, so I didn't have to wear them to school!

Above: The Miranda Magpies netball team, 1966. I'm at the far left, aged nine. My positions were goal defence or goal attack.

Left: North Epping primary school captain, 1968.

Right: Backyard golf in West Pymble, 1971. Check out the sunglasses, clogs and mini skirt!

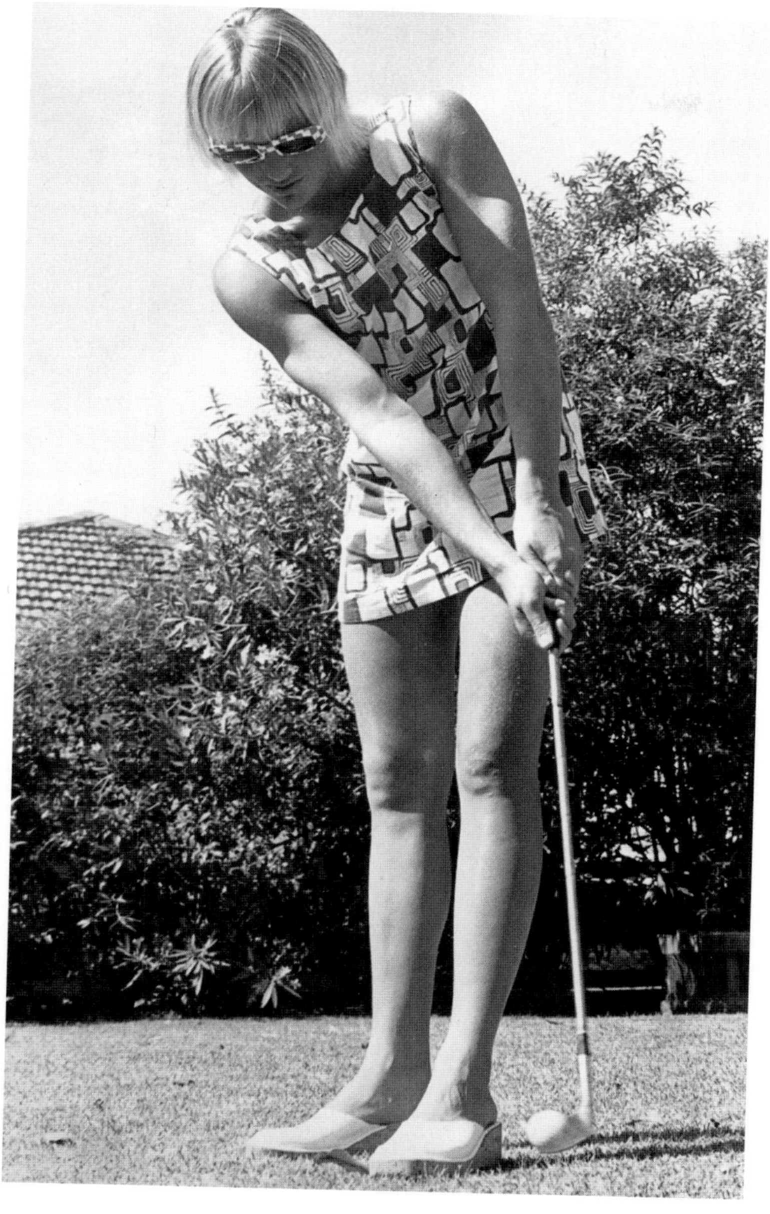

The Herald and Weekly Times

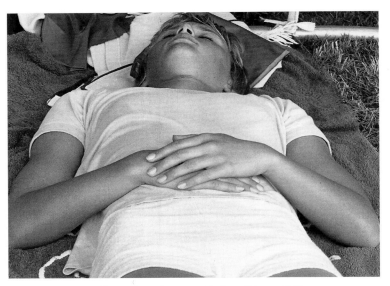

West Pymble, 1971. I didn't really like doing dry-land exercises, but they helped specific swimming muscles. I should have done more of them ...

Withdrawing into myself to 'psych up' for a race in Brisbane, February 1972.

At the Olympic trials in Brisbane, February 1972. I had braces on my teeth for 18 months —
they were removed just before the Games in August that year.

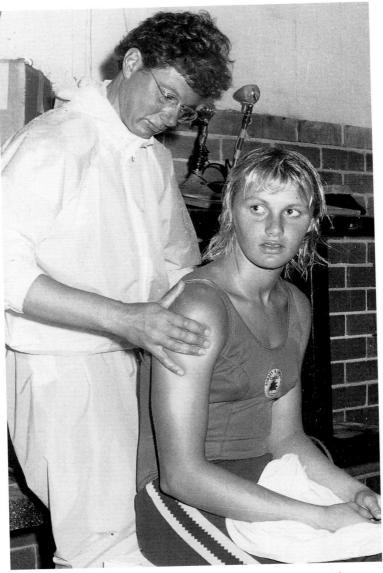

Ursula Carlile massaging my sore shoulders (bliss) before a race at North Sydney pool,
January 1972.

A pre-competition pep-talk from coach Don Talbot (left) at the Munich Games, August 1972. From right: Brad Cooper, me and Michael Wenden.

Signing an autograph immediately after breaking the 100m freestyle world record at North Sydney pool, January 1972.

'Why didn't they tell me the race was going to begin?' With tears in my eyes, embarrassed that I had held up the live TV coverage of the 100m freestyle world-record attempt by waiting in the pump room of North Sydney pool, January 1972.

At Sydney airport, 11 August 1972, departing for Munich. From left: Lynette, Leah Housman, a schoolfriend who designed the fish I use with my autograph, me and Michelle Trotter, my best friend from the Fiji days.

With my sister Jenny, holding medals at an airport press conference upon arrival home from the Munich Games.

The Melbourne reception at the MCG (it was the VFL final) upon my return to Australia from Munich in September 1972. My three sisters are in the car, too.

At the MCG reception. From left: me, Mum, Debbie, Jenny, Lynette and Dad.

Patting the police horses at the welcome-home reception, MCG, September 1972. I was happy to have a distraction from being the focus of the football crowd of about 100 000 people.

A family holiday in Port Macquarie after the Olympics, December 1972.
From left: Debbie, Dad, Jenny, Lynette, me and Mum.

Aussie swimmers at Crystal Palace, London, April 1973. From left: Stephen Badger,
Brad Cooper, coach Laurie Lawrence, me, Gail Neall and Bev Whitfield.

Just after I became ABC-TV Sportsman of the Year, Sydney, January 1973. From left: ABC-TV Chairman Mr Duckmanton, me, Dad, Mum and sports commentator, Norman May.

Being interviewed at Los Altos, California, May 1973. Swimming pace clocks like this were invented by Forbes Carlile and Professor Frank Cotton in the 1950s.

My wedding on 15 June 1975 to Neil Innes of Perth, Western Australia.

Cactus the dog, Neil and me in Perth, March 1976. Note my very blonde surfer's hair, shell necklace and homemade calico skirt.

At the opening of the Busselton High School 25m pool, 1976, with my halterneck swimsuit from the local op-shop. I didn't own any racing bathers at the time.

Above: Inside the farmhouse in Margaret River, August 1978, breastfeeding baby Joel. We used a kerosene pressure lamp (shown in the foreground) for lighting for seven years.

Right: Arriving in Darwin for an Olympic fundraising dinner. This was my first visit to the magnificent Top End of Australia, October 1998.

drinks for me. The team manageress noticed what was happening and got me away before I got drunk. I slept a sound and dreamless sleep that night.

During the swim meet in London, I had a visit from a lovely old English gentleman who had exchanged Christmas cards with my grandfather, Poppa Reid, for 20 years. Captain Grattidge was the retired captain of that famous old ship, the *Queen Mary*. I was honoured that he had come to see me. Poppa had written to tell him that I was swimming in London. I also met Rolf Harris, a childhood favourite of mine. He sat with the Australian team on the pool deck. I felt shy talking to him, but I listened to what he said to the older kids. Rolf had been a state-level swimmer in Western Australia in the 1950s. Laurie Lawrence was also there as a spectator. He got us all feeling very patriotic about being Australian by singing a rowdy song during and after the races.

We were taken on a tour of London, and history came alive for me: the Thames, the Tower of London, London Bridge, Buckingham Palace, and the hangout of the hippies, Carnaby Street. We ate Yorkshire pudding and were kept awake by the eerie twilight lasting until 11 pm. I ate my first Mars Bar in London. They hadn't yet come to Australia.

The team went on to France, Sweden, West Germany, Italy and Greece. Some sightseeing tours were fitted in between meets and training sessions. The one that I particularly enjoyed was a boat ride down the Rhine. I listened closely to the commentary, fascinated by the stories of castles being built on the river bends so as to prevent pirates from attacking from the river. It was all so long ago, and yet those fortified castles were there in front of me.

In Halsinborg, in Sweden, we swam in a saltwater pool. Steam rose from the warm water into the cold air and obscured the end of the pool. We also had a sauna, followed by a very cold dip in the icy fjord water next to it. We experienced the passion of French sports fans in

Marseilles when the Australian women narrowly won the 4 x 100 metres freestyle relay. We ate ravioli in Padua, in Italy, where I swam 59.5 in a four-lane 25-metre pool. We boated down the canals of Venice, and I imagined ancient gladiatorial contests in the Colosseum in Rome. I marvelled at the Vatican, and sat on the marble steps of the Parthenon in Athens, pretending to debate democracy. In Bonn, in West Germany, we met the Australian ambassador and stayed in the Beethoven Hotel. I swam some good freestyle times in a short-course pool — 58.1 for the 100 metres and 4.16.2 for the 400 metres. My logbook says, 'Magic did it!'

In these meets, I was meeting and racing against swimmers who would be my rivals the next year at Munich. This was my first visit to Europe, and I loved the historic buildings and the local food. I made some tentative attempts to speak German, which I was studying at school. That whole tour was a wonderful history and geography lesson for me.

Three months later, in July, I had a few more days off school to go with a small Australian team to Santa Clara, California. My parents made the trip too. (Low-cost travel was a benefit of working in the airline industry.) The Santa Clara Swimming Club arranged an International meet, inviting swimmers from Australia and Russia to compete against Americans. The event was one of the club's fundraising projects (another was selling fireworks for the Fourth of July). This enterprising club hired their coach, George Haines, for the summer season.

Individual families hosted the swimmers, and I stayed with the Ciabattari family. Gene and Marian Ciabattari had five children, Janet and Lori being about my age. We got on so well together that we wanted the visit to last longer. Dad joked, 'OK, another day here if you get a world record'. It seems so much like child's-play now. Today, the breaking of a world record would mean lucrative prize-money and highly paid commercial endorsements. As it happened, I did break the world record for the 400 metres freestyle (in the time of 4.21.1) — a record that Karen Moras had held. And I got the reward I wanted — to stay another day in California with the Ciabattaris!

Marian Ciabattari was a relative of the Mariani family, with whom I would stay in 1973. The family owned large orchards and fruit-processing plants in the Santa Clara Valley. Their products were exported as dried fruit or as fruit confectionery.

Between events at this meet, I was excited to meet the singer Bing Crosby, who had come along as an interested spectator; we had a pleasant chat together.

There was also a photographer who asked if he could take some underwater photographs, saying he was going to make a film about me. It turned out that he was really a spy for the American Swimming Association, and the film was to be analysed so that any secrets about my strokes could be used to improve American swimming. I never did see that film!

The Russians also seemed very interested in me. Their coach, a short, squarish lady, asked Mum in halting English about my daily routines.

Competing at the Santa Clara International meet was really important preparation for Munich. I was able to experience what it was like to compete under pressure, with lots of distractions and swimming against some very good American girls. Before the 400 metres, I was feeling very nervous and scared. Karen Moras, the world-record holder, was in the race and a lot of attention was on us both. Debbie Myer, the past world-record holder, and Nancy Spitz, a fast sprinter and sister of world champion Mark Spitz, were also competing.

The following day I swam and won the 200 metres freestyle, but I was so distracted by the festive atmosphere that I forgot to put my cap on. I had a lot to learn.

Two other famous names in swimming, American Donna de Verona and Australian Murray Rose, became real-life people for me when I met them at the poolside. (Murray was then working in America.)

At the party at the end of the meet, we were provided with a feast. There were cooked meats of all kinds, plus the most magnificent apricots and strawberries I have ever seen. The Russians, especially, couldn't believe their eyes.

The wonderful tour ended, and I got back into my school, home and swimming routines in Sydney. I had some weight to lose, like at the end of all my overseas and interstate trips. I seemed to battle to stay at a lean racing weight. At 172 centimetres in height, 58 kilograms was my best weight.

Winter training was all done at Pymble pool, where the water was warm. My strokes were improving, and Forbes had given up trying to change my kick from what looked like a lazy, balancing two-beat, to the more usual thrashing six-beat kick. He decided to leave well alone, while encouraging me to use the six-beat kick at the end of a race. 'And don't glide in, Shane. Push towards the wall,' he frequently advised me.

The Australian summer swimming season opened early in October, and we were then back into top-level meets, which were arranged by the NSW Swimming Association. These meets were held to enable swimmers to qualify for State Championships. Correct procedures were followed, and the officials were all fully accredited. There were three events each night unless it was the longer 800 or 1500 metres. I usually swam in all the events, whether it was the breast stroke, medley or backstroke, 100 metres or 200 metres — I did them all. Apart from the swimmers and the officials, the only spectators were parents or friends who had acted as chauffeurs for the competitors. Their main interest was to see their child swim, collect the official timekeeper's card, and then go home as quickly as possible.

The meets were often held at Drummoyne Olympic Pool, located almost under Iron Cove Bridge which spans one of Sydney Harbour's many bays. The water was often cold and the venue wasn't covered, but the races went on even if it was raining. Families took raincoats and umbrellas, rugs, scarves and woolly caps. The little shop sold hot drinks and meat pies.

At the end of 1971 and into January 1972, I had a world-record-breaking spree: three world records at the top-level meets and one at the State Championships. Looking back on it now, it was as though my life was in fast forward. It was an extraordinary five weeks.

The meet scheduled for 26 November was planned for all age groups to swim 200 metres freestyle. I had my 15th birthday during the week, which I celebrated by going to the Australian Grand Prix on the Sunday with my boyfriend, John Williams, who was also a training partner at Pymble pool. I was in full training (35 miles that week, 40 the week before) and still at school all day.

On the day of the meet, I had been at training at 4.45 am. I came home for breakfast complaining about feeling lethargic and slow in the water. I went to school for the day, had a fried rice meal at 4.30, and then went to bed for an hour's rest. I must have gone right off to sleep. Mum woke me at 6.30 to ask if I still wanted to go to the meet, or whether I would prefer to have a night off. I decided to go.

I'd missed out on the warm-up swim at 5.30, so I used my exercise pulleys instead. On the blocks, I felt I might lose my balance and topple in for a false start, so I rocked back on my heels just as the starter's gun went off. All the swimmers had hit the water before I had even started my dive! The referee called for the false-start rope to be lowered, but it stuck. By the time it was lowered, all the swimmers were clear and I found myself in the lead. I felt so ashamed of being left behind on the blocks, that I just put my head down and let adrenalin work for me. As I came into the turn for the last 50 metres, I heard lots of noise: it was cheering!

At the end of the race, the timekeepers went into a huddle to compare their stopwatches. It was then announced on the public-address system that I had broken the world record with 2.05.8. Wow! What a surprise that was! I thought I had botched that race. What a way to win a world record!

The next morning, I participated in the Ryde club's annual swimathon, where I swam 5000 metres in 60.35. After another three-mile training session in the afternoon, I went to a party at a training mate's place on the coast. It was certainly a busy and successful weekend.

I continued to train hard. Forbes was sure that I could better my time for the 800 metres freestyle, which was scheduled for 3 December. He also advised me to 'really go for the 1500 metres' on 12 December and get it behind me. He was pleased with the way I was handling the media. In my logbook, he wrote: 'Your interview with Channel 9 was excellent. You did yourself great credit, Shane.'

I was particularly keen to do well in the 800 metres freestyle time trial, maybe even beat the existing world record for that distance, because my 'uncle', Lew Hoad, and his wife Jenny had come along to see me swim and to talk about old times with my parents. Just before the race, I shared Lew's meat pie with him — matching him bite for bite through that sloppy, spicy meat encased in rich pastry with tomato sauce swirled on top. Suddenly, I heard myself being called to the marshalling area. I hurried down to the starting blocks, wriggling out of my tracksuit as I ran. I just made it in time for the start of the race. With half a meat pie lying undigested in my stomach, the 16 laps of the pool were rather hard going, but the result was great: a world-record swim — 800 metres in 8.58.1! A very sweet sequel to this race was receiving a card of congratulations from the American swimmer, Anne Simmons, who had been the previous holder of the record.

The last top-level meet for the year was the 1500 metres swim. It was held in Sydney's south-western suburb of Birrong, more than an hour's drive from home. The swimmers from this area had been travelling to Drummoyne, so the venue was more convenient for them on this occasion. The race was to be held on a Sunday evening: the previous meets had all been on Friday nights. Because quite a lot of fuss had been made about my record swims, a big crowd of people came to watch this race. Watching a 1500-metre race, 30 laps of the pool, can be rather tedious for the onlookers. The laps aren't swum at a sprinting pace; the swimmers need to settle into a rhythm and avoid going out too fast, which would leave no energy for the later laps. I really appreciated the spectators — the older people still in their lawn bowls uniforms, the parents who had brought their toddlers in pyjamas and dressing-gowns, and the journalists and TV crews. These people were behind me, I knew, and I wanted to do my best to justify their interest.

It was a pleasure to swim that evening. My stroking felt good, and the 30 laps felt easy. I was swimming with assurance. The water was my friend, carrying me along. I was in rhythm and harmony. The big surprise was that this swim resulted in a world record that was 18 seconds better than the previous one held by the American, Cathy Calhoun.

Forbes wrote in my logbook afterwards: 'The 1500m was wonderful . . . P.S. I meant to tell you Shane that we believe you have handled press TV etc wonderfully well. You well deserve the popularity you have earned with these people.'

More and more of my time was being taken up by the press and media. On 13 December, I was filmed and interviewed at home and at the Ryde pool; and the next day, *The Women's Weekly* took some photos at the pool. I also made a public appearance at a city bookstore later in the week. My logbook records all my activities: I trained, raced, went sailing with my boyfriend and partying with school friends, and slept as much as I could. At the end of the week I wasn't feeling too good. My chest was sore, I felt dopey, and I had a bad cold and an irregular heartbeat. I went to the doctor, who said I was overtired and gave me a sedative. She advised complete bed rest for me. In two days, I slept for 30 hours.

I was unaware of how tired my body was becoming. It took me more than a week to recover — a week filled with end-of-school-year activities, a lot of interviews, and several requests to open fetes or to appear on TV shows. Our postman brought over 100 letters, mostly from fans offering congratulations and requesting autographed photos. During this time, my parents switched to an unlisted telephone number.

So, here I was at the end of 1971. It had been my year for breaking records. I'd been on a roll. I had equalled the great Dawn Fraser's 100 metres freestyle record, then gone on to break the 200 (twice), 400, 800 and 1500 metres world records. It had been a year of training, training, training, and competing, competing, competing. I had given everything to swimming. And my support crew had given me all the help I needed.

At 14, my life seemed to be happening at an accelerated pace. One event followed immediately on the heels of another, so that they were no longer separate enough to savour individually. They became a collage.

I had had some great invitations during the year. Some I accepted; most I didn't. In August, I had been invited to go to South Africa with my coach either to compete or to do demonstration swims. My parents were against it because of South Africa's apartheid policy, and the Australian Swimming Association declared that it might infringe on my amateur status in some way. I didn't go.

~

After a family holiday up the coast at Yamba and Avoca with Narnie and Poppa Reid for Christmas, I prepared for the State

Championships in early January 1972. The media had taken up the possibility of my breaking the 100 metres freestyle world record. The 100 metres for men and women was scheduled for the first night.

When we arrived at the pool for the finals, we couldn't believe our eyes. It was hard to get a parking spot because there were so many people there before us. The usual small group of mainly swimmers and their families had swollen to an enormous crowd. People were actually in long queues. TV vans were positioning themselves, and there was a lot of noise and excitement. The North Sydney Olympic Pool is located almost under the northern end of the Harbour Bridge. I was told later that some of the people who were turned away went up on to the footway of the bridge in order to catch a glimpse of the races in the pool. It was scary to know that these people had come to see a world record and that I was the one they expected would do it!

Live TV was still quite a novelty then, and especially outside broadcasting. My race had been marshalled when I was told that it was being held off for ten minutes because the TV station wasn't ready. I told an official that I would be in the pump room, away from the crowds and where it was warm. I needed to have some peace so that I could psych myself up. It was rather noisy, because the pool pumps and filters were purring away, and I didn't hear the call for the race to start. A very agitated official finally found me calmly getting mentally ready. He said, 'Everyone's on the blocks waiting for you!' 'Why didn't they tell me?' I asked accusingly. I felt totally embarrassed. I raced out, tore my tracksuit off and stood at the back of the blocks, my heart racing and tears welling in my eyes. There was an electric silence. I had nearly missed the race everyone had come to see! Through great mental effort I blocked out the distractions, steadied my internal chaos and took a deep breath. I was ready, but only just.

I did manage the world record that everyone, including me, wanted on that night. The race was shown live on television, and the news of the record was broadcast at other sporting venues that night. My cousin, Ken Allen, heard the result while he was at the car races. My time was 58.5. I now held all five freestyle world records from 100 metres to 1500 metres. I was very happy. 'AT LAST!!!' I wrote in my logbook.

Recently I watched the video footage of this race on Webster's CD-Rom, 'History of Sport in Australia'. I saw that most of the race was swum in a panic. My dive was short and shallow and with very little glide, and my head was too high in the first 50 metres. It was surprising that it resulted in a world record. Then again, maybe it was the adrenalin rush that did it.

What I learned from this race, and from the rest of that year, was: I could swim fast; I felt uncomfortable being the centre of attention, though I also liked it; I was very newsworthy; and there were some compulsory extras that came with being 'famous'.

That same month, I attended the ABC Sportsman of the Year awards, and it was announced that I was the Sportsman of the Year for 1971. The award included any prizes to the value of $100. I chose a radio-cassette player. I was honoured and thrilled. In the excitement of the moment, and unaccustomed to making impromptu speeches on live television, I forgot the name of the chairman of the ABC who had presented me with the award. I said, 'Thank you, Mr ...' then paused for what felt like an eternity. I tried to get my memory to function, but it had shut down! The compere, Norman May, stepped in and said 'Duckmanton'. I smiled and carried on with my short acceptance speech, my heart pounding. I got away with it, but I was determined to be more prepared next time. From then on, whenever I went to an awards dinner or sports function, I took a written speech and wrote down the names of the VIPs. After a while I didn't need to write it all down, but I mentally prepared something to say and read the program thoroughly.

Besides this Australian award, sports writers from many countries voted me as their Sportsman of the Year. At 3 o'clock one morning a

Sydney journalist rang to inform my sleepy father that *Pravda* had just declared me the Russian Sportsman of the Year. France gave me their prestigious Academy of Sports award and two airline tickets to Paris to receive it. I didn't go, but the Australian ambassador in France accepted it on my behalf.

~

On 16 February, at the National Championships, the Australian swimming team for the Munich Olympics was announced. Two years earlier, I had missed out on being included in the team going to Edinburgh for the Commonwealth Games. But I now had the style, the fitness, and some of the fastest times in the world for the five individual events and two relays that I was entered for at Munich.

Over the next two months, I averaged 20 miles a week in training and competed in events in Brisbane, Adelaide and Dunedin, New Zealand. At the end of March, I had a two-week break from training, which included a week-long family holiday in Fiji. We were accompanied by a Channel 7 camera crew, and I swam a demonstration 100 metres in Suva.

As the Olympics got closer, more media from all over the world were in Australia doing pre-Games stories. I was on their rounds. Training was intense, with 40 miles a week over ten or 11 sessions. I was on the home run for Munich. I felt excited and focused, and a little weary of the public responsibilities.

As final preparation for Munich, the Australian swimming team attended a compulsory six-week camp at Scarborough, just north of Brisbane. It was aimed at last-minute fitness and stroke correction, and we worked with the country's best coaches. We were also fitted out with our Olympic uniforms. The girls had bright yellow wool dresses with a dropped waistline and pleated miniskirt, a dark green blazer and a cute little hat. We all had green and gold tracksuits, and a rather strange wrap-around garment that looked like a dressing-gown. (I was to wear mine to hospital six years later for the birth of my first baby!)

As a potential winner of five gold medals, I was highly sought after by the visiting media. I sensed that some of my team-mates were a little jealous of the attention I was getting, and I became self-conscious about it. Nevertheless, the camp gave me a good feeling about being part of a team. On 11 August 1972, we boarded our plane in Sydney, bound for Europe and the Olympic Games.

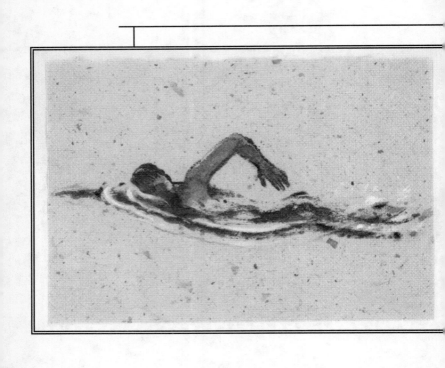

endings and beginnings

CHAPTER 7

Reflections

. . . for Shane, winning races, achieving gold medals and setting world records were all incidental to the experience of swimming.

~

Dennis Phillips, *Australian Women at the Olympic Games*

PEOPLE STILL ASK ME WHY I retired from competitive swimming at the age of 16. A cheeky short answer is: 'Because I wanted to.' But I am still unravelling the full answer to that question.

There were two Shane Goulds at Munich. The public persona looked so confident, strong and happy. Her success brought her immense satisfaction. The other, the inner Shane, experienced enormous personal confusion over being a child in an adult's world. The Olympics was a place for young adults, not a naive teenager. I feel that there is still a neglect and misunderstanding of sporting child prodigies that needs addressing. I remember comments written about me, such as 'she has an old head on young shoulders', because of my apparent maturity and confidence in speaking to reporters. The inner Shane's experience didn't mirror this picture.

I came back from the Munich Olympics to a rude awakening, to a feeling that I had somehow been robbed and used. I was now a 'thing', an 'image', not a person. I wasn't alone in feeling this way. At that time, there was no official welcome home for the athletes, so the event wasn't properly rounded off for any of us. In addition, I felt bitterly disappointed not to have swum my best in the 100 metres event, so when people said to me, 'It's a pity you missed out on getting five golds', I felt a simmering sense of guilt along with a great deal of confusion. Wasn't it enough to have won three gold medals? Did I want too much? Did I already have too much? What had my successes cost others?

Swimming had never been a sacrifice for me. I loved training hard. I loved the competition. I loved doing my best. And when my best placed me first, I loved that too. It was the others in the family who sacrificed their activities so that I could have mine. There was also the matter of my relationship with the water — the sensuous harmony I experienced. Competition had changed what had been an intimate, meditative, spiritual experience into a mechanical, technical one. Dennis Phillips, in *Australian Women at the Olympic Games* (1992), perceived this when he wrote:

> To Shane, the use of her body when swimming was somewhat akin
> to an artist painting on canvas. There was a profound purity in the
> experience itself, but this was changed when the painting went on
> sale . . . for Shane, winning races, achieving gold medals and setting
> world records were all incidental to the experience of swimming.

In the 1970s, swimming was strictly an amateur sport. Every competitor had to be on guard against the dreaded word 'professional', which would exclude them forever from competing. Sometimes it went to absurd lengths, such as when I was approached by the Burbank Nurseries in Sydney, who wanted to name an azalea after me. The Australian Swimming Association advised against it, fearing it might endanger my amateur status! (The azalea was named 'Little Girl' instead, and is a soft, pale pink colour.)

While Australians were keeping to the rules of amateurism, things were arranged very differently in some other countries. In the Soviet Union, athletes were drafted into the army; in East Germany, the parents of young athletes were given jobs and accommodation near an appropriate coach; and the Americans kept their top athletes in sport by giving them college scholarships.

In Australian sport in the 1970s, Australians were very pleased to share the glory of their athletes, but the athletes and their families were left to bear all the financial cost. Secondly, male athletes were more highly valued than female athletes. My father believes that, had I been a male, some organisation would have tried to keep me in the sport, maybe by dangling an offer of an American college scholarship in front of me as an incentive to finish school.

As described earlier, I felt under a great deal of pressure when I swam at the Munich Olympics. I think a number of other factors also affected my performance. One of these was the pre-Olympic camp the team attended in Scarborough, north of Brisbane. I was out of my normal routine, away from home, school and involvement with my family. And despite the six hours of training each day, I simply didn't have enough to do. I ate food for recreation and went to Munich two kilograms over my target weight. (At Munich I put on another two kilos.)

From my experience at Scarborough, I don't recommend long training camps for athletes under 17. Nowadays, Australia Swimming Inc. provides five-day stroke camps, often held in exotic places like Bali. The team members spend only a few days together before flying out to an international meet. There appears to be a greater wholistic understanding today of the needs of athletes aiming for a peak performance at a particular event. For instance, there is a growing consensus that athletes can train effectively at home with their own coach, without having to move into a special institute. Coaching, generally, is now also at a higher standard since the introduction of the Levels Coaching Program from the United States. Athletes today have access to more information and training aids than did athletes 20 and more years ago, in the areas of sports psychology, biomechanics, lactate testing and so on.

~

I think I posed a serious problem for Don Talbot, the Australian team trainer. At the time, swimmers were classified as either sprinters or distance swimmers. Sprinters such as the Australians Michael Wenden and Dawn Fraser and the American Mark Spitz did well at the 100 and 200 metres events. I held world records in both sprint and distance events. So, what was I, sprinter or distance swimmer? Where was my real strength? Don Talbot must have been at a loss to plan my training program in the weeks running up to the Olympics. I have a feeling he must have settled for pitching my program to the middle distances of 200 and 400 metres. I have often wondered whether he intentionally decided to forego appropriate tapering for the 100 metres event to give me a chance to do better in the other races. If so, this was a gamble that paid off in terms of numbers of medals, but at the expense of not achieving gold in the blue-ribbon 100 metres race.

The program followed by Don Talbot differed from that used by my coach, Forbes Carlile, and didn't allow me to be both sharp for the 100 metres sprint and fit for the longer distances. There was too much hard distance work, and my sprinting suffered. Forbes was recognised throughout the world as a leader in research and an innovator of swimming techniques. The swimming world respected him, but he was somehow offside with Australian swimming officialdom. He had brought more Australian swimmers into world ranking and world records than any other Australian coach. Yet, he wasn't even in Munich as my coach, but as a radio commentator!

My father was a professional manager, a superb organiser. Mum had counselling and stress-management skills and was knowledgeable about nutrition. I was used to having these professional skills available to me on a domestic, daily basis. It was simply our family's way of operating, and I didn't realise its value until it wasn't there — removed from me by officialdom.

I was the only athlete in the Olympic team who was expected to win five gold medals for Australia. The personal burden was enormous. I dealt with it by being even more self-contained than usual and by avoiding others. Anyone with any imagination or sensitive understanding might have seen that a 15-year-old girl from whom so much was expected could have used help with dietary selection, transportation to the pool, massage, or even some humorous counter to the American girls' full-on determination to beat me. The Australian officials didn't have the necessary imagination or understanding.

It is not my way to shift responsibility from myself to others. My purpose here is to try and account honestly for what happened to me at Munich, in the hope that other young athletes never have to go into an Olympic Games without an appropriate support system in place. Appropriate support for me at Munich would have eased the burden of expectation I carried. It might even have modified the symptoms that demonstrated so clearly that I wasn't at my physical best. While I thank those who helped me at Munich, I deeply regret the lack of foresight that made my task of trying to win five gold medals such a difficult one. This is my way of saying to my coach and my family: 'I missed you so much!'

In September 1998 I was among an audience of past Olympians at a lecture given by the American sports psychologist Daniel Gould in Olympia, Greece. After the Olympic Games held in Atlanta in 1996, Gould (regrettably, no relation) had studied the effects of the Olympic environment on performances. He found that:

*Successful Olympic performance is a complex, multifaceted,
fragile and long term process that requires extensive planning and
painstaking implementation. It seldom happens by chance and
can be easily disrupted by numerous distractions. Attention to
detail counts but must also be accompanied by flexibility to deal
with unexpected events.*

Distraction preparation is a critical consideration. Successful
athletes, Gould says, have plans and systems in place to deal with
distractions and implement them when the need arises. Common
distractions included 'dealing with the media, getting tickets,
transportation, dealing with families and significant others,
participating in the opening ceremonies and coping with the "hoopla"
associated with the Games'. Most of these distractions were taken care
of for me at Munich.

Another critical consideration was family and friends, who are
'either a tremendous source of support or a major distraction for
athletes'. At Munich, my support crew of my parents and Forbes was
substituted by a different coach and by officials who had been
appointed to look after the team. The officials were good, kind
people, who did their best. They weren't appointed for their travel
experience, their media skills, their dietary knowledge, their
charismatic group leadership, or their great sensitivity to the needs of
elite athletes. They were given the trip to Munich as a reward for their
voluntary service as swimming administrators!

Of the media, Gould said: 'The two media factors that most affected
performance were the amount of media attention received and
whether the athlete or team had media training and a coordinated
media plan.'

Gould further explained: 'From my studies, the factor that sets
winners apart is their ability to use skills to overcome adversity.' I
know that I used all my skills to overcome the stresses I experienced
at Munich. I *still* use those skills. Winners aren't only on the sports

field; I've learned that a winner is someone who sees a problem as a challenge and turns a negative into a positive. The sports arena is a great training ground for life challenges. That's why corporations invite athletes to speak to their employees. Athletes can motivate and inspire by sharing how they use their coping skills.

The Olympic Games in 1972 were on the cusp of a change that has led to excellence both in training and success management for elite athletes. Stars like Susie O'Neill and Cathy Freeman can now bring honour to Australia and earn an income at the same time. As Australia prepares for the 2000 Sydney Olympics, it's good to see that things are very different today.

At the time of the 1972 Olympics, I was still dependent on my parents. I couldn't drive myself to training; I couldn't pay my swimming expenses. Legally, I was a minor. In my sport I was like all athletes: constantly seeking to achieve my PB (personal best). The improvements came gradually, and eventually they splashed into the world-record books.

I became used to comments like, 'too much too soon', and 'Such young people shouldn't be competing at elite levels'. I know that *nothing* could have held me back from training and competing. There was never any pressure from my parents; just quiet acknowledgement that they would support me in the discipline I had chosen. They wouldn't hold me back.

In March 1999 at a Masters Swimming meet in Perth, I met a vital woman named Anita Eifler. Her body was flexible, her zest for life was strong, and she was a champion in her 80–85 age group. At 17 she had been selected to swim for Germany at the 1936 Olympic Games. However, her parents wouldn't allow her to join the team because there was no proper chaperonage available. They tried to comfort her by saying, 'You can swim in the next Games, in 1940'. The Second World War intervened, and the next Games were in 1948. My heart ached for this woman who had been denied an

Olympic opportunity by social constraints that had nothing to do with athletic excellence.

I was ripe for international competition from the age of 14. I'm so glad that those critics of young people in elite sport didn't prevent me from competing at the Munich Games in 1972.

Problems did arise in the mismatch of my age with the social behaviour expected of a successful athlete. At the time, I didn't realise that I wasn't coping. I soon realised, though, what was becoming increasingly evident: family life was changing, and control of the family seemed to be moving out of my parents' hands. Almost all of our family life started to revolve around me as a swimmer. Lynette wasn't so concerned; she was 16 and interested in her friends. But Debbie and Jenny, being younger, were inevitably pulled along in my wake. I had to be driven everywhere, and they mostly came along for the ride.

Dad had a busy job with East West Airlines, working in the city, so it was up to Mum to keep some sort of balance in the family. She did this by being a mother — and nothing else. Her natural path at that time would have been to get back into professional social work. My mother wasn't really very interested in sport as such, so it certainly wasn't for the love of sport that she put what could have been her own interesting career on hold. She did it purely because of her love for me. She saw how much swimming meant to me, and she was willing to give me the opportunity I wanted. I know she would have done the same for any of her daughters who had a compelling urge to do something for themselves.

So, I had a professional woman as my chauffeur, valet and secretary. She and Dad jointly acted as my manager, but it was Mum who read books on swimming and pored over swimming magazines to become familiar with the names and times of outstanding swimmers. She was starting from scratch, but she was determined to get up to speed, intellectually at least, on my interest.

Debbie and Jenny had their childhoods to live too, and the family made efforts to give them activities of their own. They both played netball and attended swimming training sessions. Dad built an aviary for Jenny, and she cared for the budgerigars and quail that enjoyed the large space, nested and produced young. There was a guinea pig called Fluffy who grew fat as a result of Jenny's generous feeding. We all took an interest in Libby, the beagle; though Debbie was the devoted carer of Tiki, the cat.

Debbie was popular at school, and Lynette and I were pleased when she started coming home red-faced, hot and perspiring. (Debbie never used to sweat!) She had at last discovered the joys of physical exertion! Both my younger sisters were good swimmers, and in another family they would have taken centre-stage for their achievements. Debbie was a very good breast-stroker, and Jenny was a competent all-rounder on minimal training. But Jenny found there was a price to be paid for being my sister. After she didn't win a particular race at a school swimming carnival, she was practically berated by a teacher, who said to her: 'We thought you could do better, like your sister Shane.' The other children made similar comments. Jenny wasn't competitive by nature, and — even more important to her — she wanted to be seen as a person in her own right, not just as an add-on to Shane Gould.

At the time, I wasn't aware of much of this. In fact, I felt that as a family, we were all encouraged to have our own activities and to share them around the dinner table at night when we talked about our day. My mother usually had some anecdote about the dog's antics; Dad had some story from the big city; Lynette spoke about school and her assignments; Debbie talked about getting a gold star for her neat work; and Jenny showed some craft item she had made. I spoke about my swimming times. My world records were given the same listening time and value as Fluffy's weight.

Jenny, who was shy and sensitive, was obviously hurt by my swimming. I certainly wasn't being deliberately hurtful, and swimming as an activity couldn't be blamed. The hurt came from insensitive outsiders. But because swimming took so much of my time, Jenny felt that she really lost touch with me from the time she was about eight. As adult women, we have become sisterly friends and I value listening to her wise words.

~

I believe that it can often take much of an adult's life to process and understand their childhood. While much of what took place in my swimming years is still a mystery to me, I can appreciate the benefits of those years. I enjoyed swimming. It was pure fun and I felt incredible in the water. I loved the sensations of burning lungs, thumping heart and straining muscles. Getting up 'a good puff' was a real pleasure.

I think of myself as a 'measuring' person. Swimming slotted well into that part of me. Through swimming I became conscious of my body's operation and competence. I used indicators such as heart rate, flexibility, stress limitation and feeling good to examine myself objectively. I became familiar with the dimensions of my body and my physical relationship to space. I liked the sensuous pleasure of feeling the water on my skin, particularly on the soft skin of my underarms and my chest and face. (When I teach adults to swim, I encourage their awareness of feel for the water.) I found that I came to know myself well as a result of all those hours spent in the water and the detailed reports I would give my coach on how I was feeling. My coaches always gave me honest, helpful feedback. A by-product of this intense athlete–coach relationship was that I quickly learned to relate to adults on a very personal level.

I was so fortunate to have excellent coaches, especially the innovators and trailblazers, Forbes and Ursula Carlile. They were superb teachers who explained to me why taking heart rates, keeping logbooks and being committed to training were important. They showed me what they were doing in their experimental training programs. They helped me to set realistic goals for times with a plan that mostly worked. They insisted on high standards of effort, consistency, and respect for oneself and others. I was drawn to them because I could see they were masters of the science of swimming. I felt privileged to be their student.

I am blessed to have been born in Australia where water sports are loved and swimmers are revered. Recreational swimming is one of the most popular sports in Australia. The well-structured system of swimming clubs — from age-group programs to elite levels, supported mostly by volunteer officials — helped me to appreciate combining efforts with others to achieve good teamwork.

Thanks to some appropriate coaching from my father, I had good press coverage not only in my swimming years, but later on as well. I learned to listen carefully to interviewers' questions and always gave answers as thoughtfully as possible. I learned to 'read' people. I loved the fans and spectators — they helped give me energy to swim to the best of my ability on the day.

All these experiences made me feel good about myself.

I also learned how to ask for help, and how to influence others in assisting me to carry out my determination to swim. My drive was unstoppable. I was persistent and single-minded about wanting to train and compete. My parents were surprised at my tenacity and could only bend to it. They gave me the support I needed. Competitive swimming enabled me to use my gifts and skills. I'm grateful to have had that opportunity so early in my life.

CHAPTER 8

A New Life

Winners are flexible. They realise there is more than one way, and are willing to try others.

~

Anonymous

'I'VE MADE A FEW DECISIONS, MUM,' I said in August 1973 when I turned up in Armidale after my aborted runaway attempt. I had decided to give away competitive swimming, and to leave home and go to boarding school at New England Girls School (NEGS), an Anglican Church school in Armidale. Mum and Dad went along with my decisions, and I was soon enrolled and outfitted for the start of the third term of the school year. The rest of the family stayed in Sydney, finishing the school year and making preparations for the big move to Armidale.

I was hopelessly behind in my school work after five months in California and found it hard to keep up, but the teachers went out of their way to help me. I was unsure of my capabilities outside the world of elite-level sport. I had always had high expectations of myself, but I now lacked confidence that I could be as good again at anything else I chose to do. Many years later I learned that this is a characteristic of athletic career transition, but no one knew of such things in the 1970s.

Despite the difficulty I experienced in adjusting, I got on well with the other girls and soon made friends. It was a relief to be out of the public eye and just be an ordinary teenager at boarding school.

After being so self-involved at Munich, then California, I lost touch with what my sisters and parents were doing. Being at boarding school exacerbated this. I only saw them every couple of months.

At school I developed some new interests to replace those I had lost. I had a go at learning to play the guitar, with minimal success (Debbie later learned with my guitar to play and sing beautifully); and I participated in the unique horsemanship program that NEGS was famous for. I didn't know how to saddle or ride a horse properly, so I had to bluff my way a bit. Many of the other girls were from farms and stations in Queensland and north-western New South Wales and were probably born on a horse!

I have high expectations of myself to be competent at whatever I do. I felt that the other girls got caught up in the competitiveness they perceived that I represented. They thoroughly enjoyed outdoing me at horsemanship, in which they excelled and I didn't. As a world-champion swimmer, being the best in the world was the measure I set for myself. I know it was quite unrealistic to think I could be the best horserider, netballer or surfer, but the thoughts certainly crossed my mind. Going into the beginners' group was okay while the lesson was private. Then I would be 'on show' doing a media story or a display for parents. I just felt that I was being judged for mistakes or incompetencies. I developed a false, over-confident bravado that I knew wasn't authentic. I couldn't stop the momentum of this bravado. I remember having raves with my friend and room-mate at NEGS, Angie Middleton, late into the night. I described to her how I had built a brick wall around myself to protect myself from others getting close and seeing that I wasn't the golden girl, the goldfish, the ideal Australian girl who was without fault. Angie agreed I had a wall around me, and encouraged me to dismantle the wall brick by brick.

I really enjoyed chapel, which we had every day. I particularly liked choir; singing hymns and old songs like 'Greensleeves'. On my own I cannot keep a tune, but with a group I can. The spiritual atmosphere of chapel stirred something in me. It gave me courage to remove another brick of the protective wall.

Then, in October, I was made an offer by Adidas, the sporting goods company, to market 'Arena' swimsuits for them. Mark Spitz, the American Olympic gold medallist, had been signed to put his name on the men's swimsuits, and they wanted my name on the women's suits. The contract offered quite a lot of money — an amount of $50 000 over five years on a sliding scale, starting with $5000 in the first year. If I signed, it would really be the end of competitive amateur swimming for me; it would mean becoming a professional. It would also mean that I would be financially independent of my family.

My parents were initially in favour of my taking on the contract, because it would include speech and deportment lessons and the sort of training that would fit me for a public life in sports promotions and marketing. I could make a career and be properly prepared and educated for it.

But then the Australian company, Speedo, made a counter-offer. Neil Ryan, who worked for Speedo, offered to find work for me that wouldn't harm my amateur status, and that would enable me to have a rest from swimming for about six months and then perhaps get back into it. Mum and Dad were swayed by Neil and now thought this the better, gentler option.

Once again, I had a big decision to make, a decision that would affect the rest of my life. I was still in a state of emotional upheaval and mental confusion. I felt resentment, bewilderment, self-pity and guilt. Was I a victim of the fame I had gained from swimming fast? Why did I have so much self-doubt when others saw me as a confident hero? Why did people expect me to perform for them, when all I wanted was to swim for enjoyment? I was beginning to feel unworthy of the acclaim that kept coming. The identity I'd been given was starting to box me in. I wanted to break out of the box because I knew there was more to me than being 'Shane Gould, the swimmer'.

Adidas was the big time; Speedo more homely. I was torn between taking a risk by getting out into the world, and taking a softly, softly approach. Betty Cuthbert and Ron Clarke, Australian track champions who represented Adidas, came to see me and tipped the scales. Neil Ryan, from Speedo, was too much like my father — too caring, too supportive; and I was rejecting any sort of parental involvement. The offer he made also seemed too loose. He was friendly with Forbes, and I thought I might be coerced into swimming competitively again against my wishes. I knew how persuasive Forbes could be!

To make my final decision, I went to a place outside Armidale where a river flowed under a bridge. Being by the water had always soothed me when I felt troubled. It was steep cattle country, with rocky slopes and stringy-bark gum trees in cleared paddocks. There were no animals or cars around. I slipped off my clothes and slowly immersed myself in the cold-flowing stream, letting it carry me gently. It was fairly shallow, and my bottom grazed over the slippery, sharp-edged black basalt rocks. I was waiting to hear a voice or to be shown a sign that would tell me what to do. But I heard only the soft rustle of leaves and bubbling water. I saw only 'Joe was here 1969' scrawled on the bridge beams. I couldn't stay ambivalent, or wait for someone else to make the choice for me. It was time for me to make my own decisions and to wear the consequences. I knew that I was possibly making the wrong choice, but I wanted to make the decision for myself. I rolled over, pushed myself off a rock and headed back upstream against the current. As I surfaced, I knew that my life had taken a new turn. I would take up the offer of a contract with Adidas.

I would go it alone. I left the water, got dressed, and went to tell my parents of my decision.

Mum just wanted me to take the path that felt right for me at that time. Dad had seen how the experience of fame had leached away my natural, youthful exuberance. While he would have preferred that I accept the offer from Speedo, he gave his qualified approval to my accepting a contract with Adidas. The money would enable me to get into a university course, which would give me a professional qualification. On 23 November 1973, my 17th birthday, I signed with Arena swimwear.

Nowadays, elite athletes who are in the same position as I was at that time are offered professional sports retirement counselling by a sports psychologist. They are helped to unscramble their thoughts and emotions, and have access to education and career planning. None of this support was available to me.

After spending just one term at boarding school, I left Armidale for Sydney and started my job with Arena. I lived in a flat in Lane Cove with Lynette, who was at nearby Macquarie University, and Dad, who worked long days in the city and spent weekends in Armidale with Mum, Debbie and Jenny. My work soon took me to Europe. In Luxembourg I met Adolf and Horst Dassler, from whose names 'Adidas' is derived. I ate *escargot* at the top of the Eiffel Tower in Paris. I visited the Louvre, attended Adidas marketing meetings, and drove through France to Switzerland. At a beer festival in Rudesheim in Luxembourg, I was sexually harassed by an Arena employee. I was frightened and scared by the experience of having my personal space invaded in such an unwelcome manner. I was young, naive and trusting, and just discovering the delights of flirting with and getting attention from men. I had no skills to know how to deal with this man's attentions, nor with those of three other men in that same year.

At the 1974 Commonwealth Games in Christchurch, New Zealand, I did some TV commentary. One evening I was invited by a married

English journalist, someone I had known for a couple of years, to have a drink in his hotel room with him and his room-mate. We all chatted for a while, and then the room-mate left. When the journalist asked me to go to bed with him, I knew I had been set up. I made an embarrassed and hasty retreat. I felt dirty, ashamed and betrayed.

At an Arena swimsuit media launch at a hotel in Sydney, a high-ranking German diplomatic official old enough to be my father came to my door late one night uttering endearments and saying that he loved me. I had met him previously at official Olympic functions, and enjoyed speaking German with him and asking him questions about Germany. I had no other interest in the man, so when he presumed more from my behaviour than I had intended I pushed him out the door and locked it firmly.

Another incident involved an English photographer who was taking promotional photos for the Arena catalogue. He asked me to pose in seductive positions long after he had all the photos he needed. I nearly vomited with fear when he asked me to go to his hotel room. I fumbled my way out of the situation by saying I had another appointment to attend.

Many young athletes are in the position of trusting adults such as coaches, officials, the media and others with whom they come in contact through their sport, and of having that trust violated by sexual harassment or sexual abuse. It is a sad indictment of the sporting scene even today that young female athletes need to be trained in how to deal with sexual harassment and to be accompanied by an older female companion to photo shoots and interview locations.

I didn't discuss these incidents of sexual harassment with anyone, because I felt guilty, as all people who have been abused feel even though they are the victims. They also coloured my perception of men. 'All men want is sex!' I thought. I was confused by the world of adults. I went into self-defence mode: I 'closed down', became suspicious of everyone, and felt even more isolated. I enjoyed my work less and less, and felt unsafe and unsupported, but I didn't know how to ask for help.

The training I had been offered by Adidas/Arena didn't happen, and I was too inexperienced to insist on it. I ended up selling swimsuits, taking orders for the next summer season from sports stores and department stores such as Grace Bros. I had to learn to find my way around Sydney in my Ford Escort, and to smooth-talk experienced, discerning buyers. Somehow, I bluffed my way through it, but there was a limit to how long I could go on pretending.

I was also given a job producing a calendar of major sporting events in Sydney. I didn't have a clue about how to type reports. (I still have a copy of my European report. When I look back, I'm surprised by my insightful understanding of marketing as a 17-year-old.) I knew very little about sports other than swimming, or about how sporting organisations were structured. I had been placed in the position with little training apart from two weeks at an advertising agency, and with high expectations placed on me. The people at the Adidas office in Marrickville didn't really know what to do with me.

In fact, it seemed that Arena didn't yet know how to use an athlete's name and image in promoting their product. Both Ron Clarke and Betty Cuthbert were employed for their work skills. Their Olympic name and fame were the reason they were employed by a sporting goods company, but they weren't primarily promotional images. I had no work skills and was relying on being given on-the-job training. My experience was at the turning point in the transition from amateurism to professionalism in Olympic sport, and athletes are now paid for the association of their name and image with a product.

I felt like there was no place where I fitted or belonged. I'd just been bought. With unsatisfying work that offered little future, I felt used and betrayed. I was a fish out of water, gasping for air.

I regretted my decision to work for Adidas, but I didn't see any way out. Pride kept me from discussing my predicament with my father.

Besides, I didn't really know how to describe the acute discomfort I was feeling.

While this turmoil was going on for me, the family move to Armidale had taken place — in time for the start of the 1974 school year. A new house was being built on two acres of land on the outskirts of town. I wasn't part of the move, but when I visited, I could see that each member of the family was thriving. The Armidale years were very good for the family. Jenny and Debbie were both school captains: Jenny at Drummond Memorial Primary School, and Debbie in her senior year at Presbyterian Ladies College.

Lynette completed her Arts degree, and followed it up with a postgraduate Diploma in Education. Debbie developed a lovely folksinger's voice; she took the romantic lead as Meg in the musical version of *Seven Little Australians*. And with her guitar, she financed her overseas travel by singing in a restaurant each week. Both she and Jenny did secretarial training, and found jobs easily. They were popular girls. They kept up their interest in netball and swimming.

Jenny indulged her love of pets. She had a menagerie of caged birds, dogs, cats, bantams and geese. The family attended the Uniting Church where the minister was Reverend Ian Fardon, an old friend of Mum's from their Student Christian Movement days at Sydney University.

While I was waking up to the commercial world, my parents were going through changes, too. Dad rode his bicycle to his administrative job at the university. He started reading sociology, and took an interest in alternative lifestyles and technologies. My mother restarted her professional life, first as a hospital and community health social worker, and then with a specific unit, the New England Educational and Diagnostic (NEED) Centre. She did some extra study in psychology, did courses in Gestalt and family therapy, and eventually coordinated a family counselling service for the New England region.

~

In April 1974, feeling alone and very unhappy, I found myself one day outside the Central Methodist Mission, in Sydney's Pitt Street. My paternal grandfather, Reverend A.J. Gould, had been associated with the Mission in the 1930s, and Reverend Alan Walker, the current minister, had written to me after my return from the Munich Olympics in 1972, inviting me to talk to his youth group about my experiences. After the talk, he had suggested that I might like to attend the group.

Two years later, as I stood outside the building, housed in the old Lyceum Theatre, I remembered Reverend Walker's invitation and went in and had a chat with him. He invited me to the youth group, which would meet on the following Friday night in a room at the Lyceum called 'Daniel's Den'. There was a typical 'seventies' atmosphere, with Bob Dylan music playing and people sitting in darkened rooms strumming on guitars and drinking coffee. A former prostitute sang songs of sadness and of hope. The people were very kind to me, and it was refreshing to be accepted by a group of people for *me*, rather than for my achievements. I felt safe in the environment and found the experience soothing.

I kept going back to the group. I enjoyed being among young people my own age who were interested in serious issues. I started to see the commercial world I was involved in as shallow and artificial. I felt I was among people I could trust. They seemed to want to know *me*, not the famous person. I asked them why they were so nice to me. They said because Jesus loved everyone for who they *are*, not for what they *do*. So as disciples of Jesus, they do the same. It was a big revelation.

Over the next month I believe God came to me. Not in a spectacular way — just quietly through verses from the Bible. I had the ears to hear. I was tired of trying to save myself from confusion, loneliness, self-deception and my disappointment in what I saw as the empty promises of fame.

When I learned that God was personal, not just an energy, and that I could relate to Him through Jesus Christ, I was comforted. Especially when I read in the Bible, 'For it is by God's grace that you have been saved through faith. It is not the result of your own efforts, but God's gift, so that none can boast about it' (Ephesians 2:8–9). It took study and time to understand how this good news applied to every aspect of my life.

~

In June 1974 I went to a camp at a church bush camp site at Arcadia, on the outskirts of Sydney, with the youth group and met a young man in his mid-twenties, Neil Innes. At this time, I was smoking cigarettes and eating junk food, and not taking particularly good care of myself. My new Christian faith had not yet become wholistic. Neil and his good friend Jill Ennever (a naturopath) invited me to eat my meals with them instead of in the cafeteria, which served greasy meat dishes. I enjoyed sitting outdoors with Neil and Jill and eating thick slabs of wholemeal bread with lashings of salad and alfalfa sprouts.

Neil, who was from Perth, was passionate about surfing, horses and ecology. He was intelligent, though undiagnosed problems with his eyes had meant he'd had a hard time at school. He was a member of the Baptist Church, and felt that his vocation in life was to be a missionary, helping people on the fringes of society such as drug addicts, hippies and surfers. Neil was so unlike anyone I had ever known. He wasn't interested in achievement or materialism. He had beautiful brown eyes and a very gentle manner. He seemed such a peaceful, thoughtful person, and he had a great physique from horse-riding, body building and surfing. He was also a vegetarian and health food addict. By the end of the weekend, I knew I was very attracted to him. When he first introduced himself, he said: 'I would like to get to know you over the weekend.' That 'weekend' lasted for 23 years!

At the camp I also met Reverend George Davies, a long-time youth advocate and youth worker in Perth. One morning I rowed him across the dam in a canoe, while he read aloud from the Bible the story of Jesus preaching from a boat on Lake Galilee. He reckoned he was safe with me if the canoe capsized! In turn, I felt safe with him as a kind of minder. George had great sensitivity about my need to fit in, for which I was very grateful.

Some Baptist ministers also present at the camp had started a community in Sydney called the House of the New World. It was called a 'para-church' group because it worked in parallel with the traditional churches and ministered to people who felt uncomfortable in the 'straight' world. One of the leaders was Reverend John Hirt. The people in this community were deeply concerned about big issues such as nuclear technology, ethics, world economics and social justice.

After the weekend 'Jesus Teach-In' at Arcadia, I started to spend time at the House of the New World. There were books and tapes in the library, and discussions about issues to which I had never been exposed. My Olympic experiences seemed overrated by comparison. I heard talks by people like the prominent trade union leader, Jack Mundey, by psychiatric social workers and the Hare Krishnas. Among the many books I read at this time was John Taylor's *Enough is Enough*, which I took along on a 'surfari' camp with the Christian Boardriders group at Old Bar, Taree. Neil had taken me surfing at Palm Beach quite often and spent his weekends on the coast. I joined in with the guys surfing. It was great to be in the water and the surf again, using swimming muscles but not having to do laps.

In *Enough is Enough*, Taylor wrote about the seductiveness of advertising — about how it encourages us to accumulate and consume goods that we don't really need. He proposed alternatives to our Western consumer society, community living and 'living simply so that others may simply live'. I was still involved in advertising, and the book's message was a shock to me. Along with the incidents of sexual harassment I had been subjected to, the book influenced my decision to quit working for Adidas in August, terminate my Arena contract in October, finish my Higher School Certificate at TAFE in 1975, and live in one of the households of the House of the New World. I realised that I needed to further my education in order to understand the real world better.

Apart from my work with Adidas and Arena, I had secured contracts with Eyeline (swimming accessories) and White Wings. (In a TV commercial for Muesli Flakes, I said: 'I wonder how they get the muesli to stick to the flakes?') The income from these contracts would be enough to live on. I realised that I felt more comfortable and safe with the Australians than the European Arena representatives.

Neil was also involved with the House of the New World and the Christian Boardriders group and we saw a lot of each other at meetings and on weekends. As well as being physically attracted to him, I felt I had a lot to learn from him intellectually. Neil saw my life differently from anyone else. On one occasion when I had to do a shopping-centre promotion for Arena in Wollongong, on the coast south of Sydney, Neil and a friend of his volunteered to pick me up afterwards and take me for a surf. They were late in arriving and found me sitting alone amongst the discarded boxes and other rubbish at the back of the shopping centre. The shops were shut and everyone else had gone home. I had told the organisers that I was being picked up and was happy to wait, but Neil saw me a 'victim' and the sporting fraternity as my 'persecutor'. He found the contrast between the sports hero who was the centre of attention, who was feted and hero-worshipped, and the young girl who was left alone when the show was over, very disturbing. He thought I was being used, that something wasn't right, that the whole thing was just for show, and that the people who were supposed to care about me didn't really give a hoot. He then took it upon himself to assume the role of my 'rescuer'. I found his solicitous concern for me very sweet and refreshing, and it wasn't difficult to succumb to his view of the situation. It was an attitude that Neil was to hold for many years, and one that I helped to promote.

In August I quit my job and started to spend much of my time hanging around the drop-in centre at the House of the New World. I read books avidly and listened to tapes on theology, philosophy, politics and social justice. It was wonderful stuff, and all new to me. Neil was doing a course called 'The School of the Prophets' with Baptist Church ministers and social workers. Sometimes I sat in on the teaching sessions. I found much of it hard to understand, not having the background knowledge of Old Testament history, Greek or theology that Neil had from his two years at Bible college and growing up 'churched' at Scarborough Baptist Church in Western Australia.

The House of the New World was also a drug referral centre and trained people who provided counselling education and crisis accommodation. Once I answered the phone and spoke with a distraught mother who had just discovered heroin hidden in her 16-year-old daughter's room. I met a teenage girl who often sought attention by cutting her wrists and swallowing razor blades. She got the help she needed from a loving and calm nursing sister called Wendy, and slowly her self-mutilation stopped. She eventually became a talented cartoonist and artist. When, some years later at age 20, she visited my husband and me in Western Australia, she had only just started to menstruate. She celebrated her newfound womanhood by going to the pub wearing a hat with tampons dangling from the brim like corks.

The main ethic of the community was sharing, and I got involved in the food co-op. A group of us would go to the markets to buy fruit and vegies in bulk, and we would haggle over the prices like everyone else. When I did the advertisement for White Wings, they offered me some muesli. I asked for five boxes, but I was given five cartons, each containing 12 boxes! They all went into the food co-op and were sold cheaply. The money raised went into the community kitty to pay the fuel and phone bills. For the next couple of months, whenever anyone asked, 'What's for breakfast?', they would be met with a chorus of 'Muesli Flakes again!'.

There were about ten households, with three to five people in each house. Rent and food expenses were shared. The drop-in centre in Ryedale Road was the hub for teaching, counselling, study, prayer and craftwork, and included an office for John Hirt. We had regular common meals. For lunch we all put in 50 cents which paid for a nutritious bread and salad meal. Many community members were involved with their own traditional church but represented the House of the New World at other church youth groups for street theatre, musical entertainment and preaching. I was involved in some of these visits.

Towards the end of the year, I turned 18. I had become interested in politics and was now entitled to vote. I was leaning heavily to the political left.

My interest in and enjoyment of surfing continued to grow through my involvement in the Christian Boardriders group, which was run by John Hirt who was also pastor of Avalon Baptist Church. Meetings would be held at different houses on the North Shore beaches, and we surfed together on Saturday mornings. We would follow this with a 'bakery bash' at the Avalon Bakery, which made wonderful vanilla slices and apple pies. At the Avalon picture theatre we would watch classic surf movies, such as *Morning of the Earth*, *Endless Summer* and *Sea of Joy*, which celebrated a romantic, soulful and easygoing view of life. We followed Alby Mangels's surfing and sailing adventures through films projected on to the walls of school and church halls.

Surfing kept me physically active and mentally challenged. It was before the days of leg-ropes, and I fell off my kneeboard regularly and had to swim to retrieve my board. I also took up skateboarding.

At this time I was a woman of independent means, living far from my family, and falling deeply in love with a man who was nearly seven years my senior and with whom I shared many of my new interests and pursuits. I felt very positive, finally, about what I was doing and about the people with whom my life was becoming entwined. My parents were concerned about the direction I was taking, which they saw as leading me away from pursuing further education and into fundamental Christianity. They were concerned about my uncompleted contracts. A hippie was not a good image for advertisers. They still saw me as vulnerable and needy, and feared that I was being exploited by my new friends — in particular, by Neil, whom they didn't know and saw just as a long-haired, bearded hippie with a drop-out mentality and few prospects. They didn't appreciate Neil's social conscience, non-materialistic values, or his missionary compassion for people on the edge of society. They were unable to understand that I regarded the experiences I was having with Neil, and within the community at the House of the New World, as an intense, personal, adult education — one that was helping me to move forward into maturity and not just sideways, away from competitive swimming. It was a difference between us that would affect our relationship for nearly 20 years.

While my path was leading me to Christianity — radical, not traditional — my parent's beliefs were turning gradually towards eastern mysticism and meditation practices. (They would later visit India and sit with enlightened teachers there.)

The move to Armidale was brilliant for the five family members still living at home. While Lynette moved in and out of student accommodation, I was the first to leave home and support myself. My move away distressed Dad deeply. He had had dreams of the family regaining its unity through the Armidale move. But too much had happened with me, and life beyond the family was beckoning.

Mum felt I had left too soon for us to enjoy an adult relationship together. She regretted that her aim of guiding her daughters towards independence had been only too successful. But both parents had to accept the inevitable. Hoping that close contact would continue, they gave me their blessings, and hoped my life would be full of travel and education. They could now concentrate on the teenage needs of Jenny and Debbie, just as they had done for Lynette and me.

alternative lifestyling

CHAPTER 9

Back to the Land

The earth is the Lord's and everything in it.

~

1 Corinthians 10:26

AT THE END OF 1974, Neil and I headed off in his panel van on a surfing holiday, bound for Western Australia. After travelling through Broken Hill in Western New South Wales to Port Augusta, we stopped for a surf at Cactus, a popular and remote surfing break near Penong, in South Australia. We camped there for a week.

I was still learning how to handle myself in the surf and wasn't yet able to turn properly or to make quick decisions, but I had the bug and wasn't content just to sit on the beach and watch Neil catch waves. I loved the feeling of riding the face of an unbroken wave, of being carried by the energy of the ocean and occasionally getting inside the barrel. One morning I got caught inside at Caves, the southern reef break at Cactus, on a shallow reef and was held down by the whitewater of 'sneak' sets. I was very scared; I thought I'd breathed my last breath. The experience gave me a healthy respect for the ocean.

I enjoyed camping. Our tent was small and cosy. We cooked on a gas camp stove and read or wrote letters by the light of a gas lamp.

At night, the only sounds were the surf and the tent flapping in the breeze.

The very cold Southern Ocean is renowned for its Great White sharks. Although we didn't see any sharks during our time at Cactus, the following week a young boy was attacked and killed by a white pointer as he swam out to his father's fishing boat.

One day on the beach we met a man who was looking for a place to bodysurf. Cactus isn't a bodysurfing spot and we advised him against it. It was a very hot day, with a hot wind that burned my throat. I could smell the earth cooking. Our new friend then invited us to join him in a picnic. He produced from an esky some cold, cooked crayfish and a chilled bottle of white wine. We made ourselves comfortable in a cool rockpool in the shade of an overhanging white limestone rock and tucked into our pre-Christmas drinks and nibblies. What a treat!

From Cactus we drove west across the Nullarbor Plain on the Eyre Highway, which at that time was still a gravel road and very corrugated. It took 20 hours to travel around 300 kilometres! Along the side of the 'highway', scrubby trees struggled to grow. A huge wedge-tailed eagle startled us as it took off from under a tree. Its wingspan was as wide as our panel van was long.

We stopped in Esperance, in Western Australia, to visit some people Neil had lived and worked with some years before at Esperancho Youth Ranch. The ocean at Esperance is the most beautiful emerald-blue and washes up on long white beaches. My surfing was improving. I learned how to climb the wave and then drop, to gather speed on the face of the wave. The Esperance region is very arid, with hardy tea-trees and scrubby banksias and mallees scattered around the perimeter of the salt lakes. The beauty of the Australian landscape gripped me, and I felt a pull to the land.

From Esperance we continued on the 400 kilometres to Margaret River, which I immediately fell in love with. The tall forests of karri trees, the rural lifestyle and the wonderful surfing beaches of this south-western part of Western Australia (300 kilometres south of Perth) promised a life far removed from the commercial world I was used to. I felt that this place could sustain and nurture me.

Early in the new year, we returned to Sydney and I started a one-year condensed Higher School Certificate course at Seaforth TAFE college. I lived in the northern beach suburb of Bilgola with a married couple, Ed and Judy Alcock, whom I had met through the Christian Boardriders group. On weekends I surfed. Neil and I planned to get married in June. He had a part-time job fibreglassing boats and surfboards and did some house-painting, too.

For the HSC I did history, English literature, geography, maths and biology. I enjoyed studying the poetry of Robert Frost, John Donne and W.B. Yeats, and the history subjects. I started to understand that I was shaping my own life history by the choices I was making. My studies, my relationship with Neil and other new friends, and surfing all helped me to begin a new life.

Neil Innes and I were married on 15 June 1975 at a small private ceremony held in the backyard of Uncle Barry and Aunt Cynthia's house in St Ives, in Sydney. Neil was 25, and I was 18-and-a-half. We had postponed the ceremony from the Saturday to the Sunday, in the hope that the uninvited reporters would leave. We wanted total privacy. As it was, the intrepid media hung in there for another day and were at Barry and Cynthia's house on Sunday afternoon when we arrived in Neil's panel van, our hair still wet from just having surfed. Neil became irritated by the presence of the media. Up until then, I don't think he had realised just how newsworthy I still was. He saw the media and my public life as intruding on our life as a couple. This was the seed that would grow and eventually contribute to the breakdown of our marriage. After some heated discussion, Neil reluctantly agreed to let the press take some photos. The arguments took the shine off the day for me.

We wrote our own vows, but also said the traditional ones. We were married by Reverend John Hirt — Baptist minister, surfing companion, teacher, prophet and friend. My grandmother, Narnie Reid, made a rich fruit cake, and friends brought food for afternoon tea. Our friend Wendy's carob cake was a great success. Friends Libby and Doug, and my sisters Debbie and Jenny, sang songs accompanied by guitars.

I wore a white Armenian cheesecloth dress decorated with blue embroidery. Underneath I wore a white skivvy, as the weather was cold and wet. Around my neck I wore a necklace of Margaret River beach shells, which I had threaded on a length of fishing line on our journey back across the Nullarbor.

The ceremony was very simple and lovely, though it was apparent that my family thought I was too young and that it was all happening too soon. Mum and Dad had little involvement in the preparations, and Dad had even threatened not to come. They were still suspicious of my involvement with what they saw as fundamental Christianity, and they didn't know Neil. The night before the ceremony, Mum and I sat outside on the cement steps in the dark, talking. Mum pleaded tearfully with me not to go ahead with the wedding. I had never seen her so distressed. I said, 'I love him, Mum'. And I did, deeply. What can a mother say to that?

For the next six months, I studied and surfed and adjusted to life as a young wife in our boatshed home on Pittwater. Neil was finishing his 'School of the Prophets' course and working part-time. At high tide, the water washed against our bedroom wall and I could dive from the windowsill straight into the water! We had a dog named Cactus — a red heeler–kelpie cross. One day I left him inside at home while I was at TAFE. When I came home, I found he had devoured a whole banana cake I had left cooling on the bench. (Cactus was an inveterate scavenger. He used to bring home smelly cans and dead fish from the beach, and although we tried some Pavlov-style behaviour modification — meatballs and safe, low-voltage electric shocks — nothing worked. He had the scavenger gene.)

I remember the banana cake incident so well because, while I was making another cake, the radio announced the dismissal of Prime Minister Gough Whitlam. Hearing Gough speak with disbelief in his voice caused me to gasp and weep with a sense of injustice for him. I feel that I lost my naivety that day about the permanence of leadership. My thoughts moved on from prime ministers and cakes to the impermanent nature of my fame. Now that East Germans and Americans were breaking my records, I realised how important it was to develop a life with skills that didn't rely on my name and my fame.

Neil and I were both deeply moved by the outspoken prophets of the 1970s who were lifting the lid on the real condition of the world: terrorism; oil shortages; crime; environmental degradation; Cold War; poverty; famine; the exploitation of the Third World; the depersonalisation of urban society; the rise of consumerism; and the failure of the church to address people's needs. I can still feel a fire in my belly about the false religion of consumption, where consuming has become the meaning of life, the criterion of existence. We felt we wanted to buck against these trends; so, with missionary zeal, we developed our personal solution.

Our plan would enable us to live out our convictions and help others as well. We would buy land in Western Australia and live simply in a rural environment. We would share our abundance with others by providing a reflective place where travellers seeking meaning could talk and be guided towards hope. It would be a community of fellow Christians who would minister to the needs of surfers and those in search of an alternative lifestyle.

I felt genuine joy and excitement about our commitment to our plan. It would get me away from what I felt was the shallowness of my sporting achievements and the associated hero-worship it bred. I had been to the top in sport and found it didn't satisfy me. Neither did earning endorsement money by being a marketable image. I knew there was something more to life — a higher cause. I found satisfaction, joy and peace in a life of 'hungering and thirsting for righteousness' and 'seeking first the kingdom of God' alongside my life partner, Neil.

In the first six months of marriage, while I was studying and Neil was fibreglassing surfboards for the basic wage, we went through the usual tensions and adjustments. Being 'Mrs Innes' took a bit of getting used to. Neil had a deep understanding of all the information and ideas I was encountering for the first time, so I interrogated him incessantly. I had then — and still have now — a voracious appetite for the *why* and *how*.

At dinner one night, after asking him about his day, I brought up a theological issue that puzzled me — the notion of sin. After asking Neil a lot of questions, I asked him how he interpreted the book *Death in the City*, by the Swiss theologian Frances Shaeffer. Neil had had enough, and said he wouldn't answer any more of my questions. I would have to find out for myself, he said, and make up my own mind. He handed me a thick volume, *A Pictorial History of the Bible*, to read. At the time I felt hurt, but now I am thankful that he encouraged me to think for myself.

I can see, too, that part of my chattering at that time came from my discomfort at any kind of silence between us. As I became more at home with Neil, I also became more at ease with just being together without needing to communicate in words.

However, there was something that I desperately needed to discuss with Neil: my growing discomfort about the advertising I was involved with, and my struggle not to 'rest on my laurels'. Typical of the behaviour described in the book *Men Are From Mars, Women Are From Venus*, Neil had a ready solution, while I just needed to talk. His solution was: 'Just turn your back on it, like you decided to before I met you.' But it wasn't simply a matter of turning my back on my past. The problem wasn't 'out there', it was within me. I kept feeling that there must be a third way, another solution. (I finally found it 15 years later in the form of sports retirement counselling.) I was upset with Neil for not seeing how deeply troubled I was, and for thinking it could be solved in such a simple, cut-and-dried way.

~

We sold my car and bought a trail bike. On our last day at the boatshed, we packed up our meagre belongings and loaded them into the panel van. Four tea chests, mostly packed with my trophies and memorabilia, went ahead of us by train. As Neil was attaching the trail bike to the back of the van, he was hit by a car and suffered several broken bones and deep wounds. Being in the hospital emergency ward and not knowing the extent of Neil's injuries was a frightening experience. He spent the next two weeks recovering in Mona Vale Hospital and I stayed with friends at Whale Beach, where I had the trail bike repaired and learned to ride a Malibu surfboard. I really enjoyed those two weeks. Neil would continue to need medical attention for a while, so we postponed our trip to the west until after Christmas.

When we finally left Sydney, with everything we owned either in or attached to the van, we drove up to Armidale. Neil could have his shoulder pinned at the local hospital, and we would spend Christmas with my family. My parents had bought a double bed for us and prepared a room to make us feel comfortable and welcome as a married couple. During the visit, Neil was wary of Mum and Dad and avoided talking about things that were important to him. My parents enjoyed in-depth discussion, so they were disappointed at being prevented from getting to know the man their daughter loved. Neil and my sisters got along well in a light-hearted, joking fashion.

The big disappointment for my family was that we were moving to Western Australia, 3000 kilometres from Armidale. There were also undercurrents of tension concerning our differing interpretations of Christianity. Unfortunately, the visit was too brief to air and deal with our mutual suspicions.

I couldn't wait to get on the road for the start of our exciting adventure. I delighted in my freedom and independence, and didn't anticipate that I would come to miss the support of my family.

~

As we travelled further west from Armidale we encountered very heavy rainfall. By the time we got to Nyngan, in the New South Wales outback, the bridge was flooded and the road closed. We would have to stay the night, maybe even a few days, in Nyngan. But we were anxious to keep going, and at the suggestion of a truck driver who was also held up by the bridge closure, we tried some gravel back roads. They were muddy but passable. Every kilometre or so there was a dip in the road to channel floodwaters in the otherwise flat terrain. The further we went, the more water was in these dips and eventually we got stuck in one when the motor died. The floodwaters were rising quickly and the van soon became half-filled with water in which floated cassette tapes and photos. Feeling greatly alarmed, we tied the roo bar of the van to a tree, gathered up our bankbooks, harmonica and Cactus, the dog, and went for help on foot. Each time we looked back, we expected the van to be gone. It was rocking in the gushing flood, but the rope held it. As we trudged down the soggy road, we had a strange feeling that we could just 'disappear' in the flood and never be heard of again. We could change our identities and start all over. It was kind of appealing to think that we could escape from the past and have a new beginning. I was becoming tired of being 'Shane Gould, the Swimmer', which was causing so much awkwardness between Neil and me due to the constant media attention. Neil had no experience of reporters' persistence in getting a story. He didn't like having his life scrutinised. He disliked having his photo taken at any time, let alone by the media. My life was already public, so either he had to adapt or I had to move away from the spotlight. I moved. I wanted to continue my good relationship with the media, and I wasn't self-conscious about having my life scrutinised. I think Dad's coaching at handling questions from reporters helped me to have good press most of the time.

A few months before Neil and I were married, a reporter came to the House of the New World to do a story on our relationship. Neil greeted him, and the reporter said, 'I'd like to see Neil Innes. He's a good friend of mine from Western Australia.' Neil, with considerable presence of mind, said: 'Sorry, I'm just going out, but Ken here will look after you.' He called out, 'Ken, this man's from a newspaper and he wants to talk to Neil Innes'. Ken played the game out and said, as Neil walked down the stairs, 'I don't exactly know where Neil is right now'.

I can appreciate how difficult it must be for a male when he is seen as just an 'appendage' of a female public figure. Our society is respectful of a woman who stands quietly by her public-figure husband, but it pokes fun at men like the inconspicuous husband of former British prime minister Margaret Thatcher, and ridicules the Duke of Edinburgh for walking three paces behind Queen Elizabeth when they appear together in public. It takes a lot of emotional fitness and confidence in one's own self-worth to partner a woman who is in the public eye.

My musings about just disappearing and starting a new life were interrupted by the sound of a car coming towards us. It was two shearers in a utility heading south for their next 'shed'. They towed the panel van out of the swift-flowing creek for us and five minutes later had the motor running again. We thanked our rescuers profusely and then drove to the highest point in the road. We spent the night on our soggy bedding in a 60-centimetre-wide space in the back of the van accompanied by what seemed like hordes of mosquitoes.

By morning the waters had subsided and we drove nonstop in order to get out of New South Wales. On the outskirts of a town in the Mount Lofty Ranges, in South Australia, we emptied the car to dry everything out. We strung sleeping-bags, clothes, mattress, car-floor underfelt and pillows over a barbed-wire fence on the side of the road. We felt and looked like gypsies. A policeman came by and asked us to leave as soon as our things were dry. A 'local' who was walking by said they hadn't had any rain in the town for ten years! While our things dried, we practised throwing a boomerang in a stony sheep paddock and read poetry.

When we arrived in Perth, we moved in with Neil's parents, Jan and Laurie. Neil had further medical attention for the injuries he'd sustained in the accident, and we looked for land around Esperance and Margaret River. Jan, married during the Second World War, was an efficient housekeeper and homemaker. Her elder son, Ross, was living overseas, so she was delighted to have her youngest son at home to fuss over. The trouble was, he now had a wife.

There hadn't been any time in my adolescence to learn housekeeping skills. Yet, as a married woman, I was expected to be competent around the house. Although I didn't place much value on domestic skills, I did my best and Jan tried to turn a blind eye to my deficiencies — until the day I burned her aluminium pots on the gas stove. I was then edged out of the kitchen. I didn't understand the vagaries of their old washing machine, so Jan took over doing our laundry. Differences over diet (Neil and I preferred vegetarian food), personal habits, politics and even theology surfaced. Because Neil needed medical treatment, he couldn't surf. And since the situation was only temporary, we didn't look for work. I virtually had nothing to do but read and dream.

I knew no one in Perth. Jan and Laurie were my new family, and it was clear that I didn't live up to their expectations in being able to look after their son. It wasn't a good start. After six months of living on and off with his family, I felt more like Neil's sister than his wife. I was keen to start making my own nest in my own space.

By April 1976, we had decided on Margaret River because of the great surf and the local community of alternative lifestyle people. We juggled our finances and, with the contract money I had saved, purchased 39 hectares of land eight kilometres north-east of Margaret River town for $22 000. What a blessing it was to own our own land within a year of getting married. I felt my job with Adidas had finally been worth it.

Neil and I began a pattern of earning that stayed with us for most of our married life. When we needed money, we found work. We rarely had savings but never went hungry. That autumn, both of us worked on a wheat and sheep farm in Pingelly run by the Lange family. I cooked lunches and 'smoko' cakes on a wood stove and made sandwiches for the shearers. I was astonished at how much they ate. I tried to slip in the occasional vegetarian meal or wholemeal cake, but they just said they would make their own. The men preferred greasy mutton and fluffy white-flour cakes and bread. I capitulated and cooked what they liked, though they still preferred to get their own dinner.

After the shearing, we helped with the ploughing, getting the ground ready for seeding with wheat. The tractors went all day and night. I did a few shifts to give the men a chance to sleep or do repairs. The wide 20-disk plough covered the ground pretty quickly. Mrs Lange was a real farmer's wife and helped with everything: raising orphan lambs, collecting spare parts from town, ordering fertiliser, repairing fences, being an extra hand to yard sheep, as well as growing a garden, running a household and raising children.

Later that year, Neil worked in a hostel in Perth for alcoholic and homeless men for five weeks. I went to Sydney and did some commentary for Channel 9 for the Olympic Games in Montreal. The contrast with my new life in Western Australia was dramatic. I stayed in inner-city accommodation with friends who were assisting street people in Kings Cross and having run-ins with police whom they suspected were reselling confiscated drugs. One of the people my hosts were helping at that time was Juanita Nielsen, who later disappeared and was presumed murdered because of the inside information she might have had! There is still a mystery surrounding her disappearance.

I met up with the Olympic swimmer Murray Rose during the Montreal Games and we shared a meal at one of the few restaurants in Sydney that served real vegetarian food. (If you wanted a vegetarian meal at a restaurant in those days, they just took the meat off your plate.) I also met up with Michael Wenden's wife, Narelle. These friendships developed and strengthened over the years, even though we usually only saw each other every four years when the Olympics were on.

Back in Margaret River, Neil and I took the advice of the former owners of our land, Roy and Pat Gray, and studied how the land changed with the seasons before deciding where to build. For three months, we lived in a caravan on the site where we thought the house and sheds would be best located. Like native women the world over, I carted water in large plastic containers from a permanent spring a kilometre from the caravan. The novelty of carrying water soon wore off.

We both played in the Margaret River Bulldogs basketball teams; I sometimes confused the game's rules with netball. Norma Guthrie (a state basketball player) quietly reminded me that I could move my feet and bounce the ball in basketball. Neil and I also joined the Gojuryu Karate Club. I won a competition in Geraldton for the best *kata* (a series of controlled movements). After this I felt confident enough to say to any potential attacker: 'Be careful, I do karate', although I only had a white belt. Fortunately I've never had to use this line. The best thing about playing these sports was meeting the great people from the Margaret River area.

~

In some ways, we didn't know what to do on the farm now that we owned it and lived on it. We didn't have enough money to build a house or to buy tools and machinery. We were highly idealistic, like many people who have romantic notions of 'going back to the land'.

One day the owners of the caravan came to take their van back to Pingelly. There had been a misunderstanding about the duration of the lease. We emptied everything out of the van on to the ground, and our home was driven away! Our kind neighbours, Andrea and Eion Lindsay, put us up for a few nights while we looked for a place to live. They had a waterbed, and I got seasick sleeping in it. Neil always reckoned I did tumble turns in bed, as I was very active in my sleep.

Finally, we secured a Forestry Department house for $12 a week rent; we spent $10 a week on food. We lived there for 18 months while we built a weatherboard house from recycled timbers. We learned everything from *The Australian Home Carpenter*. When we didn't know how to do what needed to be done next, such as roof framing or weatherboard cladding, Neil would go and work for someone else to learn how to do it. It was a huge education for me. Neil was very knowledgeable about tools and I had faith in his skill and confidence, even though all he'd built before was a doghouse. It was all a bit of a laugh, really. We were so seriously determined to do it all ourselves we nearly reinvented the wheel. But we were doing it for *society* and the *planet*. We were pioneer farmers, like the early settlers. We had no electricity — all the building was done using hand tools and mostly second-hand building materials. The house was made from rock-hard, forty-year-old seasoned jarrah that we secured from a house five kilometres south of Margaret River which we demolished and transported piece by piece. It cost us $200. Many broken drill bits lie buried in that timber. When Cyclone Alby struck the area in 1978, the house, reinforced with drill bits, survived completely intact.

When we weren't building our house, we were surfing — often for up to 40 hours a week — at Margaret River main break. I got brave and fit from surfing eight-foot waves in a big swell. Occasionally I would be caught by a wide set of waves and held down on the bottom by the whitewater. I had to really psych myself up before I could go out in those conditions. I was the only woman out there, but I didn't yet feel like a real surfer.

After living for a couple of months in the Forestry Department house and doing daily shifts of building and surfing, we realised that living an alternative lifestyle on the land was going to be a lot harder than we had thought. Like many other people who thought they could somehow make the world a better place by living a simple rural life, we did it the hard, idealistic way, learning as we went. Many people gave up after a few years. Others like us struggled on. The learning process was heartbreaking and discouraging, mostly because of our ignorance. We didn't have the years of experience that farmers have from being born on the land. When we did have success, like installing our slow-combustion wood stove and having our first hot shower (outside for a year), we were really pleased with ourselves.

By the end of 1976 I was ready to get my teeth into something that would be more rewarding than just trying to live off the land. I couldn't believe how long it took to build a house. Neil was the builder and I was the builder's labourer. He had casual jobs and I still had some contract money coming in, but we often ran out of money for building, which slowed us down even more. So I looked around for something I could do to help. I found it in swimming. Busselton High School, 40 kilometres north of Margaret River, had a new outdoor 25-metre unheated pool and I swam some demonstration laps at its opening. I didn't have a racing swimsuit and swam in a halter-neck number I'd bought from an opportunity shop! It felt strange to be 'Shane Gould Innes, the Swimmer' in my adopted home. I was just starting to feel more 'rounded' as a person and I was wary of being stereotyped. Nevertheless, I started a swim school at the high school pool in partnership with my sister Lynette, who was visiting us while travelling around Australia. Lyn had infinite patience when teaching young children and beginners. She had worked and learned swim instructing with Forbes and Ursula Carlile's swimming organisation in Sydney, earning pocket money during her university holidays.

Lyn taught the beginners and I took the developing swimmers. This was the beginning of 16 seasons of swimming teaching for me. Lyn and I worked morning and evening, staying during the day with some schoolteacher friends in Busselton where we filled in the time by watching the Test cricket on TV. We then drove back to Margaret River for the night. I enjoyed teaching swimming, improving techniques for efficiency, and overcoming problems that made swimming an unpleasant experience for some people. I bought some Speedos, too! Neil was pleased that my enterprise was boosting our income.

In 1976, Neil and I helped to re-enact the 1876 rescue of passengers from the ship *Georgette*, which was wrecked ten kilometres south of the mouth of the Margaret River. Grace Bussell, daughter of a settler, and Sam Isaacs, their Aboriginal employee, had used horses to make their way out through the waves to rescue the passengers.

For the re-enactment of this event, eight volunteers sailed in a dinghy with a makeshift mast and sail (plus an outboard motor) through the choppy waves to where the remains of the wreck can still be seen. I wore an op-shop satin nightgown over my swimsuit. Neil and the men wore shorts and dinner jackets. I think we may have mixed up Western Australian history with the sinking of the *Titanic* . . .

On the beach, two descendants of Grace and Sam, Brigid Terry and Bill Isaacs, tried in vain to get their horses into the surf. There was no way that they would venture into the breaking waves. Eventually, we six 'passengers' swam to shore ourselves. The horses stood quietly on the beach while speeches were made, photos were taken and the participants were interviewed. A reporter asked for our names to accompany the photos. Neil called himself 'Peter Rabbit', not wanting to have his real name in the paper, and that's how his name appeared.

~

I decided at this time to do some further studies. With some of my summer earnings I enrolled at Murdoch University in 1977 to do an Arts degree. I rented a room in Fremantle with some other students and spent three days in Perth each week and the other four days in Margaret River. It was a wonderful time for me, even though I missed Neil and found all the driving difficult. We only had one vehicle, a tray-back Bedford four-cylinder truck, and a 250cc trail bike which Neil had ingeniously fitted with surfboard racks. The Bedford was a tough and useful vehicle, and I drove this to Perth each week. We had no phone at that time, so we relied on neighbours, or our good friend, Ivan Clarke, who managed the tourist bureau in Margaret River, to get messages through.

On days when I was home I learned how to use carpentry tools and sawed, drilled (that damned jarrah!), chiselled and hammered the frames and weatherboards for the house. Neil had been working at the local pine mill, stacking timber, but he had to give it up when he developed a rash from the toxic chemicals the timber was dipped in after it was sawn. The rash was particularly bad when he wore his wetsuit in the surf. He spent many nights feeling extremely uncomfortable, and only cold showers and, eventually, antihistamines gave him relief.

We then bought a lawnmowing round in Margaret River. I raked grass, did edges and mowed long kikuyu grass with a Victa two-stroke mower. Neil used the self-propelled roller mower and did the finishing touches after me. With the regular surfing and physical work, I was slim and fit.

Once a month we went to bush dances at the Cowaramup Hall, where a bush band called Bungarra played great foot-stomping music. I loved these dances and looked forward to them each month.

~

The 40-year-old fences on the farm needed replacing, and new smaller paddocks needed to be constructed. We obtained a permit from the Forestry Department and cut down jarrah trees, which we split into fence posts. I used the back of the axe to debark the trees, and Neil drove steel wedges into the timber with a sledgehammer to split the logs into posts. Treated pine posts weren't then in common use. The trees we cut down were mostly affected by dieback, a fungal disease, and only lasted 20 years in the ground. Splitting posts was hard work, and the jarrah sap left red stains on our clothes and hands for weeks. The forest was a beautiful place to work, though. I would take along alfalfa sprout sandwiches on thick slices of wholemeal bread, with lashings of homemade tomato relish, and we would have a bush picnic sitting on sooty, blackened logs.

In the Forestry Department house we had a No. 2 Metters wood stove and I didn't have much success with it. I didn't know that bread needed a hot oven to cook, so my loaves made good doorstops! I had more success in the garden. I grew tomatoes, from which I made tomato sauce and relish; I sold the surplus to the local greengrocer. The Margaret River district's annual agricultural show was an inspiration for me, and the wonderful cakes, bottled produce, vegetables and handicrafts made me envious of other women's skills.

Life was a real adventure. There were plenty of books available to find out how to do anything we needed to do. Which is not to say we didn't make plenty of mistakes! Neil liked to work slowly, and his handiwork was meticulous. I wanted action, construction and results — the end product, so that it could be used. Neil was happier with the process, and I gradually learned to take a more relaxed approach.

I read and studied and travelled back and forth from Perth, working on the farm and in the bush. I liked the mental stimulation of learning as well as the quiet peace of the bush. At the end of 1977, the final lesson for environmental studies, one of my courses at university, involved a week's camp at Myalup, south of Perth. Out in the field I learned to recognise many of the native Western Australian plants and trees and to understand how they all fitted together in the scheme of things. One exercise we did was to mark out a one-metre-square plot and count the number of species in it. In the bush I counted 30 varieties; in the pine plantation there were three. The object of the exercise was to demonstrate the danger of monoculture farming: if one plant became diseased in the pine forest, one-third of all the vegetation would be destroyed. There was health in a diverse ecosystem.

Neil and I continued to read books that confirmed our choice of a simple lifestyle. Politically, I was a left-wing greenie. I went on peace marches and, with others, protested against the proposal to build a nuclear power plant in the south-west of Western Australia. We formed the Margaret River Nuclear Awareness Group to educate ourselves and others about the dangers of the nuclear fuel cycle and viable alternatives. We unsuccessfully lobbied the shire to declare itself a nuclear-free zone. I had a sticker on my kitchen door declaring our house a nuclear-free zone for a number of years, though some of the vegetarian lentil rissoles and bean dishes I made created a natural gas that was nearly as offensive as nuclear energy. Ultimately, through public pressure and environmental commonsense, the idea of building a nuclear power station in the area became a non-vote-winning proposition.

I grew our vegetables and fruit organically. I preferred putting energy into the practical, food-producing gardens and orchards, rather than into ornamental gardens. Idealism and financial constraints made me very resourceful. I made my clothes on my Singer treadle sewing machine from natural cotton and wool fabrics, and I discarded any clothing made from synthetic material. I lived in drawstring pants until I found that jeans lasted longer doing farm labouring. I recycled packaging, envelopes, paper and glass. Paper made good garden mulch. Many of these ideas are now mainstream, but in the 1970s they were part of the counter-culture. It was a heady, idealistic time and I felt like I was one of the agents of change. We spent many hours in our warm kitchen or leaning on a fence post with a cup of herbal tea or grain coffee talking with each other and chatting to our visitors.

Neil and I produced our own electric power with a wind generator. We couldn't afford a ten-metre tower as well as the generator, batteries and propeller, so we erected a three-metre tower with the generator and the two-metre propeller on the roof of the house. But the house was in a wind shadow — great for living, but not so good for catching the wind. We still needed our kerosene lamps as a back-up. The wind generator on the roof was a very effective weather indicator. When the wind blew, we certainly knew it! The house vibrated as the blades roared around like an aeroplane about to take-off. As the gusts came and went, so did the speed and noise of the generator.

It was a huge disappointment that it didn't work for us. The whole system needed more equipment and a taller tower to make it functional — but it would require money we didn't have. Instead, we purchased a diesel generator that provided 240-volt electricity. The silent fluorescent lights were wonderful after the subdued light and hissing of the kerosene lamps and the roaring of the wind generator.

We continued to pick up work wherever we could. Neil had regular seasonal shearing work, which he did for eight years. It was back-breaking work, but it paid well. The vineyards and tourism hadn't yet developed in Margaret River. Those industries now provide seasonal employment. Some couples went to the city to recharge their bank balances; others went 'up north' to work on the crayfish boats or in the mining camps.

When our neighbours, Eion and Andrea Lindsay, went to the Abrolhos Islands, which lie in the Indian Ocean west of Geraldton, for three months to go cray fishing, I volunteered to run the drive-in movie theatre kiosk for them. I had always wanted to be a shopkeeper! The drive-in showed movies two nights a week. I cooked hamburgers, and sold sweets and the usual hot and cold drinks. I quite enjoyed those nights, except when the truck broke down or its lights failed. One very dark, wet and moonless night I drove the eight kilometres home in the pouring rain, using a torch to see where I was going.

We moved into the house at the end of 1977 while it still looked like a building site, with corrugated iron nailed to the windows. (It was to take us ten years to finish building it.) We decided to have a house-warming party combined with my 21st birthday. Friends of all ages came and we raved around a camp fire and ate delicious food. It was a great feeling to have a sense of community with these 'locals'.

Neil didn't give presents often, but when he did, they were beauties. He gave me a mated heifer (cow) for my birthday. I named her Pippin. She was a Red Poll–Jersey cross and cost just $30. (Beef prices were in a slump that year!) Pippin became a part of the family. She and I were neck-and-neck having babies for a while. She won with six calves. I learned to milk her by hand; a cupful after an hour was my first effort, and that took two buckets of bran and chaff feed for Pippin to eat. Eventually, I got more proficient and could milk her anywhere, untied, as long as she had a bucket of feed to eat. We milked her once a day; the calf got the rest. I had a hand separator rigged up in the laundry, so we often got cream and skim milk. I made the cream into butter, and the buttermilk went into cakes. I loved Pippin; she was part of our life on the farm. We could keep the time by her habits. She would expect to be milked by 7.30 am. She was our alarm clock, waking us up by chewing her cud outside the bedroom window. That was before we had two-footed alarm clocks.

The summer of 1977/78 was dry — great conditions for a plague of grasshoppers. They ate everything they could sit on that was green. We tried ploughing borders of land, but they just hopped over them. We used beer baits, molasses traps and, out of desperation, some bran 'baits' with Malathion poison. Nothing worked. We got some turkeys and chickens to try and scare them off, but they slept when the grasshoppers were most active in the heat of the day, and the foxes that lived in the forest were too cunning and fast for the turkeys. Finally, we got some fertile guineafowl eggs that a lovely broody bantam hen hatched out, and the guineafowl did the trick. Over two seasons, they virtually wiped out the pesky grasshoppers. But then we had to put up with their screeching squawks. They were good watch birds if a strange dog, fox or horse came near our half-built house, but it wasn't too pleasant a noise at 5 am. The guineafowl were better guards than Cactus the dog!

Our simple, subsistence lifestyle was a lot of hard work. Until we got electric power, we had a kerosene fridge (made in 1948) to keep our food and Pippin's lovely fresh milk cold. It was a smoky old thing. It was just another part of the daily routine of the household to trim the wick, clean the chimney and fill the tank with kerosene.

Our Everhot wood stove was finally producing edible meals, mostly brown rice and vegetarian dishes. It also produced marvellous hot water. We showered outside next to the 1000-gallon corrugated-iron rainwater tank. If it was windy, we had to stand back from the shower rose to get wet. It wasn't until our first baby was born in August 1978 that we built a bathroom. In fact, the walls were being hammered on while I was in labour and after I got home from hospital. Baby Joel slept through it all.

The steady stream of visitors to the farm helped to share the workload, but eventually this took its toll. Our time and attention was taken away from the children and given to the visitors. There just wasn't enough time to give to everyone. People would stay for a day, or for months at a time. We kept one room for live-in visitors and there was always room for tents in the yard or a space for a mattress on the lounge-room floor. We had two married couples live with us for nine months. We lived as a community, sharing jobs and our lives. I enjoyed having help to share the work. I only had to cook and clean every three weeks and was able to get out on the land and help with building.

Two rather mysterious visitors we had stay with us for a week or two were wandering Christian disciples. Our house was on the Christian pilgrim's route around Australia. This couple had no car, and few possessions beyond the loose cotton clothes they wore. After a few days, we realised we were being taken for a ride. The couple gave nothing in return for the food and shelter we gave them. It took another week for them to leave such a good wicket.

One of our visitors was Marvin, a Californian Baptist minister who had spent two years in Africa with the Peace Corps. He was recovering from the news that his wife had changed her sexual preference. He stayed for about three months. Most visitors who came helped on the farm or with building the sheds or parts of the house. Marvin didn't want to learn how to use the tractor, he said. If he did, he would have to use it. Instead, he was a great help to me in the house. Marvin took a walk through the forest each morning, taking photos of the abundant wildflowers. I was astonished at the variety of species he photographed. He really opened my eyes to the beauty of the forest, which was just a broken peg's throw from my washing line.

For years we opened our house to people in crisis. We had women seeking refuge from domestic violence, state wards from Perth for holidays, and burned-out youth workers who needed to recover and reassess their lives.

~

In 1985, we set aside four hectares and planted tagasaste trees, which are native to the Canary Islands. They are used in farmyards around Australia for green feed for cows, chickens, sheep and calves, and for the prolific numbers of seeds they produce and which poultry enjoy. They are a lovely shade tree if you can prune them properly. We had ours planted by a tree-planting machine, but they were decimated by a plague of rabbits and we had to replant by hand. When Neil saw the rabbits' dastardly work, he shouted: 'God, do something!' Eerily, the rabbits caught myxomatosis within a week and our newly planted trees survived well.

We increasingly found that the financial reality of running our farm was like pouring money into a bottomless, dry well. We tried raising cattle, buying them as day-old calves from the Cowaramup calf sales. They needed feeding twice a day with Denkavit, a commercial calf formula, which was expensive and time-consuming. As our family grew, I wasn't always able to care for the children *and* do the outside farm work, though I managed to do quite a bit with the young ones safe in a pram or strapped in a sling.

The returns financially from the calves were negative once the calves grew to an age where they could be sold. Sheep seemed more promising, so in 1979 we bought some Border Leicester–Merino cross ewes and Dorset rams. The British-breed sheep did better in Margaret River with its high rainfall than the pure Merinos with their tight crimp and finer wool. We sold lambs for meat and the wool as a bonus. The money we earned was enough to pay for more fencing and tree planting.

I learned to class wool in the shed, loving the smell of the lanolin and the activity of the shearing shed. Because of the lack of adequate yards, we often had the frustrating experience of the sheep and lambs, some shorn and others not, getting mixed up. Neil and I both learned to swear when we started to keep sheep. Bessy, our sheep dog, was a great help with rounding up and yarding the sheep. Neil had trained her well, and she saved us a lot of walking and running — and yelling!

Neil had learned to shear quite well and he went on to do all our shearing unless his back became too sore from the work. In later years the children helped with the branding, tailing and castration of lambs. They stomped the wool into bales and removed the 'daggy bits' from the fleece. They liked sitting under the wool table getting covered with pieces of wool that became itchy inside their clothes. They would then have an excuse to take a long, deep bath, where I showed them the fundamentals of swimming — floating and breathing.

As time went on, the farm came to seem like an expensive indulgence. Sheep and wool prices dropped. The demand for carpet-wool looked promising so we got out of border Leicesters and into breeding carpet-wool sheep knowing we didn't have enough land for a large flock. The price of a fat lamb in 1980 was $25; in 1995 it was still $25. With increased costs and inflation, no wonder farmers went broke. We decided on Drysdales in the early 1980s, a New Zealand breed of carpet-wool sheep. With their open fleece, they were an ideal high-rainfall sheep. Prices for carpet wool were quite good and it appeared that carpet-wool sheep were going to be in demand. There was a carpet-wool factory in Albany, too, and we wanted to support a local market. We set ourselves up as Sharon Valley Stud and went into breeding. Our brand was S6V. Drysdales have a high micron count — over 35 (Merinos are 18–22) — so the wool was quite coarse to handle. It was straight — no wrinkles (crimp) — and grew rapidly, so that the sheep needed shearing twice a year. I attended breeders' meetings and learned to class the wool at other growers' farms. I loved learning about the genetics of breeding and how the wool was marketed.

To make a carpet, 20 per cent of the wool must be coarse carpet wool. This gives wool carpet its resilience — the ability to stand up and keep its shape after being trodden on. There is some brittle white fibre in carpet, too, called kemp. Too much kemp causes the yarn to snap. If you look closely at a wool carpet, you can see the kemp, as it won't absorb dyes. Just like some of the greying hairs on my head!

I often transported the wool to Perth or Albany to be batched with other growers' supplies. It was a big thing for us to have five bales of wool. To keep the wool growing consistently, the sheep needed more protein and green feed in the dry summer months. So we grew white lupins (blue lupins are not palatable to sheep) for a couple of seasons. Lupins are a nitrogen-fixing plant, so we knew that they would improve the soil naturally as they grew and then add organic matter to the soil after the harvest. We were very into permaculture and liked to do things that served a number of purposes.

We grew some magnificent crops, about four hectares of tall, lush plants. We pulled wild turnip weed out by hand rather than use chemical sprays. The children loved to play hide and seek among the lupin plants, which were often taller than they were. It was worth the sacrifice of some flattened plants to hear the giggles and see the joy on their faces as they played.

CHAPTER 10

Mothering

I think in an ideal world, everyone would have children,' I said. 'That's how people learn how to love.
Kids suck love out of your bones.

~

Helen Garner, *My Hard Heart*

ONE DAY IN THE AUTUMN OF 1978, Neil and I had a surf at dusk at South Point, Cowaramup Bay, near Margaret River. The ocean was smooth and glassy, greenish grey in colour, with the waves' whitewash tipped with gold as it reflected the sunset. The swell was just big enough to break at South Point, a left-hander breaking on a rocky reef at the south headland. Neil and I were the only ones still out. We caught a wave together. The lip of the wave threw itself over the top of both of us, forming a tube. There were actually three of us in that tube together, as I was five months' pregnant with our first child, Joel. The setting sun formed a shadow in front of the wave, making it a totally private place. That moment in the wave was like a gift. It was the last wave I caught before I entered Nappy Valley.

Pregnancy had changed my surfing patterns. It's uncomfortable paddling out on a fibreglass surfboard when you're pregnant. It's like lying on a watermelon. I heard about a kneeboard called a 'spoon', which is hollowed out in the middle, but before I could get hold of one, my belly got too big and I had to give up all ideas of surfing.

I had re-enrolled at Murdoch University that year, but I had decided to study by correspondence when I learned I was pregnant. When the pregnancy started to show, I was at first self-conscious about my body. I thought that everyone would now know that I had had sex! I was still quite prudish. I was also worried that my life would again be the focus of public attention.

I put aside my concerns and got on with being pregnant with the same enthusiasm I had for other physical activities. This was a very special activity, needing nine months of training. Birth would be like a big racing meet and the baby the winner's medal. I read all I could about the stages of prenatal growth. My bible was Dr Derek Llewellyn-Jones's *Everywoman*. I pored over the pages of the chapter called 'A Wondrous Growth' until the book was dog-eared. I also read Ina May Gaskin's book *Spiritual Midwifery*, which was an 'alternative lifestyle' view of birth.

Joel was born by natural childbirth at 3 pm on a Sunday afternoon at Margaret River Hospital. Neil and two special friends, Helen McFerran and Jill Ennever, were with me at the hospital. Jill and Helen left after a while, and Neil and I continued the back-rubbing, pushing and puffing. I would have liked to have a home birth, but at that time there were no trained, registered midwives to assist at home births. The Margaret River Hospital was like home, anyway, as I knew the two nurses who looked after the few patients.

During that first night the baby cried a lot, and I tried unsuccessfully to pacify him. The nurse took him from me, fed him water from a bottle, and then returned the now contented baby to me. I cradled him in my arms, and we looked at each other by the light of the bedside lamp. His wrinkled, old-man expression seemed to say, 'Well, hello. So you're my mother. Pleased to meet you face-to-face.'

When I became a mother I experienced emotions, sensations and insights I had never previously known. I never dreamed that having a child could have such a deep and irreversible influence on every aspect of my life, my personal identity and my social persona. I was full of wonder when milk leaked from my breasts at the sight, sound or touch of my baby. Sometimes, just thinking the word 'baby' triggered the letdown reflex. Some of my most precious and satisfying moments were spent curled up in a beanbag between midnight and dawn by the wood fire, breastfeeding the baby by candlelight and dozing in fuzzy weariness. The first ten weeks of Joel's life were the longest of my life as I became used to my new baby's constant needs and the night feeding. I felt that I had adapted to parenthood really well by the time number two came along.

I loved the harmony I felt with the baby; his sensuousness and unique smell; and the look of bliss when he fell asleep, replete, with the last dribble of milk on his tiny rosebud mouth. As I did later with all my children, I breastfed Joel on demand and carried him around wrapped in natural fibres in a sling.

Play group provided a vital network for me, and for those other idealistic new settlers in Margaret River. We were all far away from our family supports. There are many great books about birth and mothering, but nothing takes the place of face-to-face talks with other women. It was reassuring as a young mother to know that I wasn't alone in my experience of extreme tiredness, physical changes, emotional overload, and the confusing mysteries of babies' and toddlers' attempts to communicate their needs.

Our play group met once a week at the Ambulance Hall in Margaret River. We paid $1 each time to cover the hire of the hall and the purchase of paints. We all brought along our small children, old toys and fresh, homemade playdough. The women from this group helped to set up the Margaret River Community Kindergarten for four-year-olds. Some of those who still live in Margaret River are among my good friends.

~

The next 18 months were filled with building the new house and sheds for the farm. We also had to replace our old fences with new posts and ring-lock sheep wire.

Our scheme to have an 'intentional community' had brought two couples to live with us. One couple were from England. The others were good friends, Jim and Jill, from Sydney. We had a weekly meeting to discuss work rosters, followed by prayer and bible study. We had a shared food kitty and a rotational three-week job cycle — the first week for all the outdoor jobs, gardening, chopping wood and milking the cow; the second week for cleaning the house inside and out; and the third for cooking all the meals, bread and biscuits.

We worked together on building and fencing, caring for poddy calves and a hundred cross-bred sheep. We also took part-time jobs — Neil did lawnmowing, fencing and building, and I taught swimming in the neighbour's pool. Jill was studying naturopathy and she experimented on us with vegetarian raw foods. I had baby Joel to look after and breastfed him for 13 months. Our experiment in communal living was interesting and worthwhile, with some unexpected dynamics. While we had the idealistic attitude that we wanted to share the property, the other couples felt that they weren't able to gain financially from their investment of time and work while they lived with us.

~

Our second child, Kim, who also was born without the assistance of pain-relieving drugs, arrived in 1980. What a delight it was to have a daughter! Kim was safely born from a breach position, bottom first. She may have been tumbled around when, at seven months pregnant, I had a fall when I was chasing some sheep! My legs couldn't keep up with my heavier top half and I bounced on my belly. I felt a lot of uncomfortable movement and tightness for a few days afterwards.

Being a mother to two young children changed Neil's and my relationship in many ways. For one, he felt that he had lost his right-hand help on the farm, as most of my time was taken up with caring for Joel and Kim. The pregnancies had also changed my body. At 66 kilograms, I now had a woman's shape as well as muscles. I felt stronger than when I was 15 and sometimes wondered how fast I might have been able to swim if I'd kept up my training. I was generally very healthy, but one year I had a persistent cough that medication and dietary changes didn't help. My doctor finally suggested that I should damp-mop our dusty floors instead of sweeping them. Within a week, the cough was gone.

Although Neil's parents didn't share our alternative lifestyle, they generously came to Margaret River in their caravan every six weeks for a three-day weekend to help with building, fencing and, later on, childminding. I really appreciated these times. Jan brought containers of homemade biscuits, and frozen meals for Laurie, who couldn't handle the vegetarian beans and lentils. After a while I looked forward to their visits as a time when I could have a break from washing, cooking and child care.

In 1981, I was surprised to be honoured with a Membership of the British Empire. (Neil made the barbed comment that MBE actually stood for 'My Bum's Excessive'.) The investiture was to be held at Government House in Perth and the award was to be presented by Queen Elizabeth. Two immediate problems came to mind: What would I do with the children? And what would I wear? Joel wasn't quite three, and Kim was 18 months. I had never been separated from them. Neil had work to do on the farm and couldn't leave, so I decided to take both of the children to Perth and leave them at a child-care centre while I was at the ceremony. Neil's mother, Jan, would come with me to Government House. That was one problem solved. But what about clothes? Not one item of clothing in my wardrobe was anywhere near suitable! Some helpful friends supplied me with a pretty green dress, some shoes and even a hat! I scrubbed my fingernails clean and creamed my hands for a week. I was ready to meet the Queen.

The occasion was as opulent and ceremonious as I had imagined. The Queen was perfectly groomed and beautifully attired. When she reached me in the line-up, she asked sweetly, 'Do you still swim?' I replied, 'Only when I fall off my surfboard'. She gave me a puzzled look and moved on.

The children had enjoyed themselves so much playing with all the interesting equipment at the child-care centre, they were reluctant to leave when I came to collect them. The separation anxiety was all mine.

The award seemed far removed from my real life. I was so involved in being a mother that I felt I deserved an award more for mothering than for my swimming achievements. With two children, my motherhood was an intense, full-time occupation.

Neil was shearing, just locally, but he was away for long hours. A shearer's day starts at 7 am, there's smoko at 9, lunch from 11.30 to 12.30, a half-hour smoko at 2.30 pm, then they knock off at 5 pm. I didn't like to miss out on what was going on, so I would drive over to wherever he was working (we had two cars by then) to meet the owners and enjoy the atmosphere of the shearing shed. Because the mobs were relatively small, there were only one or two stands. The children got in the way when I tried to help sweep the floor or pull dags off the fleeces on the wool table. I learned enough, though, to take over the job of shed hand and wool classer on our own farm.

Neil soon found that our vegetarian diet didn't give him enough energy for the back-straining work of shearing, so we started eating more meat meals. As the main cook, I found cooking meat quicker and easier than preparing vegetarian meals. With our own sheep, we had a ready supply of meat, which was kept fresh in our old kerosene fridge. I was so proud when I could serve up a meal of meat and vegetables that was completely home-grown.

For three years I taught scripture at the Margaret River Primary School. I usually took the kids with me if they weren't too active, or had a girlfriend, or the kids' surrogate grandparents, Margaret and Leo Leslie, look after them while I had a two-hour break at the school for the class. I preferred teaching the older kids, who were starting to think about God themselves and questioning traditional beliefs. By the time I got back to my young children, my breasts were hard and full of milk — ready to feed my baby.

When I went into labour with our third child, Tom, in 1982, I was already very tired. I had been caring for our two preschoolers, and that afternoon I had been hand-sawing planks of wood to be used as cladding on the chook shed. After two natural births, I knew what to expect. I was longing to see and hold the little life that was growing inside me, but I knew how much it was going to hurt for him to come out! Tom was born after five hours of labour, during which I read some of Penelope Leach's book, *Baby and Child*. The advice given in the book helped me to relax, breathe properly and assist the baby to be born.

As a mother, I became more aware of other women with children, and of how the work we did in feeding and caring for our children was often taken for granted. A lot of it was mundane, boring and repetitive — but it was also essential.

In addition to caring for the children, I continued to work with Neil on the house and farm. I built and split fence posts out in the bush after debarking the trees that Neil felled. When Neil didn't have time, I did the daily farm walk to check on the animals, fences and water supplies. On cold mornings when the dew still lay on the wet grass,

I put the older children in the wheelbarrow and carried the baby in a sling while I fed the calves and checked for new lambs. I did the household chores, and prepared meals for our many visitors. It was often hard work, but I was young, fit and well organised.

By 1982 we were at full steam with children and farming, and we were always building something. Our earlier ideas of ministering to others were still strong, so when Reverend George Davies, the Youth Coordinator of the Uniting Church of Western Australia, asked us to host some troubled young kids on school holidays, we said 'yes' and the Department of Children's Services began to use us as a temporary refuge for women or children in crisis. One lad, David, spent every school holiday with us for three years. He became a part of our family.

Then there were the youth camps. George Penfold, from the local Margaret River Uniting Church, worked with us, and Reverend Davies brought groups of city teenagers for Easter camps for the next ten years. Part of the camp activities was to make 3000 mud bricks which were used to build a mud-brick barn.

During the 1980s, Neil went shearing every spring and summer. This was hard, back-breaking work, so I had to be sure there was plenty of hot water for his homecoming. He needed a hot shower, hot food and a restful evening.

Neil also began 'educating' horses for other people and, after a few years, started young racehorses for Ross Goulden's stud, Lindross, and later Mossmark Stud at Capel, north of Margaret River. Some of these horses, progeny of his stallion, Chestmark, were sold to Singaporean horse-owners.

Friends visited, sometimes stayed, and sometimes helped with the work. I enjoyed their company and learned how to listen to children's chat and adult conversation at the same time. Occasionally a reporter came for a 'What is Shane Gould doing now' story. Going back into the past with a reporter, or accidentally coming across photos or trophies while I rummaged in the junk room, was enough to bring on 'the miseries'. Neil, coming in for morning or afternoon tea, would notice my quiet, withdrawn mood. 'Have you been looking at your stuff again?' he'd say, irritation masking his compassion.

~

I found the monthly newsletter of the Nursing Mothers' Association of Australia a godsend — a real lifeline. My mother, bless her, gave me a subscription. It was so full of relevant information, and such a good gift idea, that I gave NMAA newsletter subscriptions to a number of friends when they had babies. The NMAA was formed in 1964, at a time when breastfeeding wasn't commonly accepted. Women had taken to bottle-feeding because they could be sure of exactly how much formula milk their babies were getting. It was a system that increased the mother's confidence and also allowed for the father to participate in feeding. It wasn't a bad thing, but it wasn't the very best thing for the baby. (Formula milk doesn't contain colostrum, which is now used by cyclists for its high human growth hormone content.)

At NMAA meetings, small groups of mothers discussed problems they might be having with breastfeeding. They also exchanged ideas about babies who cried a lot or wouldn't sleep. The involvement of fathers in the care of babies was addressed, too. It was refreshing and reassuring for young parents to find that their anxieties weren't trivialised. They were real concerns that needed real solutions. As time went on, however, some members of the association became over-zealous and came to be known as 'the milk police'.

The NMAA had some good slogans. One that struck a chord with me was: 'You have to be fit to be a mother.' After Tom's birth I was flabby and unfit, and exhausted from caring for three young children. I embarked on an exercise program that included jogging, swimming and doing sit-ups, and I soon felt better. Three months after Tom was born I swam in a marathon relay in the Blackwood River, two hours' drive inland from Margaret River, doing the one-kilometre swim in a good time. I also swam in the 1983 South West Games in Bunbury after training in the cold river and ocean a few times a week for a month. As a result of the training, I was soon physically fit again and able to enjoy my children more.

I continued to read widely about parenting, child development, organic gardening and theology. I pored over the works of Christian mystics such as Henri Nouwen. Howard Yoder's *The Politics of Jesus* and William Stringfellow's *An Ethic for Christians and Other Aliens in a Strange Land*, among other books, exercised my brain cells while I was deep in mothering land.

Like a lot of women, I felt that mothering was a job worth doing, but throughout the 1980s I struggled against the peer-group pressure to be a working mother, while also trying to break away from the stereotype of being a housewife. I consciously chose to be a full-time mother. In my kitchen I put up an NMAA poster that said, 'Mothering — a job worth doing', but Neil ripped it off the wall. 'Mothering isn't a job,' he snarled. 'Don't expect to be paid for it.' I was devastated. I had only wanted to express my pride in being a full-time mother; the idea of being paid hadn't entered my head! The poster was a cheery, motivational affirmation of a very important, sometimes rewarding but mostly thankless task. I felt totally misunderstood by Neil.

When Tom was five months old, I became pregnant again. I was distressed about having another baby on the way so soon after Tom's birth and I talked about it with a local church minister and counsellor. He helped me to appreciate the baby's life as a gift and suggested getting some help to make my job easier. As a start, I insisted that we get mains power, an automatic washing machine, and mice-proof kitchen cupboards.

A month before Kristin, our youngest son, was born, I spent three days in hospital catching up on sleep and rest. Joel, our eldest child, was just five. The Margaret River Hospital was like a rest home for people like me who were exhausted or convalescing and living far from their relatives. For the first time I contacted my parents and asked for their help. They were so surprised by my request that they immediately put their house on the market, bought a caravan, and drove to Margaret River to take over the household chores for three months while I looked after the children. Neil was out all day shearing.

With Kristin's arrival we hooked up to the electricity grid. Smelly generators and dull, smoky lights became a thing of the past. Previously, I would have the generator on for one or two hours during the day, then again at night. I'd set up the juice extractor, blender, twin-tub washing machine and the vacuum cleaner, then go from one appliance to another while the diesel engine chugged away, powering them all. If it was raining and the generator ran out of diesel, I had to light a candle, leave the kids in the house, dash up to the shed to refill the tank, then come back with diesel-smelling hands to finish preparing dinner or breastfeed a baby.

When Kristin was still very young, I used to take all the kids to the kindergarten class, where I was a volunteer mother's help. The five of us would swell the size of the group by 25 per cent. We were like a rent-a-crowd, so the Innes family didn't get invited out much!

With four children so close in age, I needed to be fit and really well organised. I think the time-management skills I learned during my busy teenage years, when I was attending school and training for six hours a day, helped me to cope with those demanding years with small children. Some days felt like a 1500-metre swim: I would be fatigued halfway through the day; then I'd get a second wind for the afternoon and push through the pain barrier of preparing the evening meal for four tired, hungry kids. Bathtime was the breather before the sprint home in the form of bedtime stories. I would often fall asleep on the bed next to one of the children after reading four or five books to them.

I tried to re-create for my children the childhood environment I had known in Fiji by creating an indoor and outdoor adventure playground for them. I turned the house over to children's activities. Our furniture was rough and tough, and the area that other people might dignify as the lounge room became a sort of children's gymnasium. I hung tyres and swings from the exposed beams, and put old mattresses on the floor for tumbling fun. The children's playthings were sand, mud, water, sticks, moss, trees, stones and animals. They had direct experiences of rural odours, such as springtime hay, Capeweed-smelling cow manure, steamy horse-snorts, kerosene lamp smells, wet wood smoke, and the aroma of the occasional dead rat! There was milk, still warm from the cow, freshly baked bread, and the 'mice' made by the children from the leftover bread dough.

I often had a baby on each hip. Or one on a hip and another on my back. Or we would all be snuggled up together reading books. The ebb and flow of the day was followed by calm evenings, with toddlers sleeping, tired out by the stimulation of the day's adventures. I was very satisfied.

As our children grew, my Olympic medals paled into insignificance. However, I still wanted to share with the kids my pride in being Australian. I began by educating them about Australian flora and fauna. At that time there were few books readily available, but I found what I was looking for in a speciality bookstore in Perth. Mem Fox's *Possum Magic*, and another book, *The Bunyip of Berkeley's Creek* were two of our favourites.

On Thursday nights on ABC regional radio, I would listen to folk music. I looked forward to the program each week. A local Margaret River folksinger–songwriter, Anna Pemberton, made a tape of songs about a mother's day with her children. The songs reflected my own experiences and reassured me that I wasn't the only woman who felt as I did. I think I believed that a 'good' mother never complains, is always capable and giving, and has an inexhaustible supply of love for her family. But mothering wasn't always bliss. In fact, there were times when I wanted to resign from my work as a mother, or to send my kids back from wherever they had come.

I withdrew from any public activities outside Margaret River between 1984 and 1989. *New Idea* visited the farm every two years to do a story. We used the $2000 payment to pay bills or to fund some overdue maintenance. There was always more media interest in the Olympic years. Unexpectedly, in 1988 a television news crew landed in a helicopter in our paddock to do a quick interview with me. I agreed on the condition that they take my children for a ride in the helicopter. The children were thrilled.

When the children were in primary school, I indulged my own love of children's stories by borrowing books from the local library and devouring them before the children could get their hands on them. Night-time was story time. I would sit on the floor in the upstairs bedroom loft area, cosy from the heat of the wood stove below in the kitchen. The light was soft and golden as it reflected off the dark red jarrah walls. Often I would get so caught up in the story that I'd stop reading aloud. The kids would prod me impatiently to keep on reading. On a few occasions I fell asleep while reading, exhaustion giving way to the warmth and relaxation at the completion of the day's work.

Astrid Lindgren's Pippi Longstocking had been my favourite book character as a child. Pippi was a nine-year-old red-haired orphan who lived alone in a Swedish village. I loved Pippi's wildness, her unconventionality and her fantastic adventures. I encouraged my children to do Pippi-type things. For instance, Joel was allowed to chop wood with a tomahawk when he was three (but only if he wore his gumboots). He occasionally managed to produce something useful in the way of kindling for the fire. Kim did her 'messy cooking' on the verandah with powdered milk, rolled oats, sultanas and water.

I would just hose her down afterwards. She could sleep anywhere as long as she had her lambskin. Kristin slept with a hammer beside him instead of a teddy bear, and Tom would disappear with the puppies into the garden to pick and eat peas for breakfast.

Like the children in the Mad Max movie, my kids were pretty feral until they went to school and had to fit into a structured system. Shopping with them was a nightmare! While Joel and Kim were at kindergarten, I would do the banking and farm business and then the shopping. By this time I would usually be tired and fed up. The two younger ones liked to slide on the cool, smooth floor of the supermarket and play hide-and-seek among the shelves. I just pretended they weren't mine. The supermarket manager dreaded when I came in with the kids. They never did any damage; they just used the area as another playground. Finally I gave up shopping with the kids and began ordering my groceries over the phone from Darnells' store at Rosa Brook, 15 kilometres away. They would be delivered on Friday afternoons. It was a great, old-fashioned service that I used for over ten years, saving both my sanity and that of the supermarket manager.

I've always recognised my need for 'soul food'. At this time when my life was so physical and taken up with practical matters, my soul was fed by women friends, books and music. With the children I enjoyed the story tapes and preschool songs put out by the Australian Broadcasting Commission. The songs were light and funny, and had easy tunes and strong rhythms.

I didn't like sending Joel to school. He was one of those boys who didn't like to sit still in class. In 1985, for his second year, we sent him to a little alternative school, the Nyindamurra Family School of Creativity, 20 kilometres away. It was a perfect environment for him. Parents had a big role in the school, in administration, as parent helpers, on excursions, and in maintaining the building and grounds. Kim also joined the school when she was kindergarten age. I loved going there, and did a stint for a year as school secretary and half a day a week as a parent helper.

The main disadvantage of the school was the driving it involved, even though the children caught a bus. To conserve fuel, I usually left the farm only once a week to do business in town. Going each week to the school meant I now had to make two trips. Schooling cost $10 a week for each child, and Neil persuaded me that we couldn't afford it.

Making money was a problem that Neil and I shared. We had chosen to live simple lives outside the fashions and consumerism of mainstream society. It was a form of voluntary poverty. We only insured our vehicles; we had no savings or superannuation. But when our children's needs increased, we knew that we needed more income. Neil frequently told me to go and get a job, and this was when conflict arose. I thought I might be able to make money by using my name and image, but this would mean going away from Margaret River for periods of time. Neil refused to support this idea. He wanted me to get a local job. Waitressing and cleaning were the only part-time jobs available.

When it was time for Tom to start school, the three older children were enrolled in Margaret River Primary School. Although I regret that all the children didn't have their primary years at Nyindamurra, the government school had other advantages to offer our kids, and most of the teachers were happy to have the help and involvement of parents.

I tried to ease the transition from home to the jungle of the playground by dropping into the school at lunchtime on days when I knew the kids were feeling emotionally vulnerable. Just sitting on a step with them for ten minutes in their school environment was enough to recharge their emotional batteries. If one of them was feeling really 'flat', I would let that one stay at home for some individual attention. I tried to stay in tune with each of the children. If they didn't quickly air a playground argument or talk about being told off by a teacher, they would become irritable, or not want to go to school, but be unable to say why.

The teachers and sports coaches were very good with my children, treating them as one of the team or class without any special privileges as 'Shane Gould's kids'. They didn't have to suffer the indignities that my youngest sister Jenny did. Their own individuality, characters and natural talents came through, so they were treated on their own merits.

I was the one with the problem. I wasn't sure what to do when they showed talent, which they all did to some degree. I played down my excitement about their achievements (though I was a proud parent) by congratulating them on their cleverness and skill, and focusing on the fun they got from participating. Despite my anxieties, the kids just got on and did their own thing. They generally enjoyed school and loved playing all sports. They are all very fit, like their parents. And they are quite aggressively competitive when they need to be.

When the children were little, people would ask me: 'Will you encourage your children to compete and train like you did?' I usually said, 'Yes, if they want to'. And then I would add that I wanted them to have good skills first and be active so that they would be fit for life. Privately, I worried about the nature of competition in elite sport.

One problem with living in a country town where there is a surfing ethic — the cruisy, 'everything's cool' attitude — is the mediocrity it encourages in kids. I'm not sure if it's because teenagers don't want to be different, or because working hard at being good at something is considered 'uncool'. The high school physical education teachers are aware of this attitude in Margaret River. My two younger boys have fortunately had the benefit of coaching and mentoring from older, successful surfers and the sports teachers. The men are like 'uncles' in a tribal village.

The hardest thing for me as a mother is to let go of my children. I'm finding that it really does take a 'village' to raise a child. The 'village' in which the children are raised will largely determine their interests and direction. I have heard that there are four elements of success: talent, skill, hard work and luck. (Luck is defined as when preparation meets opportunity.) I had all of these during my sporting life, and my children have had a lot of 'luck', too. It is yet to be seen what they do with it.

CHAPTER 11

A New Love

*Feel gives you timing. Feel and timing
give you balance.*

~

Pat Parelli

BY JANUARY 1986 WE WERE DISAPPOINTED that the farm wasn't
paying and were worn out by all our visitors. Our children were
seven, six, four and three. We decided to go to the south coast of
Western Australia for a year to assist with the camping and
horsemanship program at Esperancho Youth Ranch, 40 kilometres
north of Esperance. It would give us a chance to get a perspective on
our lives.

When we arrived at Esperancho, the camp workers were away on
holiday, so we spent some time with our friends Cathy and Trevor
Florrison, skiing and 'skurfing' behind their power boat on the salt
lake at the ranch. The 'house' we had arranged to live in was a newly
built corrugated-iron shed with a cement floor but, as yet, no running
water or electricity. It was like camping, although we had some
luxuries: power via a cord that poked through the kitchen window; a
nearby toilet block that served the whole camp site; and showers 20
metres away.

We went to Esperancho on good faith, but there was a lack of good communication between us and the camp managers as to what we all expected. At times I was restless, with little meaningful work to do besides looking after the children and doing household chores. I tried to make good use of the time by doing a stretch-knit sewing course or helping with the horses at the ranch. I soon realised how little I knew about horses and how much there was to know. I felt a lot of pressure to do 'women's work', as the chores around the place were clearly divided by gender. I also felt uncomfortable in the community, sensing that people saw me as Shane Gould, rather than Shane Innes. I was separated from my support system — the other alternative lifestyle people in Margaret River who accepted me for who I now was. My life became nuclear rather than communal. I also missed the forest trees near our house; the country around Esperance consisted of gnarled scrub and salty, sandy soil. Neil and I agreed to cut our stay short and to return to Margaret River after five months, instead of the full year we had planned.

Towards the end of our time at the ranch we moved into town for six weeks. Esperance is a port and service town for the grain- and sheep-growing farms in the area. Cathy and Trevor, who had two young children of their own, kindly opened their house to us. It was a bit cramped with six of us in one large room. Conditions became even more difficult when Neil's mother, who was still grieving over the death of Neil's dad the previous year, came to stay for a few weeks and shared the same room. We all liked different foods, and had different ways of relating to the children.

I spent a lot of time walking along the beachfront while the children played in the sand, or on the wharf watching ships from the Middle East come into port to load grain or live sheep. Joel liked to go fishing, and we sat together on the edge of the wharf and talked about the exotic countries the huge, rusty ships had come from. Sometimes the sailors practised their English with us while we fished and the other kids skidded around on the barley that had spilled on the wharf. Occasionally we fished at night for garfish and bream, in the company of gnarled old-timers and other anglers wearing layers of mismatched clothing to ward off the chilly night air.

During this interlude in town, Neil and Trevor made a steel cart to be used for wagon rides and trained a part-Percheron horse to pull it. I did some of the painting of the cart. When it was finished, and the horse had been properly trained, we hired a babysitter for all six kids and Trevor, Cathy, Neil and I rode in the cart to a local Chinese restaurant for dinner. Cathy and I went to the opportunity shop first and bought some fancy clothes for the evening. Cathy found a fur coat, which she wore with grace and aplomb on the cart. Because all vehicles had to have headlights and a tail-light, we attached a spotlight at the front, powered by a car battery, and a tail-light covered with red wrapping paper. Trevor practised some precision driving by taking the horse to the end of a jetty and then backing him up for about 20 metres. It was quite a feat, considering the cart had a turntable and the jetty was only one vehicle wide. On the way to the restaurant we clip-clopped into a drive-in bottle shop and bought some peach wine. We tied the horse to a lamppost outside the restaurant and gave it a nosebag of chaff to eat.

On another excursion, all ten of us piled into our 1968 Land Rover and Trevor's Landcruiser and we took a trek along the Noondoonia track east of Esperance, then went north towards Salmon Gums on the main east–west highway that crosses southern Australia. Trevor mentioned that some people had recently died on the track when their car broke down and they ran out of water. But water wasn't a problem for us. It was early winter, and there was water in the dams that had been built along the route in the late 19th century when the track was used to transport wool from the station country to the coast. Before there was a wharf at Esperance, ships used to moor next to the smooth-sloping rocks that dropped steeply into the ocean. Teams of horses would negotiate the heavy wool-laden drays down the rocks to the ships, where they were manhandled on to the decks. Along the track to Noondoonia Station were remnants of the hopes and dreams of those early pioneers, the rubble of homes with stone chimneys standing as a memorial to those families who had once lived there. We boiled the billy at one of these places and I thought I could hear the laughter of children coming from the walls of intricately placed stone.

I was relieved when we reached 'civilisation' at Noondoonia Station. We stayed in the shearers' quarters, which had saggy springed beds and a cement floor. Like many structures in the outback, the walls of the shed were clad with kerosene tins that had been hammered flat. They were a rusty colour, which blended in with the brown-red earth. The station was a powerfully beautiful place, with much history. I felt like an intruder into a past that belonged to other people.

Back in Esperance we packed up our belongings and headed home in the Land Rover to Margaret River and the farm. The trip took ten hours, so we stopped the night at a friend's family's farm in Manjimup. We were looking to buy a horse harness that was in good condition, and we had been told that our host, Basil, had some old harnesses. He was a very interesting man. He had been born in the area where he still lived. With his first pay packet he had bought some stamps on a first-day cover, and he continued to collect stamps and other treasures for many years. He showed us a stamp that, he said, Queen Elizabeth wanted to buy, but he didn't want to sell it. Basil also had a vase that a Dutch museum wanted as part of a three-piece set. He had bought it in a bazaar in Jakarta when Indonesia was still the Dutch East Indies.

While at the farm we celebrated Tom's fourth birthday, and Basil let me use his kitchen to bake a cake. During the evening, I went to the large chest freezer to get out some bread and Basil warned me not to be alarmed by the frozen possum and young tiger snake I would find there. He was collecting animals for the Western Australian museum.

On the farm were four small railway men's cottages full of harness tools and machinery spare parts. We admired them, not even daring to ask if we could buy anything. This man was out of our league. The next morning we went for a drive with Basil to check on some fences. Emus had been damaging them and his cattle were escaping into the forest. Basil told us stories of his life as a child in the area. There used to be wild horses around Lake Muir, which was close to the farm, and he reckoned there was still a small herd of them living in the forest.

On our return to Margaret River, we settled back into our life on the farm. We had decided to try to make a living from our growing involvement with horses. We set up a riding school, which we called Brumby Ned's Horse and Rider School. The America's Cup yacht race was to be held in Fremantle in 1987 and we planned to provide trail rides to tourists, along with riding lessons and horse starting and re-education.

Up until this time, much of my experience with horses had been vicarious, through observing Neil riding and educating young horses. Neil had bought a horse, Bucko, at auction when we first moved to the farm in 1976. We also had Spinner, a stallion. Bucko was a pretty lifeless horse, a pacer who hadn't been ridden, only used in harness. I was naive about horses at that time and impatient to ride him. One day I went on a trail ride around the farm on Bucko, with Spinner following loose. At that time we couldn't afford saddles, so I rode bareback. Bucko started to get away from me, and Spinner overtook us, which excited Bucko even more. Soon, the bush on either side was going by in a green-grey blur. I lasted for about 200 metres before I slid off and then under the horse — all in slow motion. The last thing I remember before I was knocked out is seeing a hoof coming towards my face. My face swelled up like a balloon, but nothing was broken except my pride and my enthusiasm for riding. I also lost a boot and Neil's first gift to me — a little bronze fish on a leather thong — in the accident. I later recovered the boot, but the fish is still somewhere out there under a she-oak.

We then purchased a Welsh mountain pony, Duke. (He is still in the family.) Duke could do a standing jump over a one-metre gate when he wanted to change paddocks. I had a love/hate relationship with him. When I was doing riding lessons for local children I would ride him every few days for half an hour to tune him up. He was so quick to turn if he spooked at a kangaroo. I fell off Duke more times than any other horse. He was fine with kids in a group, and he loved to pull a two-wheel cart with all of us in it for picnics in the bush.

By 1977, we had a mob of thoroughbred horses agisted on the property. There were 12 mares, a stallion, foals and geldings. These horses were an old guy's Melbourne Cup hope, and they were fabulous teachers. Observing their behaviour, especially their interactions with Neil's stallion and my gelding, was the beginning of a great appreciation of horse behaviour and how it can relate to human behaviour. Through my observations, I learned very quickly — not only about horses, but also about body language, clear communication signals and decisive leadership. Later, when I was riding and handling horses more myself, I improved my rather loose disciplining of the children as a result. (The children were happier — and felt safer — knowing what their limits were.)

Dad had sent us a book called *The Jeffery Method of Horse Handling* by Maurice Wright, a long-time resident of Armidale. The book described a method for 'gentling' unbroken horses — catching, saddling, bridling and riding them gently — all within just two hours. Neil decided to try it, and we chose a three-year-old filly who had never been ridden and had barely been handled. It took us two hours just to catch her, but within another couple of hours Neil had her saddled and bridled and was riding her confidently. It was a great experience for Neil and wonderful to watch. This was the real beginning of our involvement in natural horsemanship.

In 1987 we heard about a horse trek that would be held the following year as part of Australia's Bicentennial celebrations. The horses and carts would be supported by a convoy of trucks carrying people (including some veterinarians), food, tents and horse feed. It was planned to take 13 days to travel 600 kilometres along the water pipeline from Mundaring Weir, 80 kilometres inland from Perth, to the goldfields in Kalgoorlie. The pipeline, designed by visionary engineer C.Y. O'Connor, was completed in 1903 to supply water to the settlers in the marginal desert country. It still supplies water to the goldfields and towns along the way. We decided to participate in the trek as a family, and began our preparations.

We would need a cart that was light but sturdy and roomy enough for four kids and two adults, and a horse that was fit enough to pull us all. The 100 participants were briefed by veterinarians from the Murdoch Veterinary School and officials from the Western Australian Endurance Riders Association on matters of fitness training for the horse and riders. We also consulted with Mike Thill, the driver for the Carlton Brewery team, who was in Western Australia on a visit to Bunbury. (Mike later competed in four-in-hand harness driving at the 1992/93 World Equestrian Games.) One of the Carlton Brewery Clydesdales liked beer, and one day when we were talking with Mike at a local pub, he brought the horse inside where it was served beer in a bucket from the bar. I sat on the horse's back with two other people. Clydesdales are very tall and broad!

Neil and I followed the advice of our advisers carefully. We also drew on our own experiences of fitness training. We prepared our grey part-Percheron mare, Matilda, for the trek. She was 15 hands high and weighed 550 kilograms. We rebuilt a four-wheeled cart with motorbike tyres and made a canvas cover like a mini covered wagon. To get Matilda fit, Neil drove her in the cart twice a week, and I rode her three times a week when the kids were at school or kindy. Each session lasted two to three hours and covered 20–30 kilometres.

We did 2000 kilometres of training in three months. Matilda had a steady twelve kilometres an hour trot, which was easy to sit to, so I could relax and enjoy the ride with her.

Matilda's training had some very pleasant spin-offs for me. It gave me some time to myself — a craving every mother recognises. And I discovered some great tracks around the Margaret River area, as well as river crossings and beautiful areas of the forest that I hadn't seen before. One day I got lost, which made me feel like an explorer. I was dislocated from my ordinary life, but I was also lost in my thoughts. I was brought back to reality with a start when I was nearly run over by a farmer fooling about on a motorbike on his way to bring in his cows for evening milking. I arrived home two hours late and found the children wondering where their mum was, and Neil about to send out a search party. I was still shaking from my encounter with the motorbike and tired from being five hours in the saddle.

When the trek got under way in September 1988, we travelled about 40 kilometres each day, which was four to six hours of driving, depending on the terrain. We were slow on the hills, and often all of us except the driver got out to lighten the load. It was hard going for all the horses, some of which became chafed from their collar or harness. The vets travelling with us were pretty strict and insisted that some of the horses be rested. These horses would be placed in horse floats and driven along the route until they were fit enough to proceed. Our mare developed sore shoulders on about the eighth day, so we changed collars and used talcum powder on the swollen areas. We also used an Amish collar pad that had been made from deer hair, and Matilda was fine for the rest of the journey. Her tempered and hardened shoes lasted her the whole way, and we were pleased to have properly prepared her.

The horses were penned in small yards each night of the journey, and many of them developed swollen, fluid-filled legs as a result. To reduce the swelling, we walked Matilda a couple of times during the night and let her graze on any grass that was around. The broken night's sleep meant that we weren't always good-humoured travelling companions the next day.

The inevitable conflicts soon arose from living closely together with all the other competitors and their support crews. Some were drinkers and liked to party; others were trekking to appreciate the countryside and the region's history. Still others seemed most interested in publicising their horse-related businesses. Of the 100 riders, 20 carts and 20 cyclists, the cyclists seemed to have the best time. It took only two hours to cycle from one town camp to the next, which gave the cyclists time to see the town sights and wash their clothes at the laundromat. Their bikes didn't need feeding or watering either.

One of the best lessons my kids learned on that trip was how to pack light and keep their things in order. If they lost a shoe in the bedding, they didn't get it back until the end of the day. All they needed for the 13 days fitted into a pillowcase, which doubled as a pillow for the night. The cook on the trek, Margaret, took a fancy to my kids and helped me out by doing my family's washing a few times and taking one of the children for half a day in the cook's truck. The children — then aged ten, eight, six and five — ran for much of the way along the top of the pipeline. They slept very well at night. Sometimes they disappeared at a food stop, only to reappear an hour down the track in someone else's cart. If the main job of a parent is to help their children become independent, then we made the right decision in taking the children along on the Kalgoorlie trek. A daily newsletter was printed and distributed to keep us informed, including major news headlines and Seoul Olympic Games results.

By the 13th day we were glad it was the last. The other carts had seemed to be in self-destruct mode, and ours became a kind of Red Cross van. We picked up a wounded trekker who had been flung out of a cart, and later a rider who had been run over by a driverless, galloping horse and sulky. It came flying towards where I sat in our cart, and I could have reached out and played a tune on the spokes of the sulky's tall wheels with my fingers as it passed by. Little moments of inattention were the cause of most of the accidents. Neil did most of the driving of our cart and was exhausted at the end of each day because of the concentration needed to keep us and the horse safe.

The last two kilometres were the scariest of the whole trek. At about 4 pm each day, underground blasts took place in the goldmines close to town, and this unsettled some of the horses as we passed through the area on the last afternoon. This was exacerbated by a police escort who was driving too fast. We ended up cantering nearly out of control at 20 kilometres an hour over gravel speedbump mounds, with a railway line on one side of us and towering mine tailings on the other. Fortunately, we arrived intact at the showgrounds, where we were to spend the night. Neil collapsed in a nervous heap, vowing never to harness up again. We unhitched Matilda, washed and fed her, put the harness away, and helped load the cart on to a truck to be transported back to Perth by road. On the way back to Perth, a wheel fell off the cart when the axle snapped. Thirteen days and 600 kilometres was enough for us in the cart, and we took the train back to Perth. It took only six hours to cover the distance.

After the Kalgoorlie trek I got more into riding. I had been put off harness driving a bit because of the accidents we saw during the trek, and by the time it takes to harness the horse and hitch it to the cart. I preferred riding, because it enabled me to be closer to the horse. I watched the Australian horse sport of campdrafting and studied some of the basics of the sport. The adult riding taught at pony clubs in Australia is based on English riding disciplines, but campdrafting is Australian riding. It's like the difference between a violin and a fiddle.

Campdrafting developed in the Australian outback where stockmen challenged each other to draft (or cut out) a beast from the main herd and move it to another holding yard. Competition campdrafting is very fast and exciting and requires a great deal of skill on the part of both the rider and the horse. A great partnership is needed between them if they are to successfully control and herd the beast. When done properly, it's a stirring sight. It's also a terrible sight to see a brutal rider and a fearful, confused horse. The secret to successful campdrafting is to have a horse that has some herding instinct, like working sheep and cattle dogs. My horse Starlight was a trier, but her destiny was not to lie in competition campdrafting, or cattle work, or dressage for that matter.

All of the activities involving horses that I had a go at brought alive for me the Australian pioneering way of life. Campdrafting was hot and dusty work. I learned to 'read' the movements of cattle, and became knowledgeable about breed types and the grazing and station farming of cattle. And I loved to camp out and listen to others spin great yarns by the camp fire. The stories would get taller as the night wore on.

I enrolled the children in the Margaret River Pony Club and became an assistant instructor with the beginners. Neil instructed, too, and became president for one year. My experience in teaching swimming was easily transferable. I also took lessons myself on Tuesdays with the Ladies' Riding Club, run by Margaret River instructors Cheryl Pateman, Ros Brennan and Jane Morrison, and Zoe Harrison from Perth. My horse at that time was Lalinka, a bay Anglo-Arab mare. I would often ride her the eight kilometres through the forest and into town for these adult classes. I quickly understood that I had two things to consider: what my own clumsy body was doing, and how that influenced the animal I was sitting on. The prime question for me was how to relate to horses and develop a harmonious partnership with them. I learned to trot and canter, and picked up some finer points so as to be able to do a dressage test and manage low jumps.

We had a lot of fun at the club, too. One of the best parts of the lesson for me was the morning teas. We would all share a luscious, rich cake and have a good chinwag about horses and life. Each year we conducted a Golden Oldies one-day event. Low jumps and simple dressage tests challenged the brave and the not-so-brave. Strong fruit punch calmed our nerves. Riders in fancy dress added to the festive atmosphere. The pony club riders got experience in conducting the event, as they were the judges and marshals. In spite of all the mucking around, rules were abided by, points were scored, and the winners and participants were rewarded.

I had a go at other riding events, including the Blackwood marathon relay — a 16-kilometre ride, usually at a gallop across the beautiful hilly countryside near Bridgetown. It was a team relay of five legs — an eight-kilometre run, a 12-kilometre paddle, a one-kilometre swim (which I did twice in different years), a 16-kilometre ride (which I also did twice) and a cycling leg of 20 kilometres. It was a fun, community-based fundraising event that helped motivate people to keep fit or challenged athletes who wanted to do something different. It wasn't unusual to have 300 teams from all over the state participate.

Another horsy event I participated in was a choreographed musical ride at the Margaret River agricultural show with nine other women from the riding club. We decorated our horses and wore beautiful black-and-white outfits with red bandanas. The music we rode to had a lively rhythm, which the horses seemed to tune into along with the riders.

Because of my elite sports background I had high expectations of myself in whatever sport I tried. I usually failed to meet these expectations, because of the years of training and practice that are required to excel in any activity. There simply wasn't enough time with four children who needed me to meet their own ever-present needs.

From around 1987 I was able to devote a bit more time to learning as much as I could about horses. I became hooked on the possibilities of what humans and horses could achieve together. In practice, however, I was still often unable to get my horse to do what I wanted it to do and suffered all the usual injuries, such as bruised shoulders, wrenched ankles, broken ribs and squashed toes. Swimming seemed much safer in comparison, but I was determined to learn.

My two favourite smells became horse manure and horse sweat. The scent of horses stimulated a memory for me that seemed to go back further than my years and, thinking that it might be a genetic memory, I searched within my own family for others who had loved horses. My father told me of his experiences as a teenager. In the 1940s he and a friend, Bob Arthur, used to go to the Flemington saleyards in Sydney and hang around until they got odd jobs handling the horses and shovelling manure. At 14 they planned to run away from home and become jackaroos in the bush. Pooling the pocket money they had earned at the saleyards, the pair bought bridles, a halter and a saddle. They drilled holes in sixpenny pieces and replaced the spiked spurs with them. They then arranged to meet secretly at Croydon railway station. Somehow my father's mother heard of the plan, intercepted them at the station, and hauled an embarrassed son home for a lecture from his Methodist minister father. This put an end to his plan to spend his life on horseback.

My father's friend Bob did manage to become a jackaroo, but during a severe rainstorm, when he attempted to cross a flooded creek on his horse, he was swept from the animal and drowned. Although he was a strong swimmer, he was weighed down by the heavy woollen army greatcoat he was wearing. He was only 16.

The other family connection I found was my great-great-grandfather, Jonathon William Fish (1827–1893), who migrated from Nova Scotia in the 1850s to work as a foreman blacksmith for the Cobb and Co. coach company in Melbourne.

From some old books I found at the library I learned about the original natural horsemen, the 19th century 'horse whisperers' of

England, Ireland and America. The art of horse whispering was then apparently lost until the 1950s and 1960s in the United States, when a number of Californian horsemen such as Troy Henry, Tom Dorrance and Ray Hunt, and later, in the 1970s, Pat Parelli, Monty Roberts and Buck Branneman, came to public attention as practitioners of the art. In Australia, horsemen such as Jimmy Wilton, Kell Jeffery, Steve Brady and Maurice Wright had the 'gift'.

The American Pat Parelli became the most important of these teachers for me. He and his Australian wife, Linda, developed a systematic training program in 1991 that is easy for anyone who loves horses to learn and which is now taught by selected, carefully trained instructors. I was very fortunate to become an instructor in Parelli natural horsemanship. What I liked most about Pat's program was his assertion that his was a people-training, not a horse-training, business.

As my knowledge of horsemanship increased and my riding skills improved, I did more pony club instruction. In 1992 I coached the Margaret River junior riders and they came second in the Western Australian State Championships. Two of the riders were Innes kids and three of the five ponies were Innes ponies.

The pony club placed a strong emphasis on sportsmanship. Their motto in competitions was: 'Win with a grin and lose with a smile.' However, many of the kids and their parents lost sight of this when ribbons were being strived for, and I became rather dismayed about children's equestrian competitions. Horses don't care what colour ribbon they win, but people do.

I also started to assist Neil more at home with our riding school. I really loved seeing kids have fun on the ponies. Our own children didn't really go for the competition or show side; they just liked going on bush rides and playing games on horseback. On weekends we would take the children in the cart for picnics in the forest. I preferred to be a passenger in the cart. Though I sometimes did the driving, wearing my Akubra hat, I preferred to imagine myself as a grand lady of olden times, carrying a parasol. It was lovely to leave all the domestic chores behind and enjoy the rhythmic sound of Matilda's hooves on the track. We smelled the aromas of the damp forest floor and watched the flirting of the exquisite little blue wrens. The slow pace of the cart and our elevated position gave us a good view of the bush. I breathed it all in deeply. This was soul food for me. Later, we would picnic on scones, jam and cream.

The children were usually more active than introspective on these excursions. They would jump on and off the cart and gather gumnuts, and unusual leaves and feathers. They marked patterns on the sandy track with sticks. We often had a turnaround point at a special swimming hole on the river in the Bramley bush. Sometimes we camped out by the river or at our favourite freshwater swimming hole, Canebrake pool.

As the children grew, they eventually took up other sports and spent more time surfing than riding. They all like horses — and they earned good pocket money feeding horses and shovelling manure — but they're not *horse lovers* in the way that I had become.

~

Most elite athletes participate in what are known as 'linear' sports. Achievement in such sports is measured by time, distance covered, height scaled, or the number of goals shot or points scored. At the end of their sports career, many of these athletes find that their mental attitude to their sport changes. Their passion for it cools, and their excitement diminishes, but their body still craves physical activity, so they take up 'extreme' sports such as rock climbing, sky diving or surfing, where the physical challenges are posed by nature. I was one of these athletes and my new passions were surfing and horsemanship. My body had sought its own outlets.

As my mind began to catch up with my body in the early 1990s, I came to see that horse sports require a special kind of partnership between a skilled rider/handler and a horse with talent for the job. I learned a lot from top-class stockmen and equestriennes, but I still needed a decent horse if I was going to have any success in competition. What I needed was a well-bred stockhorse, but I couldn't afford to buy one. I decided to have a go at breeding my own and, to this end, I joined the Australian Stockhorse Society, the largest breed society in Australia. Four foals later, and still not a good horse among them, I decided that I needed to learn even more about horses and riding.

Around this time, Neil and I took the children to the Boyup Brook annual agricultural show. Boyup Brook is a small township near the Blackwood River. Nestling among tall trees and gentle slopes covered in good grazing grasses, it services the local farming community. While Neil was giving cart rides, I wandered over and watched the end of the Ploughing Championships where Cecil Noakes, from Rosa Glen near Margaret River, retained his title. I started to move off in the direction of the jams and preserves, when I heard Cec call out, 'Shane! Come and have a go!' Cec isn't someone you can say 'no' to, so I took the handles of the plough while he held the reins of the horses. It wasn't easy. The following year at the show I had another go, and this time I found my interest was aroused. When Cec offered to coach me, challenging me to enter the novice event the next year, I succumbed. I would learn how to plough.

I knew what coaching would involve for Cec: a huge commitment of time and a lot of sacrifices on his part. I felt humbled by the old man's offer — and grateful. Once again I would have a mentor.

Cec had won his first ploughing competition when he was 15, with a pair of Clydesdales who had completed their first season of contract ploughing. He hadn't planned to enter, because he wanted to do well in two riding events — jumping, and the walk, trot and gallop. He won both competitions that day and 50 years later he won the State Open Ploughing Competition at Boyup Brook several years in a row.

During my first lessons with Cec, I made hard work of it, treating the plough as if it were a wheelbarrow to be turned and pushed along. With Cec goading me on, I wobbled my way along the crooked furrows I was making. A furrow is the shallow trench left by the plough shear after it digs into the soil, which is then turned over by the mould-board.

There are many criteria for judging competition ploughing. Furrows should be even in depth and width, and straight. The soil turned over should be firm and evenly laid on the previous sod. The 'ins' and 'outs' (start and finish of a 'run') should be accurate, so as to form a straight line between the ploughed and unploughed ground. Once the last furrow is done, all the ground should be turned over and no weeds should be visible. The top of the soil should be level, with the rows straight, and even in width and depth, to give an overall appearance of uniformity and neatness.

Cec had been a physical fitness trainer in the Australian Army during the Second World War and his standards were high: he insisted on accuracy and perseverance — two qualities I respected from my years of mastering swimming strokes. Cec's commanding authority, and his deep, resonating voice, made both me and the horses stop immediately whenever he called out 'WHOA!'

Cec, with his friend Ross Willmont, taught me how to plough a decent furrow using a single-furrow walking plough, where the operator walks behind the plough which is pulled by a pair of horses. There are other ploughs where the operator is seated. That takes a lot of skill.

With Cec and Ross's encouragement and advice, a lot of practice, good, steady pulling horses, an accurately adjusted and set plough, a ploughwoman's lunch and lots of laughs, I gradually got the hang of it. The trick was to let the handles of the plough 'float' in the hands, relax the shoulders, put one foot in front of the other, and keep looking ahead between the pair of horses. At the same time, I needed to keep a feel for the width of the cut and watch out for stumps and rocks in the ground. It was wonderful to hear the sound of the share slicing into the sandy soil, the jangle of the chains connecting the plough to the horses, and their snorts of pleasure, and to smell the rich smells of the newly turned earth.

I continued to learn to plough, which I saw as linking me to the pioneer farmers of the past. And I loved those wonderful old men, Cec and Ross, who had such faith in my efforts, who pushed me to my limits and then carried me beyond them. (In 1994 and 1995, I won the Western Australian State Open Ploughing Competition at Boyup Brook. The trophy — a horseshoe nail sculpture of a ploughman, a single-furrow plough and a pair of horses, mounted on a small block of wood — is one of my most prized possessions.)

In 1993, Neil and I also became very involved with Parelli natural horsemanship, which has had a profound effect not only on my understanding of horses, but also of myself and other people. My involvement has been like an accelerated personal growth course. As I started to apply the principles, I got amazing results with my horse, Lalinka, and had a lot of fun in the process. I learned to do even more with horses than I had seen others do. It is the most blissful experience to confidently ride bareback and bridle-less, or to have Lalinka attach herself to me as her herd leader and follow me or my car without being on a lead or coerced in any way.

Pat Parelli is a charismatic communicator with a showmanship style of teaching. Many Australians are turned off by this, but I'm not concerned by it when I can get remarkable results with horses by using his methods of natural horsemanship. Unlike Neil, I have no inborn talent with horses, just a love for them and a desire to be in harmony with my mount. This harmonious partnership is possible even though humans are 'predators' and horses are a 'prey animal'.

I can get my horse to go willingly into a narrow space like a horse float; I don't need to force her or to use tranquillising drugs. If my bridle breaks, I can safely direct and slow my horse without it. I can catch her using an invisible string. The mental connection between us is such that my horse respectfully and willingly submits to my leadership. When I go to spend time with my horse, I go to play with her because horses love to play. I have found that I can now control my emotions better, thanks to the 'horse savvy' I have gained. This emotional fitness is combined with mental fitness, where I am constantly thinking of creative games to play with Lalinka and trying to understand why she does what she does and what I am doing to influence her. The physical fitness is a bonus.

I have found that when I am emotionally, mentally and physically fit, I am able to be more assertive while at the same time I have a less predatory attitude to life in general. Playing with horses has taught me that synergistic cooperation between people and horses can produce outstanding and creative results. Lalinka's life is expanded through my using my leadership skills, while my life is expanded through her using her physical capabilities.

My dream with horses is not just to ride into the sunset with my hair flowing behind me, although I do have that romantic ideal — especially if there's a handsome hero involved and some stirring music, too.

I had observed how beneficial being around horses is in the organisation Riding for the Disabled (RDA). I had assisted RDA classes at Bunbury Pony Club when I was studying the Level I course for the Equestrian Federation of Australia. So I designed a horsemanship program for high school students who were having trouble fitting in with the education system's requirements. Using the principles and system of Parelli natural horsemanship in which a lot of time is spent on the ground playing seven basic games with the horse, groups of four students came to the farm for two-hour weekly sessions for ten weeks. There was a theme each week with a worksheet to take home. We looked at subjects such as authority (the right and wrong use of it), discipline, boundaries, fear and assertiveness. I put into practice Pat Parelli's assertion that 'the PNH program, using horses as a metaphor, teaches us so much about developing positive human qualities'. Many of the students improved their use of school time because of what horses taught them.

Playing with horses seemed to help not only my students but also my own feel, timing and balance. As a result, I was relating well with my children, my horse and myself. But the relationship that still sorely needed attention was that with my husband.

~

It was Neil's many talents and characteristics that attracted me to him. He had a gentle manner and a moral character. He was a deep thinker and a patient listener. He was very good at answering my questions (and those who sought him out for counsel) with a question I have noticed that the best teachers and counsellors do this to empower a person to find answers for themselves. Neil's non-competitiveness and self-confidence (sometimes irritatingly arrogant to me) meant he didn't need to demonstrate how much he knew or prove what he could do.

I respect Neil for his do-it-yourself skills, his commitment to his ideals and his gift with horses. When I first saw him on a horse, Spinner, a four-year-old stallion, the sight of the harmony he had with the animal brought me to tears. He looked on the horse like how I felt in the water. I spent a lot of time sitting on the fence rails or shovelling manure near him, watching and learning how he related and responded to the horses he was training. I learned so much.

He now specialises in 'starting', not 'breaking', young horses giving them their kindergarten education. He also has a talent for re-educating difficult horses. Back then I found myself explaining in detail to Neil's customers what he was doing with their horses, as though I had the experience myself. It is wonderful when a married couple becomes one, but it is not healthy when one lives through the other. After a friend pointed out to me that I was expressing other people's opinions, particularly 'Neil reckons. . . ', and not my own, I realised I had been living vicariously. I immediately started remedying this by concentrating on my own experiences and formulating my own opinions. As I drew from all my life experiences, including the famous years, my opinions and insights slowly emerged as being different to Neil's. My fame had coloured my life and my ideas.

I am sure that he struggled with being the husband of a famous person. We both felt oppressed by 'Shane Gould the famous one' and dealt with it in our own ways. We spent hours and hours and hours talking, trying to understand each other and resolve our differences. Despite the tensions and problems between us, we had a mostly good life together.

I tumble-turned into his life and when I tumble-turned out of his life, it was into a different pool. I am glad about the things we shared together — surfing, playing with horses and being the parents of our four fantastic children.

CHAPTER 12

Family Times

*The harmony and unity in riding both a wave
and a horse is about that one particular moment —
when time stands still.*

~

Shane Gould

MY CHILDREN HAVE BEEN FORTUNATE to have the parents they have! As a family we had lots of adventures together, which took us close to nature, challenged our physical abilities and were a lot of fun. The beach and the ocean became my children's adventure water playground. The kids learned the rudiments of swimming in the bath, then learned swimming strokes in the calm, salty water of rockpools and freshwater holes in the bush. In the process, they gained an awareness of waves and tides and of water safety. When they went to school they participated in the Education Department-run swimming lessons. I taught swimming with the Western Australian Education Department during the years my children were going through the various levels of the program. Before the Margaret River Aquatic Centre opened in 1998, these lessons were held in ocean conditions at the protected bays of Gnarabup and Cowaramup. Seaweed, stingrays, and the murky, turbulent water after a storm added to the challenge of teaching the kids. When the aquatic centre finally opened, my two younger boys started to improve their technique, fitness and flexibility during physical education classes, as well as their paddling ability for the sport they love best: surfing.

Over the years, all of our boys became addicted to surfing, just like their parents. Neil and I would always be watching the wind direction. Often a trip to 'check' the windmill was really an excuse to find out the wind direction. If the swell was big, we could hear it — even 15 kilometres inland where we were. Surf conditions and horses dictated our lives for a long time.

I didn't like getting stuck with four children in the house while the surf was good, and Neil was always very reluctant to look after the children while I surfed. So my children came to the beach, too. When Kristin was still a baby, I would place him in the shade of a rock on a lambskin with a mosquito-netting tent over him and then spend 20 minutes letting loose in the surf with the kids while an obliging beachgoer kept an eye on the baby. It was reasonably easy for me to paddle a board out through the whitewater, as I still had good underwater pull and shoulder strength. I always had a few great waves.

Because of our interest in surfing, we made sure that our kids were safe and competent in the ocean at an early age. But they needed constant supervision until they were about ten.

Our family had a favourite secret spot where we spent some wonderful times together — a long white beach with crystal-clear, turquoise-blue water and big red-brown rocks on which the waves crashed. It was our haven, a place to energise our busy lives. We caught scary, big waves and perfectly shaped little ones, and sometimes got pounded into the sandbank. We were sustained by apples, water and homemade Anzac biscuits. The children would grizzle on the long, hot trek back to the car. (We insisted on the children carrying their own gear to and from the beach. They soon learned to be selective about what toys they took with them.) During the 20-minute drive home, everyone was cooled down by the breeze blowing through the old blue Land Rover's sliding windows.

It was never hard to motivate anyone to get ready for the beach. It meant fun, relaxation and thrills. But Neil would sometimes disappear at the busiest family time — from 7 to 9 am and from 4 to 7 pm — when the surf was best, leaving me with all the children. I felt it was unfair of him to leave the work of looking after the kids to me, when he knew how much I would have liked to go along.

As the boys got better at surfing, they went out at places that were too scary for me and for a longer time than the hour or so that satisfied me. It also meant that, if I went with them, dinner wouldn't be ready until 9 pm. So I started to stay at home more often. Kim would stay with me or visit her girlfriend who lived not far from us. Kim and her friend enjoyed climbing haystacks and playing in the creek in the rain, as well as the usual girls' activities. With a houseful of boys and a tomboy mother, she needed some other feminine influence. I would spend the time with my horse, Lalinka, or wander through the empty house tidying up, with my choice of folk music playing. The shoe pile needed regular tidying. With each of us owning at least two or three pairs of shoes and our no-shoes-on-in-the-house policy, they were constantly getting jumbled. When the shoes had been tidied, the laundry swept of sand and mud, the three dogs fed and petted, and the kitchen floor swept for the third time that day, I would reward myself by enjoying a good book while dinner sizzled and bubbled on the wood stove, the warm heart of the house. I was prepared for the return of the cold, hungry surfers when they tumbled into the kitchen and excitedly described their best waves while warming themselves by the stove.

Animals were a big part of family life on the farm. Apart from the horses, we had dogs, tadpoles, lambs, bantams, ducks and guinea-fowl, along with the bush animals. Neil and Joel both had a special feel for animals, and for wild ones in particular. I think that Joel's totem was a bobtail lizard. He used to bring home a bobby regularly from his farm wanderings. He called them all Fred. He would pick the kangaroo ticks off from behind their ears, then hold them on his lap and stroke them while he watched TV. He often had his fingers bitten, but it didn't put him off. One day he brought home a big, fat lizard. He made a home for Fred in a cardboard box lined with leaves, and put some fruit in it. ('Just for one night,' we said.) To our surprise, in the morning there were two lizards. Frederika had given birth to a live baby, half her size. It was a great first-hand nature lesson. Neil had a great interest in nature, particularly in creepy-crawly things like beetles. He had a large collection of beetles. I learned to appreciate the wide variety of living things in our back-yard from Neil.

We used to see at least one snake each summer, usually a deadly dugite looking for mice or a mate. I don't like snakes, so I kept well out of the way while it was removed. Snakes have a place, but not in my yard! One hot Christmas, Neil brought home a snakeskin. The next day, while playing ball in the house with Grandad, four-year-old Joel said: 'Nake, nake.' 'Yes, Joel, that's a snake skin,' I said. Then the 'skin' moved. We all raced outside, leaving the tiger snake in the house. It must have been looking for its own, or its mate's, skin. Neil grabbed a shotgun and killed it. In the process, he blew a golf ball-sized hole in the wall in the bathroom. The hole wasn't repaired until ten years later when I renovated.

One morning when the kids were eating their breakfast, a pink and grey galah flew inside and on to the table. It waddled up and down the table, tasting each bowl of Weetbix and flicking cereal all over the table. The kids loved it. It danced and talked, and came and went as it pleased. It just took over the house. It terrorised my sister Lynette, who was staying with us at the time, by picking at her feet. She couldn't go outside without a length of poly pipe to protect herself. I teased her about it until I saw how sly and vicious the bird was towards her. One Christmas I made Lyn a pink and grey galah stuffed toy, which she tied to a length of strong cord and hung from the ceiling. She could then bash it as much as she liked.

I became keen on sewing on the Singer treadle machine which I used for ten years, then with an electric Singer that was another of Neil's 'you beaut!' birthday presents. I sewed most of the kids' pants from a simple pattern when they were little. Most of their jumpers, shirts and dresses I bought cheaply from the opportunity shop. The op shop was a good source of dress-up clothes, too. (Incidentally, my Olympic uniform hat ended up in the dress-up box.)

When the children developed sporting interests, I took them to training and games. They participated in gymnastics, ballet, basketball, netball, little athletics, junior hockey, pony club, soccer and surfing, and they all collected trophies and ribbons in local and district competitions. Neil would come to watch their most important competitions and matches, but he had no interest in organised sport — I suppose because he had no childhood experiences of it. It was another point of conflict between Neil and me.

The children's excellent coordination and boundless energy needed directing. They swung off balconies, climbed roofs and trees, jumped off the trampoline into our above-ground pool, skateboarded endlessly up and down the verandahs, and rode their BMX bikes around the driveway tracks. A favourite activity in the winter, after a big rain, was to take old boogie boards to the creek and slide over the slippery weeds and the sheets of water. They came back shivering and very muddy, but it was nothing that a hot, deep bath and an automatic washing machine couldn't deal with.

In 1990 we steered the children into a non-competitive activity — the Crash Bang Circus. They loved the fun things the circus offered — juggling, stilt-walking, tightrope-walking, diablos, cartwheels and somersaults, and the unicycle. I learned to juggle using little beanbags in the kitchen while dinner cooked, but I gave up trying to learn to ride the unicycle we bought. The three boys managed this very difficult stunt better than I did.

I found great pleasure in watching the kids learn these tricky circus skills. The teachers and parents, including Fatt Matt (who later worked with Circus Oz and a children's circus in Victoria), helped the local kids, most of them still in primary school, to put on a circus performance in the form of a play about the conservation of the forest. The children performed the play four or five times in the major towns of the south-west. Kim did a solo tightrope-walk, and the boys mostly rode the unicycles. The Crash Bang Circus members were all very skilled and very good little performers onstage.

When all the children were in high school, we joined up with other families and went on adventure holidays. One time we went on a camping trip to Mt Augustus in central Western Australia, and then drove across to the coast to a remote surfing spot. The exposed, windswept coast was a stark contrast to the quiet inland riverbanks.

Another family trip that we worked hard and saved for was a surfari with another family in 1996 on a chartered yacht in Indonesia. We sailed around the Mentawai Islands, off the west coast of Sumatra, surfing any break that was surfable. It was an interesting time, but unpleasant for those of us who got badly seasick. The kids particularly enjoyed surfing the barrels. We had a grandstand view from the yacht and got some great photos and video footage. I surfed a few times, but I wasn't fit or brave enough for the speed and energy of the waves. I enjoyed swimming around the reefs, playing cards and watching the others. And it was wonderful not having to cook for two weeks. For me, this time was the calm before the storm.

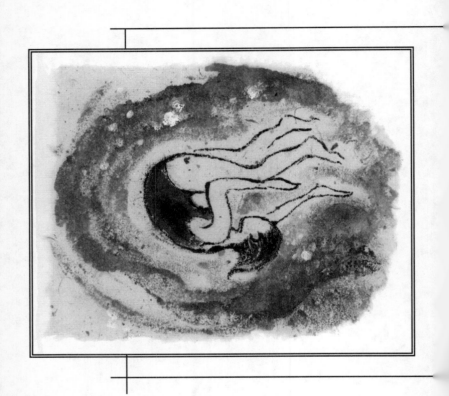

transformation

CHAPTER 13

The Tumble Turn

In this whole damn place, where do you fit?

~

Anna Pemberton, from her song 'The Specialist'

WHERE ONCE I HAD BEEN SIMPLY 'Shane Gould, Swimmer', I was now, at age 33, 'Shane Innes, Wife', 'Shane Innes, Mother', 'Shane Innes, Horse Lover' and 'Shane Innes, Surfer'. But the identity of 'Shane Gould, Swimmer' refused to be put to rest.

Identity had been a difficult issue for me even in my teens. During my long hours of swimming training, strange thoughts would go through my head. The most disturbing of these thoughts came to me when I trained with Stephen Badger at North Sydney Pool in 1971. Although Stephen was a 16-year-old top male swimmer and I was a 14-year-old female swimmer, we were doing similar times in races. The thought hit me: 'Maybe I'm not female. I know I'm not male — so, what am I? Do I belong to a third sex?'

In Munich the following year, all the female athletes were subjected to a compulsory sex test. This seemed weird to me, and then very worrying. My 15-year-old mind was thinking, 'What if they find out I'm not female?' The sterile room and the intimidating officiousness of the testing procedure was made easier for me by the frivolity of the older girls — particularly Bev Whitfield and Karen Moras. Athletics sprinter Raelene Boyle was sounding off about the insult of the testing and asking why it had to be done. Bucking officialdom was something new to me. It was like looking through a window I had never noticed before — the window of human rights and the right to question authority.

While Raelene made her comments, the other girls made fun of the procedure, trying to speak in husky voices, and squashing their bosoms flat. A medical assistant plucked a hair from our heads. The hair root was needed for testing. It stung a bit.

A week later (and a worrying one for me), we all got certificates declaring that we were female. Although I was relieved, I still didn't believe that they, or I, knew the whole story about my sexual identity. That uncertainty was somewhat justified for me. I hadn't at the time discovered the delights of my female sexuality, the rhythms of many menstrual cycles, or experienced the sexual desires and the form of the mature woman.

Of course, I found out later that my teenage identity queries were very normal. I had focused on gender because my apparent exceptional physical abilities seemed more usual in boys. So many questions had flooded through my mind: If I am female, should I have muscles? Is it right for a female to be a high-achieving athlete? Should I be instead a soft, caring person, supporting others? These private thoughts were similar to those examined by the feminist writers of the past 50 years. But as a 15-year-old, like others of the same age, I was certain that no one had ever raised these questions.

I was finally and irrevocably convinced of my femaleness after the birth of my first child, Joel, in 1978.

~

I like order: everything in its place and a place for everything. My household was systematic and orderly — hygienic, but not always neat. With four young children to care for and outside farmwork to be managed, housework wasn't a priority for me. But I knew where everything was. Most of my swimming trophies, medals and memorabilia were stored in tea chests and boxes in the 'junk room'. (To get to this room, I either had to climb up a ladder or clamber up one of the structural support poles — an old telegraph pole — in the lounge room and then pull myself up into the hole in the wall where we kept our suitcases, papers, old books and outgrown toys.) It never occurred to me to display the silver platters, crystal trophies and other memorabilia in the house. They simply didn't go with the decor. The tea chests were sometimes used by bush rats to build their nests, and I would find rat urine stains on the silver and rat-shredded paper inside the trophies.

I kept my Olympic medals, still in their original boxes, in the bottom of my wardrobe. I brought them out for visitors if they asked to see them. Sometimes I let the children play dress-ups with them. They called them 'gold metals'. Every four years when an Olympics was held I was asked to talk at local schools, so I took along the medals and other memorabilia such as programs and uniforms to show the students.

I love to read biographies and books on social history, and I can become quite sentimental when I see old sepia-toned photographs, but I seemed to have little regard for or pride in my own history. It actually disturbed me to look through my swimming stuff. Neil noticed that whenever I looked at the evidence of my past life — the trophies, medals and ribbons, the press clippings and photographs — I would become withdrawn and reflective and remain so for a few days. Neil called it 'the miseries'. I realised that while I could still remember it all clearly, it was distressing to look at my swimming stuff because it felt like I was looking at *someone else's* life. My experiences as an elite athlete had shaped my life and continued to affect me, and yet there was no place for those experiences in my married life. Although there was a place for everything else in the house, I literally couldn't find an appropriate place for my swimming stuff. There was no place for the trophies in the farmhouse, and there was no place for Shane Gould the swimmer in the farm-life of the family. I knew the trophies didn't belong in the junk room, but I didn't know where else to put them. I finally decided to send a tea chest full of medals, ribbons and trophies to the NSW Sports Museum, which is now at the 2000 Olympics site at Homebush, in Sydney. The museum curators catalogued and stored them much more respectfully than I had kept them.

Shane Gould the swimmer kept intruding uninvited into my life at unexpected moments. I tried to ignore her, but I found I was unable to do so: she had influenced too many people as well as myself. Sometimes I got angry with her for disturbing my peace. Or irritated, because she hadn't found her rightful place in my life. I couldn't resolve this duality, which became increasingly painful over the years.

Whenever the media (usually women's magazines or, in an Olympics year, a film crew doing a 'Where are they now?' series) came to the farm, Neil would usually make himself unavailable. Only very occasionally would he agree to be photographed or filmed. In 1977, Neil and I had been filmed by a crew double-dinking on a pushbike on a gravel track. When we fell off the bike, they asked if we would do another take and fall off on cue this time. Neil became very intolerant of these visitors. He said he had better things to do with his time. I became the meat in the sandwich, trying to please the reporters and stay real with Neil. Throughout all the years of our marriage, he came with me to only three or four public events. Most of these occasions were in the early 1990s when, to his credit, he made a genuine attempt to take an interest in Shane Gould, the swimmer. Up until then, she just didn't exist for him. He thought this was the way I wanted it.

In early 1990 I had a phone call from the producer of the TV program 'Burke's Backyard', asking if I would be interested in them coming to the farm to film my family. There would be no payment. I quite liked the show, so I discussed it with Neil and he agreed to be involved on the condition that we would present ourselves as a family and not just as one individual, 'Shane Gould', plus her 'attachments'. I was happy to do the interview on that condition, and we agreed on a day with Don Burke for the filming.

When Don and the film crew arrived at the farm, we talked to them about the best aspects of our backyard. I explained to them how my backyard included the whole farm and 10 000 acres of bush around it. The house yard was grazed by horses, lambs and the house cow. With the sandpit, trampoline, cubbyhouse and an overgrown vegie garden, I emphasised to them gardening was not my passion at the time. We wanted to retain control over how our lives would be depicted. I thought that maybe this time it would all work out fine.

Unfortunately, the farm wasn't looking its best. It was early May, the driest and bleakest time of the year for my garden. It was a few weeks before the break in the season when a week's rain transforms the paddocks from brown to green. The water table is at its lowest at that time and we had cut back on watering the gardens. We'd had a cold snap, too, so the above-ground pool hadn't been used in a while and the water had turned green from lack of chlorine. I'd decided to leave the pool as it was, though I did mow the grass with the help of a friend prior to the arrival of the crew. I thought that these city folk would appreciate (as our many other visitors did) the warmth and friendliness of our cosy home and wild garden in a bush setting.

The day turned into a disaster, confirming all of Neil's preconceived ideas and my worst fears. Misunderstanding erupted between us, as Neil was called away while I spoke on camera. He thought I had decided to appear on my own without consulting him, while I thought he had stage fright and had decided not to be included in the filming. It was not going the way we had hoped. I felt ashamed about the way I thought our family was going to be portrayed, and disappointed to have lost an opportunity to convey what our lifestyle meant to us. Neil's critical view of the media worsened and our relationship soured.

After six hours of filming, the camera crew packed up and left. Before they had even reached the end of our 400-metre driveway, I was on my bed crying my eyes out. 'This can't go on,' I said to myself, when I'd calmed down a little. 'You can't let this ruin your life or your marriage.' I had been reading C.S. Lewis's *The Lion, the Witch and the Wardrobe* to the children around that time, and I suddenly had an image of being chased by a huge, yellow lion. I sat up in bed and said aloud in a determined voice: 'Stop! I'm not going to run anymore. I'm going to face you and the terror I have of you. In fact, I'm going to make you a part of my life. I'm going to embrace you!'

I immediately felt a sense of peace come over me. As I sat there, a word popped into my mind: 'debriefing.' At first I didn't know where it had come from, but I then remembered hearing it in a radio news item about Anzac veterans who had returned from a government-sponsored trip to Turkey for the 75th anniversary of the deaths of British, Australian and New Zealand troops at Gallipoli during the First World War. The announcer had said that the men were offered 'debriefing' as part of the experience of confronting their past.

The word struck me. I thought of my own peak experiences 18 years earlier, and suddenly I felt sure that I had found what my problem was. I wasn't clear on what debriefing actually was, but I knew that I hadn't been offered it when my career as a competitive swimmer went belly-up! I quickly arranged a referral from my doctor in Margaret River to Dr Bob Grove, a sports psychologist at the University of Western Australia in Perth.

Dr Grove wrote to me, introducing himself and asking whether my concerns might not be related to a normal transition stage in life. I was full of anticipation after getting Dr Grove's letter. I wrote back to him, trying to give him a deeper understanding of what I was feeling.

I told him that I was dealing with an identity crisis that involved a lost heritage. 'It's more than a life-stage transition questioning the value of life now,' I wrote. 'I'm like a disenfranchised, fringe-dwelling Aborigine who has lost her heritage and yet doesn't fit in with the new culture. Neil describes me as having one foot on the wharf and the other on the boat that's not tied to the wharf . . . My aim is to have my identity integrated with my personality. With this information, can you shed any light on my ideas or guide me to possible solutions to my dilemma? . . . I'd like to see the issues through to satisfactory comfortable-to-live-with solutions.'

I gained a lot of strength from just deciding on some positive action. I felt in control of my life again and no longer afraid of the power of the fame of Shane Gould.

I thought back on the visit to the farm by the 'Burke's Backyard' film crew, which had triggered the whole episode. I even wrote a long letter to Don Burke, which I never posted.

I wanted to express that for someone to appreciate 'our backyard', they needed to be comfortable with the idea of living simply; that while our house and land could never be described as 'spectacular' in the usual sense, our lifestyle in the bush kept us in touch with much more than the land we occupied. It embraced not just the physical appearance of the earth and trees, but the sounds and smells, too. 'Our backyard' wasn't just the 40 or so hectares that were in our immediate care, but also the forest in which we walked and rode; the ocean in which we surfed and swam. Our household pets and farm animals, and the cultivated gardens that produced our fruits and vegetables, were only a part of the diversity of fauna and flora that we came across daily in 'our backyard'. I had been disappointed because I felt that the film crew failed to understand and convey the richness of our life to the program's viewers.

It is very hard for an outsider to understand how it made me feel whenever I saw my four-year-old son Tom's head bobbing up and down among the scraggly trellised peas in the garden with puppies following as he grazed on his favourite breakfast. Or what it meant for Neil and me to be able to ride on horseback through the forest in the moonlight. Or how cosy we were in our house — a house that our friends and visitors had helped to build — when the winter storms raged outside. Or how at peace I felt as I hung nappies on our clothes line on the edge of the bush or baked Anzac biscuits in our wood-fired stove.

The program on our backyard ended up being fine, with a bit of tongue-in-cheek comment about the green water in the swimming pool. But I missed the opportunity to show the bush and farm backyard I knew like the back of my hand and in which spent so much time. A television program cannot capture or convey any of this, and yet *this* was our life, *this* was our backyard — *this* was who we were. Our backyard might have seemed messy and old-fashioned — even peculiar — to some, but to me it meant more than any amount of fame or any number of gold medals.

~

In July 1990, I made an overnight trip to Perth where I spent two valuable hours talking with Bob Grove. He thought I might be suffering from empty-nest syndrome. We went on to rule that out. All my children were still in primary school. The nest was still abundantly full. He commented that I needed to work on my relationship with Neil. I affirmed that. Bob then gave me some literature to read on the subject of sports retirement stress. I put it aside for when I got home. Our appointment ended soon after.

At home, I took out the material and settled myself in the bedroom to read it. As I read, a feeling of rage developed deep inside me. I felt so angry. The articles described *exactly* what I had experienced following my retirement. I mentally checked off the list of symptoms: I had felt at a loss, because I no longer had a goal. I was unsure about my capabilities in other areas. I lacked the confidence to get involved with other activities. I had unrealistic expectations about performing well in other activities. I experienced a sense of emptiness when I stopped training. I felt like I had to live up to an image. I had a need to be what I called 'authentic'. I felt dissatisfied with my last competition results. I had unfinished business with my coaches and felt alienated from my parents. I found I couldn't please anyone, whereas previously I had pleased everyone with my performances. I became suspicious of people's motives in befriending me when I moved away from my friends in the swimming scene. I downplayed my achievements in order to build others up. I was frustrated by not being able to work to my fullest capacity. I had to learn how to give attention to others at a time when I was now receiving less attention. I missed getting the 'red carpet treatment', while at the same time I questioned the genuineness of the acclamations I had received. Had I been used?, I asked myself. Had I been a pawn in a game? I felt angry that, after all the effort it had taken me to get to the top, *being there* wasn't as good as I had been led to expect. Finally, I felt responsible for the financial burden my parents had carried in order to enable me to swim.

'Why didn't anyone tell me that this can happen to athletes when they retire?' I lamented to myself. 'If I'd known this, I could have gone on with my life instead of feeling so confused all these years.'

I looked at the dates on the articles. Most of them were written in the 1980s — I had come up through the ranks before anyone who might have helped me knew that such a thing as sports retirement stress even existed, let alone how it might be alleviated.

As I read the accounts of other athletes who had experienced difficulty after retiring, I began to relax in the knowledge that I wasn't the only one who felt they were in limbo and were confused by their emotions. It was an enormous help just being able to put a name to how I felt. But as I read on, I decided to give my 'problem' a more positive name than 'retirement stress'. I would call it 'athletic career transition'. The problem would then become a manageable challenge.

Some days later, I went 'taddying' (tadpole catching) in the creek with Kristin and Tom, then aged seven and six. We caught some tadpoles that weren't tadpoles any longer, but they weren't yet frogs either. I saw parallels with the transition I was still undergoing in my sporting career. I did some research and learned that they were in what is known as a liminal state. They were no longer what they were, but they were not yet what they were going to be. That was easy for me to understand and gave me hope. I felt I was finally on my way to becoming a 'frog'! I have since taken quite an interest in frogs. I have a frog fridge-magnet, frog-picture calendars, glow-in-the-dark frogs on my dressing table and computer, a frog bookmark, and a pair of socks with frogs on them. Apparently, frogs need a healthy environment to survive, too.

I got really excited about my discoveries. I wanted to learn more about other athletes' retirement experiences. I hoped their experiences would validate mine. It would also give me a real point of connection with my peers. An opportunity arose for me to talk to other retired athletes later in 1990 when I went to Melbourne as a guest of the Olympic Bid Committee, when the city started its bidding for the 1996 Olympic Games. At the dinner table over an informal meal, I asked past Olympians Bev Whitfield and Kevin Berry if they had experienced any problems after retiring from swimming. They said they hadn't. Kevin, in fact, was far from sympathetic about the whole matter, which upset me and I had to leave the table for a while. Michael Wenden, who was also present, seemed to be the only person who understood how much it meant to me to have discovered what had been ailing me.

Following the trip, Michael and I continued our discussion by correspondence. Michael's own retirement hadn't been stressful. He had eased out of training and competition over a period of years, while he began to explore other career options.

About six months later I was at a function on the Queensland Gold Coast, and I met up again with Michael, who was managing a council swimming pool and swim school business at Palm Beach. Michael had suggested that I talk with Dr Ian Lynagh, a sports psychologist in Brisbane. He drove me to the appointment and then waited two hours to drive me back to the Gold Coast. I really appreciated having an ally! Ian Lynagh was a great listener. Although he had little experience with the issue of career transitions in sport, he was able to appreciate how I had been feeling. I found him very empathetic. After I had talked myself out, I asked him what he thought. He replied, 'You know, Shane, I think you need to celebrate your achievements!'

My immediate reaction was to reject the idea. I'd had all I could take of being the focus of attention. How could I 'celebrate' without bringing all that up again? Besides, I'm not a party person. What did he mean by 'celebrate'? He said calmly, 'You'll know how when the right time comes'.

I reread all the material I had collected on sports retirement stress in search of a way to celebrate what I had achieved in my career as a swimmer. During the life cycle of my career, a lot of attention had been paid to the training and competition phases. But little or no attention had been given to the transition phases of detraining, and easing out of sport and into another life. There were no informed support services to help the athlete with the process of retiring. So many athletes like myself were helped and guided to the top of the mountain, but we were then left to find our own way down. I had stayed only briefly on the mountaintop, enjoying the view. Then I had run helter-skelter down the mountain by a different route, finding my way as best I could.

When I quit competitive swimming at 16, I actually experienced a loss, like a bereavement. But I hadn't grieved and then accepted that loss. Whenever journalists came to interview me about my view from the mountaintop, I would be reminded of the climb up and the amazing, though brief, time I had spent at the peak. There was still a part of me that missed the excitement, the acclaim and the exhilaration of the physical effort. The sense of loss these reminders provoked brought on a feeling of sadness and the whole range of confusing emotions that grief brings. Raelene Boyle told me that she missed running very badly. She found that retirement was like losing a leg, thinking it was still there and then finding that it wasn't.

When an athlete loses their sporting career, they lose many other things in the process, including their identity. 'Who am I,' they ask, 'if I'm no longer an elite athlete?' As I continued to search for a way to celebrate my achievements, as Ian Lynagh had suggested, I kept coming up against the things I had lost. However, by naming and acknowledging my losses, I was gradually able to see that I had also gained many skills from training and competing as a swimmer that I was still applying in my life on a day-to-day basis. I celebrated this realisation by making a list of what I called my 'Transferable Life Skills'. As I kept thinking of skills to add to my growing list, I became more and more excited. I was thrilled to find that I was actually a very skilled person. I had the ability to set goals and to work hard to achieve them. I had excellent time-management skills. All the physical training had taught me to 'stick with' things when part of me wanted to give up. I also knew what my capabilities and limits were. These and other skills had helped me to become who I now was, and I started to see my sporting experiences in a new light.

One of the things I had gained from swimming competitively was the ability to swim well. I reminded myself that I loved to swim. So, the second way in which I celebrated my achievements was by writing a little book I called *Water Delights: A guide to teaching your baby to swim in the bath.* The book was based on an article I had written in around 1987 for the local newspaper. The book was published by a friend in Fremantle, and I did the marketing and mail-order sales myself. Although I didn't earn much money from the book, I could now add a new skill to my list: author.

I also did a series of biographical audio interviews with Tracey Holmes of ABC sport radio. We compiled a tape from the interviews, which the ABC published, called 'All That Glitters is Not Gould'. I enjoyed working with Tracey, and it was helpful for me to talk.

The next thing I did was to speak out about excellence in sport generally and the joy that comes with mastering a physical activity. I became passionate about encouraging people to express themselves creatively through being physically active. I talked with Charles Billich, who had been appointed the official artist of the 2000 Sydney Olympics, and we shared the view that sport can be art, with the athlete a moving sculpture.

I was a guest at the Prime Ministerial Sports Awards dinner in Melbourne in 1991, where I spoke about the joy of physical exuberance. I said that one didn't have to be the winner to feel satisfaction and pleasure in sport. Just doing it was its own reward. I was given a standing ovation, which rather stunned me.

In the same speech, I touched briefly on my experience of sports retirement. In the audience was Deidre Anderson from the Victorian Institute of Sport, who had planned to do her master's thesis on athletes' career transitions. But she was considering switching to another subject as she was getting little encouragement from her supervisors for her research. Months later, when she came to Western Australia and interviewed me, she told me that my talk had motivated her to stay with her original subject. I learned a lot from Deidre, who went on to complete her thesis and to add her insights to the Institute of Sport's Athlete Career and Education program. There are now ACE programs at all the state sports institutes, with athlete career counsellors who are knowledgeable about the retirement needs of athletes. In 1997, Deidre hosted the first World Congress of Athlete Career Transitions, held in Canberra. By that time, largely through Deidre's efforts, Australia had become the world leader in researching the subject. David Lavallee, a sports psychology student at the University of Western Australia, chose sports retirement as the subject for his PhD. He interviewed me at length as part of his research, and quoted me extensively.

I continued to want to share my own experiences with others. While on a visit to Sydney I approached the television program 'A Country Practice', which often dealt with social issues such as homelessness, drug abuse and various forms of discrimination. I thought that career transitions in sport might be an appropriate topic for the show to deal with, and I spoke with the producer about it. Unfortunately, the show was cancelled soon after. I then contacted the ABC and suggested that the issue might be dealt with in their program 'GP'. They misunderstood my intent and thought I was suggesting that I write an episode of the show. I now knew that I had a lot of skills, but scriptwriting wasn't one of them. I put that in the 'too hard' basket.

I had a business card made up. I think I was the world's first Sports Retirement Consultant. It was a bit presumptuous of me, but I wanted to set up some way of helping other athletes, some way to help them avoid the same painful adjustment process that I had gone through after retiring from competitive sport. In offering a consultancy service I was continuing to celebrate and complete my own sports career.

I can look back now, in 1999, and see how the management of career transitions has changed since the early 1990s when I first was able to put a name to my problem. Football clubs, cricket associations, the surfing bodies and others are now providing career planning and training for their athletes. Companies like Quiksilver,

Rip Curl and O'Neill now provide regular training camps for their young sponsored surfers. They are coached in public speaking and industry awareness, as well as physical fitness and nutrition. They don't want surfers who are just good at surfing; they want athletes who are role models, who have a positive attitude both in and out of the waves and who are equipped for life after competitive surfing. I applaud these companies and clubs who are going out of their way to do this for their young athletes.

Wayne Pearce, the Balmain Rugby League Club coach, told me that the club includes regular 'social awareness' events, to give footballers an appreciation of other aspects of life. They take gifts to children's hospitals, work alongside Wesley Central Mission helpers, and recently spent a day painting a women's refuge. Elite athletes are very self-focused to the point of selfishness, so doing things for others helps to keep a natural balance.

The ACE program pamphlet explains: 'It's important to have goals, to put your natural talent to the test, to pursue excellence. But while you are giving your sport the dedication of time and effort that it demands, remember that it is unlikely that your entire life will be sport. There's another side to your life, and it's most important to win in this as well! . . . It is vital and possible to prepare for life after sport whilst achieving your goals.'

CHAPTER 14

Dark Night of the Soul

It is our light, not our darkness,
that most frightens us.

~

Nelson Mandela

BY 1993 I FELT LIKE A JACK-IN-A-BOX that had been sprung free. The changes in my life were rapid and profound, making it impossible to squeeze myself back into the confines of my old relationship with Neil. My swimming fame had always driven a wedge between us, but now my growing interest in sports psychology was increasingly taking me away from the farm and our life there. Neil had been patient for a while. 'Just give me a year,' I'd begged him. 'Then I'll drop it and get on with our life.' But I couldn't. I was changed forever. However hard I tried, I couldn't find a way to remove the wedge that was now threatening the very fabric of our life together.

I was torn in two. Neither of us knew what to do. Neil was fed up with all the attention my swimming career was receiving again, even though my swimming years were now so long ago. His resentment of the media attention stemmed from his belief that I was being held back by my own past. 'Just get on with your life and leave all that behind!' he would argue. But I now felt that I was, finally, getting on with my life. Whenever I was asked to comment on sports matters, I tried to avoid putting any focus on my past achievements and concentrated on more current topics that interested me. I never wanted to go back. I didn't want to limit my identity to just that of a talented swimmer. But I did need to acknowledge and affirm the positive contributions of those experiences. And there lay the main point of conflict between Neil and me. Neil disliked sporting competition, while I enjoyed sporting activity and saw competition as just a small part of it.

One day I mentioned to Neil that I was thinking of competing in the Australian Masters Swimming Championships in Perth. I had just returned from an interstate trip and the idea had been suggested to me. I thought it would be a bit cheeky and fun to do as a one-off thing. I was still in celebration mode. But Neil wasn't at all impressed with the idea. He thought that I was planning to 'get back into' swimming. 'Don't expect me to stop my life and support you!' he said. It hadn't occurred to me that that was how he would see it. I obviously hadn't explained to him very clearly exactly what it meant for me — that it was just something I was considering doing as part of my process of celebrating my swimming life. Tensions between us built, and another cold war started.

A day later, I had saddled my mare Lalinka and was mounting her in readiness for a bush ride. The children were playing inside. Neil was preparing to train a young horse. We started arguing again about the swimming event. Neil pulled angrily at Lalinka's reins, scaring both her and me, so I quickly jumped off and let the horse go. I then 'pulled a finger' at him (which was something quite out of character for me). As we argued, my body language and defiance really angered Neil and he responded violently with three hard hits across my face. I was knocked to the ground and momentarily lost consciousness. I was stunned and deathly scared that he would harm me again as he stood over me, but instead he looked concerned and asked: 'Are you all right?' It seemed incongruous. I didn't know whether or not to accept his help, or whether I could ever *trust* him again. My face hurt, and my split lip was bleeding. I let him help me to my feet and walked unsteadily towards the house, saying: 'You've really blown it now.' The concern left his face as he said harshly, 'I suppose you'll tell the police'. In the time it took me to say 'No', I realised that, although I loved Neil (or at least the idea of a loving partnership) and our lifestyle, I felt trapped in my relationship with him. I also felt ashamed of what I had done to provoke his violent outburst. I felt responsible for the incident and didn't mention it to anyone for two years.

I have been physically scared of Neil ever since that day, even though he later apologised and I forgave him. I felt frightened of doing something that might displease him, in case he became angry and violent. I have read quite a lot about domestic violence since that incident. My experience is mild compared to what many women endure, but my response in feeling somehow responsible and keeping it to myself was typical. I should have reported the incident to the police and talked to a friend about it. I should have insisted that Neil have counselling in anger management. Even though it was the only incident of physical violence I experienced with Neil, I think he was just as scared of his behaviour as I was.

The previous year, I had had my long hair cut short after attending a weekend seminar in Perth with Christian feminist author, Miriam Therese Winter. I wrote in my diary on 27 July 1992: 'The act of having my hair cut short is: A symbol of solidarity with all the women who have been humiliated and denied the right of their humanity. A symbolic act to commit myself to work towards learning and living as a whole woman.'

Neil was shocked. He accused me of becoming a lesbian and moved out of our bedroom. I saw this as being symbolic of him moving out of my life. I experimented with referring to God as 'She' and this greatly offended him. He made it very clear that I was 'wrong' to have my hair cut and if I adhered to that 'heresy', then I wasn't welcome in his life. I worried that he might try to squeeze me out of our house. I had nowhere else to go, so I vowed that he wouldn't succeed in turning me out of my own home. I prayed for the strength to communicate lovingly with Neil while we tried to work things out.

When I looked at my financial situation, I realised that I was totally dependent on my partnership business with Neil. We worked together in the business of horse handling, riding lessons, firebreak ploughing and sheep-raising. We worked long hours for a subsistence income, and were unable to afford some much-needed capital improvements. (I had finally painted the house interior and renovated the bathroom myself.)

I looked into starting up swimming lessons in Busselton and investigated other enterprising activities, but I hit a brick wall. Neil had told me that he wouldn't let me stay at the farm if I tried to use the name 'Shane Gould' to earn an income, as it would involve extended absences in a world that he had no respect for or interest in. I made some tentative steps into the sports arena, but I decided the risks were too high. This was very frustrating, because I thought that I had some valuable insights to contribute in the area of sports retirement and career planning.

I did some wildflower picking and thought about getting a school bus driver's licence, but I refused to clean houses for $8 an hour. I did do some surfing instruction, both privately and with Leaps and Bounds Outdoor Adventures for Women, and I continued to run the household, and do the sheep and horse management. To do the surfing instruction, I decided I needed to learn to stand up properly on my board. I was 35, not too old to learn. I retired my kneeboard and got hold of a new sort of surfboard made from a soft rubber in Margaret River by Resurf. (It was softer on hip bones and bosoms.)

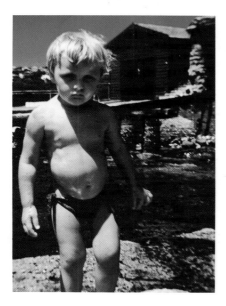

Left: At Vaucluse, Sydney, 1959, aged two. I still had the scalding scar on my chest from an accident with boiling water six months previously.

Below: My other mother, Tima, and my three sisters in the backyard in Nadi, 1964. Lynette (left) is nine, Jenny three months, Debbie three, and I'm seven years old.

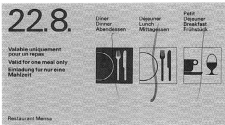

Clockwise from top left:
The official poster for Munich
— the colours and modern
design were new and exciting
for me; my identification tag;
a meal ticket sample; and the
closing ceremony ticket for
10 September 1972.

At Munich in the official green and gold swimsuit — nylon with low-cut legs and a skirt.
A commercial poster was made from this photo. No permission requested from me and I saw
none of the profits!

Above: Munich, August 1972, in harmony with the water and feeling good. New lane ropes had been designed to reduce wash. If you weren't in the lead it was like swimming in the surf!

Top right: Holding the 1956 Olympics kangaroo mascot thrust into my hands by Dawn Fraser at the medal presentation for the 200m individual medley. At left is American Lyn Vidali (bronze) and right, Kornelia Ender, East Germany (silver).

Bottom right: Medal presentation ceremony for '200m Lagen Damen' ('women's medley'). The medal is engraved with 'Gould Shane'. With colour TV the Olympics became a world spectacle.

Above: Bev Whitfield in our Olympic Village room at Munich with our first three medals. It was the best congratulations I have ever had, thanks to two rolls of toilet paper.

Left: Coach Tom Green (right) and Forbes Carlile giving me pre-race instructions during a warm-up at North Sydney Olympic pool in January 1972. I'm in my favourite swimsuit.

Right: These are the original Arena swimsuits that I endorsed with Mark Spitz in 1974. The swimsuit fabric was like paper, a little bit stretchy — there wasn't much lycra around back then.

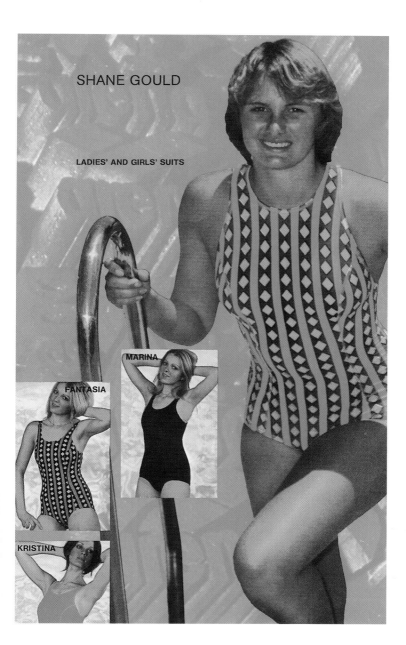

SHANE GOULD

LADIES' AND GIRLS' SUITS

MARINA

FANTASIA

KRISTINA

On the way to a new life with Neil, drying the contents of the panel van after being flooded out in Nyngan, New South Wales, February 1976. The district hadn't seen rain for seven years!

Pregnant with Kim in our no-dig garden, January 1980. The paddocks in the background were brown and dry until the April rains.

Kneeboard riding in a vest and homemade shorts in 1976 at Left Handers, near Margaret River. My upper shins still have 'board bumps' on them — from the bruising of kneeling on the board.

The hippy from the bush, dressed in borrowed clothes, receiving the MBE from Queen Elizabeth II in 1981.

Above: May 1984. From left: Kim aged four, Kristin eight months, me 27, Tom 22 months, and Joel five.

Left: The Quirks wind generator on top of our timber-framed weatherboard house in Margaret River. When the wind blew hard it sounded and felt like an aeroplane taking off!

Family picnic at Kilcarnup near Margaret River, 1988. We all loved camping in wild places and feasting on sausages, salad, fruit and homemade cake with billy tea on the fire.

At a family reunion in Byron Bay, 1990. With my three very different, wonderful sisters: (from left) Lynette aged 36, Jenny 26, me 33 and Debbie 29, who was pregnant with her second child, Aaron.

Heavy horse farming demonstration in Boyup Brook, 1993. Cecil Noakes (right) is setting the plough adjustments with a spanner for the Massey Harris plough, as Ross Willmott and I look on.

IOC President Juan Antonio Samaranch after I was presented with the Olympic Order in Sydney, April 1994. I interrupted my three-mornings-a-week ploughing training to attend! It was a great honour.

Heavy horse farming demonstration in Boyup Brook, May 1994, the first year I won the WA State Open Ploughing Match. It took about 1½ hours of precision ploughing of a 60 x 10 yard plot. It was a team effort with my coaches Cecil and Ross.

With my four bloody marvels. From left: Tom aged 11, Kim 14, Kristin 10 and Joel 16 at Margaret River in 1994.

Left: With Michael Wenden at the World Swimming Championships in Perth, January 1998.

Below: Opening of the Sydney International Aquatic Centre, 1994. I joined with Olympic swimming legends (from left) Dawn Fraser, Murray Rose, Lorraine Crapp and John Konrads for a historic 50m swim.

Above: With Mark Spitz at the Perth World Swimming Championships, January 1998. I learned a lot from him about speaking concisely for sports commentary.

Right: Running with the torch at the Opening Ceremony of the Sydney 2000 Olympic Games under the watchful eyes of over 100,000 spectators in the stadium and billions of television viewers worldwide. I felt comfortable in front of the crowd, like my athletic life had come full circle.

Astride my mare Lalinka in the Ocean at Rockingham (a horse beach in Perth), helping her to feel more comfortable in the water.

Milt and me, learning to trust and love again.

I soon learned to stand up in reasonably sized waves. One session, I caught 50 left-hand waves in an hour. It was offshore and I was the only person out. Yeah!

Neil and I reconciled after three months, but there was still a coolness between us. To avoid further conflict, I no longer shared with him the things that mattered to me. I went underground into the shadows to do the things that stimulated me and fed my soul.

~

Over the years I have had regular contact with my former swimming Coach, Forbes Carlile. On his recommendation, I read Andrew Jennings's controversial 1992 book, *Lords of the Rings*. Forbes also sent me articles by Professor John Hoberman, an academic from the University of Texas with a special interest in the sociological history of swimming, about the history of the Olympics. I also read in Professor Hoberman's book, *Mortal Engines*, his analysis of drugs in sport. At this time I had been thinking more positively about my Olympic experiences, so it was disturbing to read criticism of the Olympic organisation. From the extensive information presented, I gleaned some simple facts about the Olympic principles — if I was to become involved again in public promotion of the Olympics and elite sport, I needed to work out the rights and wrongs of the state of affairs for myself.

My personal experience confirms that the Olympic Games is more than a festival of sport. While sport is the focus, there are two other aspects of the Games: cultural exchange and global diplomacy.

There is a mystique about the Olympics, too. I think that's because it is, as Hoberman calls it, 'an inspirational internationalism'. I believe the principles and the role of the Olympic Games are worth preserving and enjoying. In my mind, there is one proviso to this: the IOC needs to be reformed, just as many large corporations have been restructured over the past decade or two. The IOC needs to be accountable, both in its financial arrangements and organisational structures.

Part of the reconceptualising of the Olympic Games means more involvement of women at an executive level, and the coaches and athletes in the decision-making and profit-sharing. I strongly feel that coaches are treated as second-class citizens in Olympic sport, often seated far from the start and finish lines at events, and often inaccessible to their athletes. Athletes have been described by some high-ranking swimming officials as 'just the performers'. Sounds like performing seals at the circus.

The modern Olympics will not be a circus if athletes and coaches prevent themselves from being treated as just performers, mortal engines and marketable products. Professional sports like the AFL and Australian cricket formed players' associations to protect their interests and maintain their human dignity as individuals, not just excellent biological organisms open to exploitation and abuse.

In my reflections I saw that the 1972 Olympics and swimming at an elite level was without doubt an amazing experience for me. Without discussing it with Neil or anyone else in 1993 I was quietly accepting Shane Gould the swimmer and the years of fame as a treasured part of myself.

So with my eyes wide open, I was ready to say 'yes' to an invitation the following year to receive the Olympic Order from the President of the International Olympic Committee, Juan Antonio Samaranch.

In April 1994 I flew to Sydney for the presentation — a simple and dignified occasion shared with Herb Elliott. After the ceremony I rang Neil to tell him how honoured I was feeling to receive this award. He had no congratulations for me; he reminded me that he was looking after the children while I was swanning around in the city. I was deeply hurt by this.

In September, when all the bids for the 2000 Olympics were being considered, I was invited to go to Berlin as the guest of a television company that was putting together a show to help the Berlin Olympic bid. I awkwardly negotiated a fee over the phone with a pleasant German man who spoke broken English. Neil was like my pimp, urging me to negotiate a higher fee, as we needed a new car. He said that if I 'had' to go, that I should make sure I was paid well. I had trouble explaining to the German that I didn't have enough money to get a passport or appropriate clothes, and that I would appreciate getting an advance. In the end I negotiated a fee of A$6000 but no advance. I felt like a poorly dressed, high-class hooker.

In order to get the $100 needed for a passport, I found a good patch of tea-tree, which I cut and sold to the local florist. Then I approached Liz Davenport, the Perth-based designer, for clothes. She gave me two beautiful outfits in exchange for my photo in their catalogue. I now felt like a well-dressed, high-class hooker! I dusted off an old suitcase, had my hair cut, bought a $5 lipstick and I was ready! I had $150 in cash on me. I didn't own a credit card. I wasn't a good credit risk.

When I arrived at the hotel in Berlin after 24 hours of travelling, I had a sleep and then went to the gymnasium-cum-TV studio for a rehearsal. It was one of those hurry-up-and-wait situations that are all too common in the entertainment industry. I wasn't enjoying myself until I got talking to some of the other athletes who had been invited. One track athlete was writing a book about cover-ups of positive drug tests in American athletics. I can't remember who it was, or if the book was ever published, or if the man still has a life because of his incriminating evidence!

We were all soon hungry, but we had to buy our own lunch. The sandwiches didn't look too good, so I filled up on sugared coffee to preserve my money. While I was drinking my coffee, some autograph-hunters gathered around. Some of them had travelled by train from the south of Germany just to secure autographs. I was looking for some human connection, but all they wanted was a signature. I was offended. I felt like an object, not a person, to these pimply-faced, sweaty young men. When I said I didn't sign autographs anymore but that I would be happy to shake their hand and talk to them, they became irritated. I sensed that these people didn't value themselves very much and that they wanted my signature in order to feel good about themselves. Soon they turned nasty and demanded that I give them an autograph. I was scared, so I signed a few before excusing myself to go to the bathroom. That was the closest I'd been to an angry mob.

I got a chance before the show in the evening to walk down the main street of Berlin to the Kaiser Wilhelm Church, which had been bombed during the Second World War and left unrepaired. A service was just starting, so I sat down and listened to the familiar songs and a German sermon that I didn't understand. I was saddened by the state of the building, the walls of which seemed to speak to me with the voices of people made homeless by war.

The TV show was very disappointing. I thought that I would have time during my interview to say something of value, something to inspire the German audience, or to tell them something about Australia. But it was a shemozzle. I was treated as just a name and a face. An interpreter was used for the two-minute interview, and I had to wear headphones in order to hear the questions in English, though I understood some of them in German. There was a small but pregnant three-second time delay for the interpretation, which made the English-speaking guests look ridiculous. Furthermore, the compere didn't ask any of the questions he said he would. It was a complete waste of time and left me feeling very let down emotionally. I sobbed uncontrollably for an hour afterwards while the set was dismantled around me. A kindly producer sat with me until I recovered.

I didn't know what I was meant to do after the show, so I went back to the hotel and ate a room-service dinner. I noticed an advertisement in the room for bus tours and decided to take a bus trip around the united city the next day, to see the remnants of the Berlin Wall and gain something valuable from the trip. I wanted to see history come alive.

The next morning when I went to check out of the hotel, I assumed that the TV company had settled my room-service bill. But I was told that I would have to pay it myself. It was more than all the money I had left. I was going to have to offer to wash dishes. I had received a cheque in US dollars for the TV show job, and I thought I might be able to cash it. I found a bank, but they couldn't cash it until it had been cleared. I went back to the hotel and agreed to pay the account when I returned to Australia. By then I had just enough time to get to the airport to catch my plane. In disgusted defiance, I decided to do the bus tour as planned and catch a later plane, and to stay overnight in London at a $10 a night backpackers' hostel.

The tour of Berlin was well worth changing my flight for. The most sobering part was the memorial graves for the 80 people who had died trying to escape from communist East Berlin before the Wall was demolished in 1989.

When I got to London late that evening, I enquired about accommodation. I didn't have enough money for a bed, or even the taxi fare to get there. Ten dollars a night for backpackers' accommodation was the Margaret River price, not the London price. I was about to retire to the Qantas lounge for the night when a woman asked if I would answer some questions for a survey she was doing about airport services. I agreed. I was resigned to calling the airport 'home' for the night, so I was happy to talk to someone and fill in some time.

After we had finished with the survey questions (I suggested that one service that was needed was cheap accommodation near the airport), we carried on talking. The woman said she had a number of Australian friends, and asked me about where I lived. She also had a daughter who was into horses, she said, and they lived on a farm too. I was feeling a bit reckless and desperate, so I cheekily asked if she had a spare bed for the night. She happily invited me to stay. Her shift was nearly over, so I didn't have long to wait.

It was nearly midnight when I got to bed. I didn't meet the rest of the family until the morning. The branches of a huge oak tree scratched at my upstairs dollhouse window during the night. The bed was cosy, and the house had an old, musty smell. It was glorious.

I got up early to explore. The house was 'only' 300 years old. The 200-acre farm was near Windsor Castle and had full Thames frontage. A grey stone castle perched proudly on top of a hill across the river. It was the manor house of the farm. The farm used to support 30 families, but now it couldn't even support my host family who leased it. It was beautiful, but run-down. I asked lots of questions when the farmer came out to feed the beef cattle and check on the barley crop that was nearly ready to harvest. The manure smells were wonderful, and the dry, crunchy grass looked as old as the barn that sheltered calves and pigs in the snowy winters.

Back at the house, a primary-aged boy was getting ready for the first day back at school after the summer holidays. I showed him my Olympic medals that I had brought with me for a possible 'show and tell' in Berlin. He was more concerned about whether his school friends would still like him after the holidays.

We dropped the boy at school and then drove past Windsor Castle, where we caught the end of the Changing of the Guard, before going to some stables where my angel's daughter was mucking out a pen. It was a grand tour with a very generous woman. I was humbled and thankful. It was the best part of the whole trip.

When I was dropped off at the airport I went to check in my luggage and get a seat allocation. The assistant queried me on my ticket, as the name on the ticket, 'Shane Gould', didn't match the name on my passport, 'Shane Innes'. She asked me for proof of identity. I didn't have my marriage certificate with me, which was the only thing that could prove my identity. I panicked, and my face went a hot red. I just wanted to get on a plane back to Australia. I fought back tears, and then started to giggle at the absurdity of the whole thing. It was the middle of the night in Margaret River. We didn't have a fax machine, and the closest one in town wouldn't be checked for another six hours. Neil probably wouldn't have been able to find our marriage certificate anyway, because I'd rearranged the filing cabinet and couldn't remember where I'd decided to file it: under 'F' for 'Family', or 'M' for 'Marriage', or 'C' for 'Certificates'? I might even have put it under 'I' for 'Ideas'.

I put my cabin bag down on the ground because it was heavy and I heard a jangling, clunking sound. 'Aah,' I said to myself. 'I *do* have proof of my identity!' I asked the airline assistant, 'Would five Olympic medals engraved with my name be sufficient identity?' She was rather stunned at first, then smiled and said 'Okay' as though it was a dare. I spread them out on the counter like a hand of rummy. I showed her my name, 'Gould Shane', engraved in small lettering along the edge. She squinted to read it and then relaxed. With a smile she took one of the medals out the back for her supervisor to approve it. There were some laughs and 'oohs' and 'aahs' from the back room. She then returned with a big grin and let me through. Phew! 'Take me home, British Airways, take me home,' I sang as I strode towards the departure gate.

Some years later I was at Sydney airport checking in for a return flight to Perth with Shirley de la Hunty (nee Strickland) when Shirley was asked to produce proof of her identity because her ticket was in her maiden name. She pulled out her tattered marriage certificate, which she carried with her for just this purpose. We laughed together about the situation when I told her of my experience in London. At the same time, we were indignant that sponsors still showed a lack of sensitivity towards women athletes who had married after ending their career, by booking tickets for them in their maiden names. When Neil and I finally separated, I changed my name and all my documents back to my maiden name, so that I wouldn't have to endure another 'getting-out-of-London' ordeal.

In 1989 I went to Melbourne to be inducted into the Sports Hall of Fame — one of 100 athletes to be honoured in this way. Before I left, Neil and I had a huge argument. He said that I was going back to the womb and that I just wanted my ego stroked and to be idolised. I was torn apart by his comments and felt guilty about wanting to attend such sporting functions. I couldn't agree with Neil that what I did as a swimmer was wrong, but by God it was a burden I carried. Trips away were also a strain financially, even though most of the big expenses were covered. They disrupted our family routine, too, even though I was usually only gone for two or three days at a time. Neil's parents would come and keep the house running and care for the children while Neil worked the farm. Despite all the problems and tensions these trips caused, it was a relief to get away and receive some positive input and to be valued without being judged.

Neil is an interesting man, but I lost the ability to understand his perspective on life. He had always asked me lots of challenging questions about everything I took an interest in, which had been enormously beneficial to me and I thank him for that. It encouraged me to research my ideas thoroughly. However, competition, heroism and the Olympic Games were three subjects we continually clashed on.

At a conference in Canberra in 1992 titled 'Bradman, Barellan, Balmain and Bocce — The Culture of Sport in Australia', I was asked to speak on the subject of heroism in sport. I called my presentation 'Athletes Burp and Fart, Too — The Importance of the Ordinary'. The handout of my speech included a photocopy of the Mona Lisa picking her nose. The conference was excellent and I made a number of valuable new contacts, including Professor Colin Tatz. Colin, who knew my parents well, wrote editorials for the magazine *Inside Sport*.

While I was in Sydney I sometimes stayed with my sister Debbie and her family. She warmly opened her home to me. She helped me by advising me on the business world I was about to join (Debbie was an office manager) and gave me emotional support when I was away from home. It was terrific to finally get to know her as an adult.

After I returned to our life on the farm, I continued to seek answers to the conflict that existed between Neil and me about my sporting life. My biggest tumble turn had been finding out about sports retirement stress. It had opened up a Pandora's box for me. (In Greek mythology, Pandora opened a box that released all the evils of human life. The only good thing in the box was hope.) Neil had thought my 'debriefing' would be a simple matter that would be over quite soon. But as time went on, it became a mission and then, for a while, a sort of crusade. I felt I had a personal quest to help athletes and sport in Australia. I was getting positive feedback from everyone I spoke with about sports retirement. Besides, the children were all at school, and I had the organisational ability to pursue my research while also making sure the farm and house continued to run smoothly. But Neil became impatient with me for directing my interests and focus outside of our life together on the farm. He wanted me back. I dug my heels in and continued accepting speaking engagements. The Pandora's box I had opened had given me hope, but it plagued our marriage.

Why couldn't the man I loved just accept my swimming achievements? We had intense discussions about the moral dangers of fame, hero-worship, popularity, pride and competitiveness. It was a time of prolific reading for me. I was searching for answers and found some in books such as M. Scott Peck's *The Road Less Travelled*, Andrew Jennings's *The Lords of the Rings* and Clarissa Pinkola Estés's *Women Who Run with the Wolves*. I also devoured *God, the Holy Father*, by 19th-century theologian, Peter Forsyth, referred to in the inspired writings of South Australian theologian, Geoffrey Bingham.

Neil's arguments always sounded convincing, but they didn't offer me a way to live with myself. I would actually have to deny my past and 'repent' of my involvement with swimming and the hero-worship I received and accepted. By allowing myself to be hero-worshipped, would I inevitably, as Neil believed, become self-centred and self-deceiving? I didn't want to be 'idolised', but I wanted — and needed — to accept and be accepted for who I was. I knew I wasn't a 'bad' person, that I didn't do 'bad' things. I have a strong Christian faith, but I have always had a problem with the notion of sin. Forsyth and Bingham put that to rest. I found a great deal of comfort at this time from talking with the Margaret River Baptist Church minister, Brian Arthur, and his wife, Dorothy. With some great teaching and eager searching for solutions, I had a marvellous renewal of faith. In two separate, middle-of-the-night experiences, I had revelations that helped me to understand grace and freedom. I experienced a freedom that *Jonathon Livingstone Seagull* alluded to. We can rise above ordinary love to holy love, which is grace. Grace can endure hate and transform it. In this action there is freedom. Freedom to love. Somehow, I could not convey this to Neil.

~

During 1995 I realised that the key to Neil's and my alienation from each other was the lack of loving communication between us. I was still committed to my marriage. I felt that if Neil could accept my love and understanding, we could be reunited. But by that stage, Neil had closed himself off from everything I was learning and was married to his surfboard. The door was firmly closed. Maybe our love had too many conditions on it.

On the surface, life went on as usual. The children were absorbed in school, soccer, hockey and surfing, and there was a regular busy rhythm of family life. I had finished doing the surfing instruction and taken on managing an established but run-down blueberry plantation. (I was to manage it successfully for three seasons — profitably for one. In my third season, I worked for $2 an hour when New Zealand dumped tiny but cheap berries on the Western Australian market. They were no match for my fresh, fat, sweet berries, except in price.) I taught beginner riding lessons after school three afternoons a week. I was a weekend surfer, and played with my horse for about ten hours a week.

During this time I hosted champion surfer Pam Burridge when she competed in the Margaret River Surf Classic. It was good to hear Pam's stories of her surfing successes and how she had overcome experiences similar to mine as an elite athlete. Pam is wise and has great strength of character — a great champion.

I caddied for Pam in the finals. The surf was large, so Pam needed another surfboard out near the wave lineup in case she broke a board, as others had done earlier in the day. Sure enough, on her first wave she snapped her board. I was enjoying the view from the sidelines with other girl caddies, when a piercing wolf whistle brought me to attention. 'That's me. Pam's snapped her board!' I said. I quickly paddled over to her, gave her the spare surfboard, and she gave me what remained of her other board. I started swimming for the shore, about 400 metres away, wishing I was a bit fitter, as the drift from the whitewater washing across the reef was pretty strong. Fortunately, the Sea Search and Rescue guys, who volunteer their time at surfing competitions in Margaret River, picked me up in their rubber duckie and gave me a ride to the beach. I raced up the beach and then up the steps with Pam's bit of surfboard. Out of breath, I urged one of my kids to go and get another one of Pam's surfboards. In five minutes, Kristin was back, pushing through the crowd with the board. I raced down the steps and paddled out the back to watch the last 20 minutes of the 45-minute final. And Pam won. I was so excited for her. She surfed brilliantly in the powerful eight- to ten-foot waves.

Pam gave me her red competition vest as a souvenir. It's something I treasure.

At this time, horses were terrific companions and teachers for me. I continued to study Parelli natural horsemanship, and the results I was getting gave me hope that the same kind of harmony I was experiencing with my horse might be possible in my other relationships — and particularly with Neil. In order to get some perspective on my emotions, I regularly rang my mother to ask, 'Am I reading this situation correctly, or am I crazy?' Mum was very encouraging and supported my commitment to my marriage. In Margaret River, I turned often to Brian and Dorothy Arthur for advice and comfort whenever my frustration reduced me once again to tears.

For about a year I felt overcome by despair and hopelessness. My tears often turned to racking sobs of grief. One morning, after working in the heat of the blueberry plot repairing irrigation pipes, I joined Brian and Dorothy for a cold drink. Brian asked me if I thought I might be depressed. 'No,' I said. 'I think depressed people are just weak. Depression's just a cover-up for unresolved emotional issues.' Brian tenderly said, 'It's OK to be weak'.

If I were a cat, my hackles would have risen. I felt defiant. 'No, I'm *not* weak!' I thought. 'I'm strong!' I had an image of myself as being brave and bold, capable and confident, able to overcome any adversity. No way was I weak! But I also doubted myself. I sat on my sweaty hands and braced my back 'It's OK to be weak, Shane,' Brian repeated. 'You don't have to be strong. In fact, asking for help shows strength of character. Perhaps you also have a chemical imbalance that's causing you to be depressed.'

I suddenly felt very tired. 'Maybe I *am* weak,' I thought. Immediately, my strength drained out of me. 'I can't hold it together anymore,' I said to myself. 'I need help before I do myself harm or get chronically ill.' I had accepted that I was weak, and that it was OK. I felt like a piece of heavy fluff. I gave up the fight with my mind and emotions, and went to see my doctor who prescribed antidepressant's.

I took the tablets for three months, during which time my emotions became dulled by the chemicals and levelled out. Blueberry picking and marketing took up to eight hours a day. I carried on with the routine of life, sharing only meals and a bed with Neil. I tried to shield the children from the tension, but their instincts were highly tuned. Neil and the boys usually went surfing without me, and I felt excluded from their excursions. Even when I did go, I wasn't pleasant company. I spent a lot of time with my horse.

In the spring of 1996, just after the Atlanta Olympic Games, I started having uncontrollable weeping bouts again. This time, I didn't fight it. I allowed myself to be weak, which helped a bit. I slept a lot and tried to be around positive, loving people.

One day I was in the garden doing some weeding, my red, tear-swollen eyes concealed behind sunglasses. I heard a voice speak to me. I looked around, thinking a horse-client was talking to me, but there was no one present. Then I clearly heard the words, 'Why don't you just give up? Life isn't worth living.' Now very alert, I stood up tall, looked around and said out loud in a defiant voice: 'Piss off! It *is* worth living!' I was really angry. Later that day I played REM's song 'Everybody Hurts' over and over. It became my theme song for the next few months, until I finally resorted to taking antidepressants again towards the end of the year.

I didn't like taking them, as they dull every sense. I kept looking for other ways to change how I was feeling and sort out my life. I came across Tony Robbins's book *Awaken the Giant Within*, which helped to restore my self-confidence and provided some 'tools' that I felt I could work with. I had thought that if I could just get right, my marriage would be right. But I decided just to get on with my life and try to put energy into positive things. Any thoughts of suicide were firmly pushed aside. I had too much to do.

Nevertheless, I was scared of my own power and of what the future might hold. I felt I was holding myself back, but didn't know why. I read this from the contents of South African President Nelson Mandela's inaugural speech, as I confronted my fears for my future:

> *It is not that we are inadequate. Our deepest fear is that we are powerful beyond measure. It is our light, not our darkness, that most frightens us.*
>
> *We ask ourselves, 'Who am I to be brilliant, gorgeous, talented and fabulous?' Actually, who are you NOT to be? You are a child of God. Your playing small doesn't serve the world.*
>
> *There's nothing enlightening about shrinking so that other people won't feel insecure about you.*
>
> *We were born to make manifest the glory that is within us — it is within everyone. As we let our own light shine we unconsciously give other people permission to do the same.*
>
> *As we are liberated from our own fear our presence automatically liberates others.*

I gave myself until Easter 1997 to see if my attitude towards my marriage and circumstances changed. During Easter I suffered a bout of pneumonia. Neil gave me no support and refused to care for me while I was ill, and I concluded that there was no love left in the marriage. I was desperately disappointed and felt totally neglected, particularly when I was sick. If I was going to survive, I had no choice now but to move out of our home and into a more positive environment.

Neil and I went to a counsellor to discuss a separation and arrangements regarding the children, but I don't think he really believed that I was going to leave him. However, I now felt very determined about my decision. I had been reading the book *Too Good to Leave, Too Bad to Stay* by Mira Kirshenbaum, which had clarified some issues for me. Instead of trying to weigh up the bad against the good in our relationship, I asked myself what I would really miss. My answers to questions posed in the book — Do you get excited when you see each other? Has there been any violence? Do you feel unsafe? What do you like about him? — satisfied me that it was definitely too bad to stay.

So I made plans to leave. I stayed in the house for another month while I finalised arrangements to go to the United States to do accelerated personal development training courses with Tony Robbins in California and with Pat Parelli at his International Study Centre in Colorado. I felt that I needed a radical change in my life, and spending three months in the United States was as good a way of doing this as anything else I'd come up with. I knew that I would be among positive, progressive and affirming people, and that I would be forced to stop feeling like a victim. I had faith that Tony Robbins and Pat Parelli could help me regain my self-confidence and emotional fitness, which would equip me for the next phase of my life. I felt I couldn't do it on my own, even with the wonderful help I had in Margaret River.

The children were numb with confusion, not really sure what was happening to their secure world. Neil was in a similar state, I think. I took my last antidepressant tablet the day I made the decision to leave the marriage. I did feel down at times after this, but it was just the normal sort of blues and grief that accompanies loss and change. The antidepressants had helped me to stabilise my emotions so that I could think rationally. Having made the decision to throw off my immobilised state and take action, I no longer needed them.

My decision to leave was not made lightly. It was the hardest decision I have ever made. I could no longer concern myself with what other people might say or think. I had to do what I needed to do, without worrying about other people's opinions or even about my husband's and children's emotional state. It was a desperate situation that required desperate measures. I know that it may have seemed selfish — the children were encouraged to think so — but a selfish person doesn't willingly spend over 20 years raising four children on a low income in an environment where everything was done the hard way. I decided I would just have to pick up the pieces later, which I am still doing — but at least I am alive and thriving.

In addition to being called 'selfish', I was told that I was a 'quitter', and always had been. 'You quit swimming when the going got tough, and you're quitting again now,' I was told. 'You're running away again, just like you did when you were 16.' The 1972 headline after I won my bronze medal at Munich, 'Shane Fails', flashed through my mind, mocking what little confidence I had left. I felt utterly misunderstood. No one seemed able to see that I had been in the pit of despair, but that I had chosen life. I tried to block out the 'noise' and listen to my inner voice.

In May I went as a guest to the Gatton Heavy Horse Field Day in south-west Queensland where I was to conduct a natural horsemanship demonstration and compete in a single-furrow ploughing match. My hosts extended generous hospitality in their Queenslander house built on stilts. I practised ploughing for a couple of hours the day before the competition with the pair of Clydesdales I was to use, then again at the showgrounds where the competition was held, but the horses responded to different commands than I was used to. After I'd established some rapport with the horses, I checked the plough and found that the shear was too sharp. It was skidding around like ice skates in the compacted rodeo ground. My host found a blacksmith who fixed the shear for me. It worked much better in the practice ground and even better once the soil had been harrowed through the hard clay pan.

When it was time for my event, it started to rain. I donned my raincoat, licked sweaty drips from my hat and got into it. I wasn't at all impressed with my performance, but we managed to get some semblance of a furrow and about eight runs. I was happy to score second place.

During my visit I enjoyed hearing about local history, seeing the wide variety of horse-drawn vehicles and feeling the warm friendliness of the country people.

After Gatton, I went to stay with my parents for a couple of days to get some much-needed mothering and emotional refuelling in preparation for the long months ahead. It was a warm and loving time; I appreciated their support. Their beautiful cosy cabin was an ideal place for reflection. I found the steep, tree-covered hills and the bubbling waters of the Cataract and Clarence rivers soothing. Mum and Dad's cooking and 10 o'clock smokos were great, too.

I felt shaky about going away, but I was committed to taking the step I had chosen. I had faith and trust that somehow everything would work out and that the breakdown of my marriage would have a positive outcome.

CHAPTER 15

Alive and Thriving

The future has several names. For the weak it is impossible. For the fainthearted it is unknown. For the thoughtful and valiant it is ideal.

~

Victor Hugo

I WENT BACK TO MARGARET RIVER to remove some of my personal possessions from the house and say goodbye to the children for the three months I planned to be in the United States. One of the children was very angry about everything that was happening. In an attempt to bridge the distance between us, I left a card on which I had written some words from a song by Troy Cassar-Daley that I had heard on the radio:

I carried you inside me.
I carried you in my arms.
I'll carry you in my heart for the rest of my life.

It was a painful time. The transformation process of combining my identities, triggered by my experience with 'Burke's Backyard' in 1990, seemed to be nearly complete. I was gaining my whole identity, but losing my marriage.

I was concerned about storing my sporting memorabilia and other personal items at the farm while I was away. I was fearful that Neil might burn my clothes. I heard that he had smashed one of my plaques with a sledgehammer on the wood-chopping block. He must have really hated Shane Gould, the swimmer. I left my Olympic medals with the friend from whom I had borrowed the money to finance my trip. We had a formal legal agreement: my medals were used as surety that I would repay the debt within two years. This agreement caused a lot of controversy during Neil's and my property settlement negotiations.

On 2 June 1997, I started my solo adventure when I took a flight from Perth. While in transit at Sydney airport, I had a meeting with Rob Woodhouse, a director of the sports marketing company, Elite Sports Properties (ESP). Rob had won bronze in the 400 metres individual medley in the 1984 Olympics. He knew swimming and swimmers. There was an instant trust and understanding between us.

It was arranged that Rob would be my manager; that he would negotiate commercial opportunities for me with the Olympic sponsors in the run-up to the 2000 Games in Sydney. Moving back into the commercial world was yet another of my 'tumble turns'. Rob knew of my aversion to and avoidance of a prominent public life. After relating some of what I had gone through to get to this point I told him that I felt I could go ahead now.

There was a nice synchronicity when, during the transit, I met Susie O'Neill ('Madam Butterfly') for the first time. I warmed to Susie's modesty and admired her self-confidence. I had some twinges of envy that Susie had Rob Woodhouse and ESP to manage her commercial life while she was still competing. The old amateur-versus-professional times were well and truly over.

As the plane climbed out of Sydney, I felt the enormity of what I had done. I'd removed myself from my husband; I wouldn't be seeing my children for three months. Joel was 19 and working. Kim was 17 and living away from home. Tom was 15, and Kristin 14. They were all well on the way to becoming young, independent adults. All the same, I felt some anxiety about being away from the younger boys in particular.

Then came a bubble of excitement. Depression had gone. I was alive, and I was sane. I was on my way to making my life strong and worthwhile. I was giving myself the chance to grow and learn and to feel free. I believed I had a positive future ahead of me; I just needed some new skills and tools to make it come about.

I had no income I could survive on, no job, and no fixed address. But I had an unshakeable conviction that what I was doing would eventually have a beneficial outcome for all the family, including Neil.

Los Angeles airport was a shock. Perth airport was like a terminal in a country town by comparison. The airport was huge and impersonal, with armed security guards every 50 metres. I felt tired and lonely. I gave myself a talking-to and refocused on why I was making the trip. When I eventually found my way out of the terminal, I caught a cab to Laguna Beach where I stayed overnight with a friend of a friend. I slept for a blissful 12 hours.

I then moved in with a couple who lived closer to the venue of the Tony Robbins Life Mastery course. These people confirmed my view of American generosity and kindness. They drove me to the course each day, and picked me up in the evening — often well after midnight. Having decided to undertake massive changes in my life, help seemed to be there at every turn.

The Life Mastery course was marvellous. Hugely challenging, it enabled me to break through a whole set of self-limiting beliefs I'd been gathering for years. It was such a relief to drop the lot. In a state of happiness I hadn't known in a long time, I was open to taking in the information I was looking for. Out of a host of useful concepts, I singled out the idea of identifying my basic needs. These were: the need to grow, and the need to contribute. Then I analysed how I had tried to meet these needs in the past; I hadn't always been successful in the methods I'd used. 'It'll be different from now on,' I thought as I wrote checklists for the future.

I gained a clear understanding of something I hadn't wanted to face: that I had been in a negative relationship for a long time. As Clarissa Pinkola Estés describes in *Women Who Run With the Wolves*, I had felt that I had to cringe, flinch, grovel and plead for the life that was my own to begin with. I had felt wrong for being myself, as I didn't fit the image Neil wanted me to fit. I had often been shunned by him; shut out, ignored as if I didn't exist. Perhaps by withdrawing his love and concern he was trying to make me conform to another image.

This treatment, observed by the children, was humiliating. I would then creep into the shadows, hurt and bewildered about what was wrong with me. But I didn't conform, and I never lost my enthusiasm for life. Soon I'd be devising some idea for a new business venture, or planning a home renovation. Neil never welcomed my plans: 'It's your idea, you do it,' he'd say. So I'd throw myself into the new project — 'over-functioning' — while Neil 'under-functioned' and criticised. It was always wonderful to make a trip 'back east' where I would fall into my family's unconditional love. However, pride kept me from telling them of my difficulties with Neil until after 1990.

A further realisation during the course was that for 25 years I had 'felt sorry for myself' for winning five Olympic medals — I had seen myself as a victim of fame. It was time now to emerge from the shadows, to put aside self-pity, and to acknowledge my achievements and the life-skills I had gained from them.

I came away from the course with new energy. It was like changing into a different person. My mood was lighter, optimistic and confident, and ripples of happiness gently touched everything I did, felt and thought. Seeing myself honestly and clearly, I was grateful that I was a woman blessed with many talents. I knew I would continue to grow, and that I was capable of making a positive contribution in the world. I knew I wasn't a victim.

~

From Los Angeles I went to the Parelli ranch in Pagosa Springs, Colorado, where I planned to continue my studies of Parelli natural horsemanship. I lived with other students from all over the world: Australians, New Zealanders, Swiss, English and French. It felt like the Olympic Village. We had chores to do, plus theory classes and practical lessons. They were long, ten- to 14-hour days, but I thoroughly enjoyed Pat's progressive teaching methods, which stimulate accelerated learning.

My ploughing experiences came in handy at the ranch. With fellow students Calvin, a Navajo Indian, and Don, a Canadian, I worked with two big bay Suffolk Punch horses, carting hay and collecting manure. My other jobs included meeting and greeting new students, working in the kitchen, and running free weekend workshops for the local kids. One day I helped to remake a boundary fence, and the Colorado landscape took my breath away. There were snow-capped mountains to the north, and steep hills covered with scrubby oak, aspen and pine trees to the south. On the ground nearby I saw the droppings and tracks of bears, elk and deer. I was a long way from Australia.

Most of the days were spent playing with and learning more about horses. It was sheer joy to connect with horses that accepted humans as their lead-horse. They would willingly walk on to a horse-float 'at liberty' (no ropes attached). We rode, rein-less. We raced the horses sideways, and followed cows on the run. We took the horses swimming in a dam, and played horse games that exhilarated the riders and kept the horses so alert that they were eager to know what was coming next.

Pat and Linda Parelli are master-teachers, and their main technique was to make learning into a game. Playing games removed tension, and took us beyond our imagined limits, time and time again. It was accelerated learning, and it felt effortless. I noted the contrast with some equestrian teaching I'd seen before — a serious, military-type approach with boring routines that make horses apathetic. This type of teaching turns kids off. They want fun, not regimentation, so they gravitate to other sports.

As the days flew by, my confidence grew. I was given positive feedback for my efforts, and I felt stronger in every way except one: I was homesick. I ran up a big telephone bill keeping in touch with my children and friends back home. It felt rather strange to sit in the warm afternoon sunshine in the mountains of Colorado and talk with the boys before they went off to school in Margaret River the following morning.

A new student, Andrew Booth, arrived, and brought out some photos of his family's farm in New South Wales. Tears came to my eyes, and a shiver ran up my spine when I saw the distinctive grey-green eucalypts, low hills and vast landscape that was so unmistakably Australian. This sudden rush of emotion surprised me. Far from home, I knew where I belonged. My place was Australia.

We often had a camp fire and singalong under the stars. One evening, Andrew — who could play a vacuum cleaner pipe like a didgeridoo! — thrummed an eerie tune on the pipe didge while I led some kids in a dance around the crackling camp fire, mimicking the movements of emus and kangaroos. There were also some talented musicians who played guitars and sang country-and-western-style songs.

Sometimes after a long, hard day of riding, we would all pile into cars and go to the nearby hot springs. We sat in the bubbling springs, moaning with pleasure as our strained and aching muscles started to relax in the hot sulphur waters. Luxury! There was an outdoor 15-metre pool nearby, which was warmed by the spring water. The water was too hot to do laps, but it was just right for learning to swim and I got a lot of satisfaction from helping the wife and daughter of one of the course instructors to improve their swimming.

For a few weeks I went swimming at the Pagosa 25-metre pool with some other Parelli students who also wanted to improve their swimming. (It was hard to get air into our lungs when we first got in, as the pool was at an altitude of 7000 feet.) I enjoy teaching adults, because small improvements such as efficient kicking and proper breathing can make all the difference in being able to swim competently. Most children are taught to swim in order to be able to survive in the water, rather than to swim for its own sake, and many adults still swim like they did at their last swimming lesson at around age 12.

Andrew Booth sometimes joined us at the pool and I noticed he swam pretty well for someone who had been raised in the country. His stroke looked familiar, too. When I commented on it, he told me that Gail Neall, my fellow high school student and Olympian, had been his primary school teacher and she had taught him to swim. A further Olympic connection was with Peggy, another student at the ranch, who had been a reserve in the US Olympic figure-skating team in 1972. Her current profession of physical therapist had also placed her with the US Olympic ski team. She was an excellent therapist as well as having a sharp, quick wit that kept us laughing. I sprained my ankle pretty badly at one stage when I leapt exuberantly over a railed fence, and I sought help from Peggy. She gave me 'muscle memory' exercises to do that would help prevent further injury — similar to teaching someone how to fish rather than just *giving* them a fish.

Pat Parelli also taught us to train our muscle memory for horsemanship by using a bucking barrel to simulate a bucking horse and the trampoline to simulate falling off a horse. It was a lot of fun. We used beach balls in our morning wake-up aerobics to develop our peripheral vision for handling horses on the ground. Horses can move very quickly and in unpredictable ways.

My days at the ranch were very full, with a rich and challenging physical life and plenty of chores to do. Sometimes I felt lonely and introspective and on the brink of slipping back into depression. I felt guilty at times about leaving my children. Depression was a paralysing place, I reminded myself. I had too much to do to give into it. I resolved to just keep looking forward and trust that all would be well.

I could see that my years of intensive mothering were coming to an end and that I needed another worthwhile goal. I felt that I had done my job well enough to make myself redundant as a full-time mother. I had come to the United States in order to re-skill myself in at least two areas: I wanted to participate in the lead-up to the Sydney Olympic Games in 2000; and I wanted to gain the skills needed to become a Parelli natural horsemanship instructor. Just before I left Pagosa Springs, I graduated from the student instructor program and was awarded private instructor status. It was an honour to be one of Pat Parelli's instructors, and a very satisfying reward for all the effort I had put in.

During my time in Pagosa I read Victor Frankl's book, *Man's Search for Meaning*. I realised that it was my choice as to how I responded to any given situation, and that positive, productive responses are an indication of 'emotional intelligence'. I knew that my life, my health, and the opportunity I might have to make a valuable contribution, would depend on my developing my emotional intelligence. The freedom to choose one's attitude in any given set of circumstances — *to choose one's own way* — is the last freedom that can be taken from a person, Frankl explained. He used the example of prisoners in concentration camps. The survivors of such camps were those with a positive attitude, a hopeful outlook, and forgiving compassion towards their captors and fellow inmates. Frankl quoted Dostoevski who said of the concentration camp prisoners: 'The way they bore their suffering was a genuine inner achievement. It is this spiritual freedom which cannot be taken away that makes life meaningful and purposeful.'

The depression, bitterness, anger and self-pity I had experienced during my marriage hadn't given meaning to my suffering or alleviated it. I thought about all the time I had wasted in brooding and not taking action. I accept now that it was all part of my growth towards emotional intelligence. As Dostoevski described, I wanted to be worthy of my sufferings.

In the early mornings before I fed the horses, I sometimes sat on the steps of the little cabin that was my home in the mountains of Colorado, feeling like a stranger in this land. At the same time, I felt at home and at peace with the wildness of nature, the untamed power of the oceans and with Mother Nature's finest animal, the horse. I was becoming more at home with myself. The feeling of being at home was very important for me at that time, because when I returned to Australia I wouldn't have a home to go back to. I was both apprehensive about and excited by the prospect. I now knew that I had the inner resources to deal with anything that was thrown my way, as well as the emotional and practical support of friends in Australia. One of my main needs is to feel that I belong somewhere. I knew that my journeyings were part of the process of finding out where that was.

At the end of three months I was ready to come home and get on with my life, no longer living in the shadows but out in the open. I no longer needed to ask the 'real Shane' to stand up. Despite my broken marriage and long separation from my children, I felt confident about moving into the next exciting phase of my life. The question now was how to fully express that self in all my dealings with others and create positive, joyful outcomes in the process.

In September, soon after I returned to Margaret River, I signed a three-year contract with Channel 7, the broadcaster of the Olympic Games, as one of their seven 'Olympic legends'. I was in very distinguished company with Dawn Fraser, Murray Rose, Shirley de la Hunty, (nee Strickland) Ron Clarke, Marjorie Jackson and Herb

Elliott. I stayed with friends until November, when I rented a house near the beach. After six months of having no fixed address, I was Shane at home.

It took a couple of months to re-establish a relationship with the children, who had been told that they 'no longer had a mother'. This gross untruth was painful for me, especially when I experienced the boys employing their father's shunning technique. I would choose the physical pain of a hundred childbirths before the emotional agony of being shunned by those I loved.

In the three months I had been away, the children had grown up, too. They were more independent and self-reliant, and their relationship with their father had strengthened. I felt as if my absence had allowed them to go through a kind of initiation into adulthood, in the way that young boys in tribal societies are taken from their mother's house for initiation into manhood.

However, I wasn't a tribal mother. At one stage, I was like a raging mother bear or a she-wolf with her cubs, needing to give my children the care and attention I felt they needed. In February 1998 I had a physical and verbal argument with Neil, because he refused to tell me where the boys were. He took out a restraining order against me. The case ended up in the local court. After the hearing, the judge basically told us both to go away and grow up, and try to work things out in a more mature way. We were both given a misconduct restraining order. I felt angry, frustrated and humiliated.

Separation and divorce are messy, ugly things.

While I was still in a state of raw adjustment to my life as a separated person, I undertook my first major public engagement — the 'Olympic Journey' street parade in Perth in September. The idea of the parade was to demonstrate that all of Australia was hosting the Games, not just Sydney. I enjoyed getting into the spirit of the parade. I was now involved in a series of jobs for Channel 7, Holden and Telstra. These three companies are Olympic Partners — the official name for companies who have bought the right to use the Olympic rings and their association with the Olympic Games in their advertising. I entered the commercial world feeling like a migrant from another culture.

On Boxing Day, 1997, I had the privilege of starting the Telstra Sydney to Hobart yacht race in Sydney. The start of the race was very exciting, with the yachts looking magnificent as they tacked back and forth, their giant sails billowing in the breeze. I love Sydney Harbour. Whenever I'm in Sydney and have the time, I like to take the ferry from Circular Quay to Manly. I buy a muffin or a packet of hot chips to munch on the way. I really feel like I'm in Sydney then.

In January 1998, Perth hosted the World Swimming Championships. I was present as a guest of Ansett, one of the main sponsors, as well as having a media pass to do special commentary for Channel 7. I was familiar with the Challenge Stadium, as I often swam there when on visits to Perth, but I was intimidated by the huge media entourage and the now-unfamiliar language of competitive swimming. I felt quite uncomfortable, again as if I were in a foreign culture, and yet I was expected to make reasonably perceptive comments on what was happening. I listened to what the other commentators such as Mark Spitz and Murray Rose were saying. I watched the coaches with their athletes in the warm-up pool. And I asked questions. I soon started to see what the experts were seeing and picked up the language of swimming again, but I felt as if I was bluffing my way through it.

I was conscious that I was out of touch with modern elite swimming. Learning to swim, yes. And I could talk confidently about surfing, farming, animal breeding, horse psychology, ploughing and cake-baking. But I wasn't au fait with competitive swimming, 1998-style.

Surprised by the warmth of attention given to me in my public appearance at the Championships, I wanted to justify my welcome and give a good performance. I found that trying to catch up on 26 years of changes in swimming was mentally taxing, and emotionally and physically draining. I slept nearly every afternoon before the finals at night. This reminded me of my routine during my racing years.

Early each morning I relaxed from the stress of learning and participating in this new, unfamiliar world by spending time with Lalinka, who was stabled only a stone's throw away from the swimming stadium. I would talk with her, feed her and have a smell of her, get sand in my shoes and smudged dirt on my cheek. We rode together along the soft, sandy tracks to the north and east of the stadium, up through the jarrah and banksia scrub hills towards the ocean. From the top of a hill in Bold Park, to the east all I could see was an ocean of treetops and the high-rise buildings of Perth's central business district. To the west I saw only hardy coastal scrub and the ruffled Indian Ocean. I was astonished not to see houses or people only eight kilometres from the city.

By the last session of the Championships I felt more at ease at the pool and made some reasonably intelligent comments about the swimming and the swimmers, but then it was all over. I was pleased that I had had the chance to meet Mark Spitz again. Mark was very experienced in talking to the media. He had strong views, and spoke clearly and simply. He knew how to give television reporters their five-second 'grab' and then expand on it for the print media. I tend to go for the long yarn or an in-depth discussion rather than a short, pithy comment, and I realised I had a few things to learn about commentating. It's very difficult for me to say something profound in just a sentence or two, but I'm working on it.

I learned a lot from Mark Spitz. Another 'teacher' is my favourite cartoonist, Michael Leunig, who is adept at expressing a complex concept simply. It seems that the more you know on a subject, the more easily you can simplify it. I am determined to do a good job of giving special comments at the Sydney Games. I'm in training for it now.

One thing I did feel confident in speaking about at the World Swimming Championships, however, was the issue of drugs in sport.

During the Championships, it was all over the newspapers that four Chinese swimmers had been disqualified for testing positive to using diuretics, a masking agent for steroids. In 1997, Chinese women had posted world records in swimming, and media inferences at the time pointed to drug-assisted performances. At a Telstra Swimmer of the Year Award lunch in Melbourne, I had asked Don Talbot, the Australian team coach, how he would be able to motivate the Australian girls to rise above the situation. Don was almost despairing. He said that all he could do was to tell the team to ignore their competitors and focus on their own strengths. He was also distressed that FINA, the world body governing swimming wasn't taking action.

'What can I do?' I wondered. I thought that positive peer pressure would work best to encourage athletes to swim clean. An art teacher from a Perth high school helped design a T-shirt that would make a positive statement. Jenny Day and Barry Cable of the WA Football Commission's Community Service division assisted me, too. The Western Australian government agreed to fund the printing of 500 T-shirts and caps carrying the slogan, 'Clean Sport'.

Just before the Championships began, I had a meeting with the swimmers. I took three gifts. First, I handed out some of the T-shirts. Next, I gave them little fabric packets of sweets labelled 'Excellence Pills (not detected in urine or blood) Revealed in Cool Attitude and Superior Performance'. The third gift was a handful of large silk butterflies on sticks. These were to remind the swimmers to get their pre-race 'butterflies' to fly in formation.

The swimmers were awesomely fit and they glowed with good health. The beauty of these athletes in their prime was stunning. They had great team-spirit, too. The big surprise for me was the size of their support crew. Besides coaches and managers, the entourage included physiotherapists, masseurs, media liaison officers and psychologists. It was another learning experience for me about the ways of modern sport.

The swimming results for the Australian team at the World Championships were exceptional — maybe my 'Excellence Pills' had helped. The disqualification of the Chinese swimmers became big news and the West Australian newspaper provided comprehensive, open and informed reporting on the issue. I heard that the FINA officials were astounded by the forceful anti-drugs stance of the Australians. FINA rules didn't allow swimmers to be banned from competing for using diuretics, whereas the International Olympic Committee rules do.

I believe that there were attempts to whitewash the findings, but FINA couldn't ignore the evidence, or the passion of those opposed to the practice. I think these powerful officials got a taste of Australian fair play — a bellyful, in fact. Australians love their sport. They want clean sport and will not be patronised or sweet-talked out of what they know makes for fairness in competition.

Reporters covering the story were helped by three outstanding men: Forbes Carlile, Peter Daland and John Leonard, the drug taskforce members of the World Swimming Coaches Association. These men were as persistent as Australian flies, and action was taken because the decision-makers had to take notice. Europeans can't ignore flies. The World Championships in Perth proved to be a valuable testing ground for the Sydney 2000 Games in more ways than one.

On 31 March 1999, FINA boldly introduced tough new rules for doping in swimming at an extraordinary congress in Hong Kong. The new rules comprise four-year bans for the use of steroids and similar substances, and cancellation of all swim results six months prior to a positive test result. These and other strong sanctions are setting a benchmark for doping control rules for all sport.

I felt I had a small part to play in this excellent legislation. At the World Championships, I distributed the 'Clean Sport' T-shirts in the media rooms, to some of the American athletes, and to the Swedish and Canadian teams. Some of the 'POOS' (Parents of Olympic Swimmers) welcomed the opportunity to make a stand for Clean

Sport and wore them. It was good to talk to people who were really concerned about the use of PEGs, and it spurred me on to make a more public stand. I use the acronym 'PEGs' for performance-enhancing drugs. Pegs are useful for hanging out the washing. They are also small, weak and often break. No athlete needs a peg's support to display his or her achievements.

~

Each evening of the Championships, during the finals, one of the sponsored swimming legends was presented to the spectators. These legends were Dawn Fraser, Murray Rose, Mark Spitz, Kristina Egeseki, diver Greg Louganis and me. The evening on which I was presented was after the Chinese swimmers had tested positive to diuretics and the human growth hormone vials had been discovered. I obtained a bunch of blue and yellow helium-filled balloons and wrote 'CLEAN SPORT' all over them. I took them with me out in front of the crowd and let them go one by one. I stood on block 4, while the electronic advertising screen below the block flashed the drug-free message.

I really wanted to do a 'bomby' into the water and encourage others to come in too. I wanted to fill the pool with bubble bath to further make the point that we Australians wanted clean sport. The bomby and the bubble bath didn't happen, but it would have been good, clean fun if they had. Maybe another time. The POOS proudly wearing their 'Clean Sport' T-shirts provided another great example of positive peer-group pressure.

After the World Championships I made plans to 'train' for my work with Channel 7 and associated public events in the lead-up to the 2000 Olympics. I was nervous about being involved once again with the international media and important people and commercial sponsors. Occasionally I confessed to friends: 'I just want to go home to my wood stove and bake some scones!'

I knew that I had to change gears and learn to move and think faster, so I set myself some specific tasks. I wanted to be well prepared, so that I would be able to work and 'perform' to my maximum capacity. The first thing I had to do was improve my public-speaking ability. Several times when I was in Sydney, I arranged to practise speaking on camera at the Channel 7 studios in Epping. The cameraman and soundman gave me some valuable tips. I did a public-speaking course organised by the AOC Olympic Communicators program. That was hard, but again valuable. Successful athletes are expected to be able to speak confidently in front of a camera or a roomful of schoolchildren or business executives. But it's a skill that has to be learned.

I had voice-coaching lessons with Earl Reeve of ABC Radio fame, too. Earl is a patient teacher, and his lessons are excellent. I found, though, that my emotional state can really affect my voice strength. Neil and I were involved with the Family Court at the time, and my voice quality suffered along with my emotional equilibrium.

To help me lighten up a little, I joined a local women's singing group. That was fun. We played around with sounds and songs, experimenting with harmonies.

To let go of my attachment to the farm, I had a little ceremony in the bush with some close women friends. I was missing the land I'd lived on for over 20 years. My spirit was wandering, needing to find another place to make a home. I also needed to let go of anger, give thanks for the good things I had shared in during my marriage, and forgive myself and Neil for our failure to live out our lives together.

We women met in the misty rain at the designated spot before sunrise. In my oven at home I had heated some smooth granite rocks for us to sit on. We built a little fire and threw on some herbs. The smell of damp wood smoke and earthy aromas wafted over us. We sang a few songs of praise and thanks. We shared prayers and poems, and broke some homemade bread that was dunked in hot peppermint tea. It was a very moving way of letting go, forgiving and giving thanks. When the sun rose and shone through the dripping branches, I felt that I had finally put a lot of things to rest. My voice became stronger and my concentration improved.

In my new work, it was important for me to be able to think quickly. I practised speaking concisely and getting my point across quickly. I was used to being in cruise-control mode, so it was like doing repeat sprints when I was used to a slow-paced rhythm.

Another area that needed attention was my knowledge of today's swimming. I needed to learn fast. My understanding of accelerated learning suggested that I do it practically, in a fun way. I asked Pauline Pratt, who coached the Cambridge Swimming Club at Bold Park in Perth, if I could get in at the back of her training squad. She kindly agreed. The ten- to 13-year-olds in the training group stretched my fitness capabilities. By listening to Pauline give instructions and doing the drills and sets, I quickly gained a better knowledge of modern swimming. I also went to Forrestfield, where a friend's daughters trained. Brett, the coach, was terrific, giving me encouragement and stroke tips. He didn't think much of my old-fashioned dive, though. I liked using flippers for underwater drills, as I could no longer do butterfly without them. Now, wherever I go on my travels, I try to do a training session with a local club.

Just as I had known I would have to be physically fit to be a mother, I knew I would have to be fit for all the travelling in my new work. In addition to my swim training, I started swimming a few times a week for fitness. I bought a thin wetsuit and swam in the ocean at Gnarabup Beach where I used to teach swimming. I also did a few long walks or jogs each week. I built up enough fitness to be able to jog four kilometres around Lake Monger in Perth. It nearly killed me, but I did it. I still find it much easier to swim four kilometres than to jog the distance. I rode my horse several times a week, too. One day I had a very jarring ride and a disc in my lower back collapsed. I was in a lot of pain and worried that I would never be able to ride again or exercise vigorously. After seeking medical attention, having some X-rays taken and experimenting with a number of different therapies, I found that I could manage the pain and damage. The cure was to keep moving and do flexibility exercises. So, I did more swimming and more walking and jogging, along with gentle riding.

During this time, the local shire asked if I would be involved in the opening of the new 25-metre indoor swimming pool at Margaret River, to be held in July 1998. I offered to swim a fast lap to demonstrate what a swimming race was. I knew that my kids and other local people hadn't seen a live pool race. It would also keep me motivated in the cold weather to keep swimming and do some systematic training. I had two months to prepare. To accelerate the fitness process, I learned how to use the gymnasium. Three times a week, Carol McCarthy kept me company and guided my strength program. I would need instant muscle strength for a 50-metre sprint.

I was nervous and self-conscious on the day of the opening of the pool, partly because I saw myself as a 41-year-old woman standing semi-naked in front of my friends and home town. I was also conscious that no one in Margaret River had ever seen me as 'Shane Gould' and yet, here I was, assuming that persona. Despite my nerves, I felt as prepared as I could be.

To raise money, the other seven lanes had been auctioned. My dentist swam in a lane next to me. And in lane 8 was the local writer of outspoken letters to the editor, dressed in a polka-dot, neck-to-knee swimsuit. I finished the race with a time of 29.4, an Australian record for my age group, 40–44.

I continue to swim at least three times a week, doing three to three-and-a-half kilometres each session. I enjoy doing ins and outs at the beach, too — running down into the waves and across the sandbank, diving through the shore break, then bodysurfing a wave in and running back up the beach. I do all of this with some Margaret River Aussie masters swimmers. It's much easier — and a lot more fun — doing it with others. On my own, I sometimes think: 'What am I doing this for? I don't need this pain in my lungs and arms!' But I do enjoy the feeling of health and wellbeing that it gives me.

I try to stay focused by eating properly, getting enough sleep and nourishing my soul. I often take a siesta in the afternoon — it really refreshes me and gives me a second wind. I have started to take nutritional supplements, even though I eat a good balanced diet with plenty of complex carbohydrates and 'slow' foods. I nourish my soul with quiet times of prayer and reflection. I read books that nurture a positive frame of mind, and I spend time with my friends. I have always loved the natural beauty and wildness of the south-west coast of Western Australia and love to walk on the beach and over the rocks or up on the ridge among the hardy coastal scrub. My relationship with my horse is very sustaining, too. Manure, sweat, flies, dust and horses have a way of keeping me real and grounded.

I am looking forward to being at my second Olympics. I will be there as a senior Olympian doing special comments for Channel 7 at the swimming events, and enjoying the athletics as a spectator. Our Games will give the world an opportunity to gain a more accurate understanding of Australia. I bet there will be more people wanting to migrate to this fantastic country after the Games!

And after the Olympics, my children will continue to be my prime motivation for everything I do. I also have a mission and a program to assist athletes to develop as whole people.

As Shane Gould, I won five Olympic medals at the age of 15. Being an Olympian is like having a brand burned deeply into my body, mind and soul. It is a lifetime description. I will never *not* know what it is to be an Olympian. But, so what? As a mother, the best legacy I can give my children is a love of the outdoors and of physical activity, of health and fitness, for their own sake. Sport is just a means to this end, not an end in itself.

~

My life so far has seen me through many tumble turns: leaving Australia at three and returning at nine; fitting into nine different schools; becoming an Olympian; escaping from being an Olympian; joining a Christian community; marrying at 18; mothering at 21; living an 'alternative lifestyle' in voluntary poverty; learning farm skills; awakening to my denial of 'Shane Gould, the Swimmer'; researching sport retirement; experiencing depression; separating from my husband; attending the Life Mastery course; becoming a natural horsemanship instructor; divorcing; re-skilling myself for the commercial world; and getting back into age-group swimming.

During some of these tumble turns it felt as if life was flipping me over. In others, I deliberately took the turn that set me on to a new path. I'm grateful for all my tumble turns. They have shown me that I am not just an accumulation of accomplishments and achievements. Rather than what I've done, it is who I have become in the process.

Rather than asking myself, 'Will the real Shane please stand up', I can ask a more powerful question: 'How can I fully express the special person I am in all the places I go, communicating the joy and wonder of the world?' Come on the next 43 years!

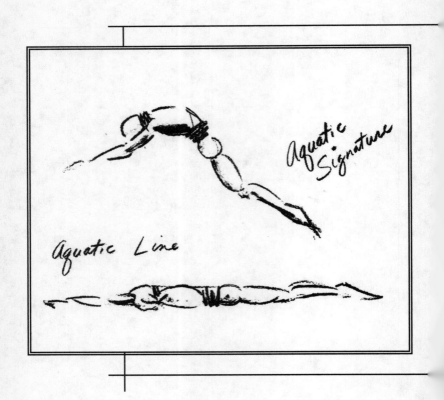

Aquatic Signature

Aquatic Line

PART SIX

reformation

A Note from Shane Gould

April 2003

IN MAY 1999 WHEN I TYPED THE last words of my autobiography, I sat at my computer, elation alternating with deflation. Elation from the achievement; deflation from the end of the project. I had written a book about an Australian woman's life. I knew it wasn't a regular sports biography. I wanted my story to be in the vein of an Aboriginal tale or myth — a record of history and, embedded in the story, some moral precepts or hints for living.

The many messages I received from readers (thank you for your compliments and appreciation) demonstrated that the first edition of *Tumble Turns* achieved that. People told me they had changed their minds about swimming — some had got back into the water and rekindled their love for swimming. Some people had changed their life and relationships. Others had affirmed their life's struggles, seeing them as having a positive effect on their personal growth, and stopped feeling like victims, helpless and powerless. Many people compared their successes and life transitions with mine — especially the difficult times where I was reinventing myself! Others identified with the ordinariness of my life. Being a parent and a wife is so undervalued in our society, so I wanted to affirm the importance of this role, and the series of recipes in the back of the book symbolise the nourishment and nurture I gave to my family.

After I delivered my finished manuscript to the publishers, I thought, 'I'd like to do some more writing.' Be careful what you wish for! Shortly afterwards *The Australian* newspaper invited me to write feature articles for publication in the lead-up to and during the Sydney 2000 Olympic Games. After some consideration I agreed, eventually penning about 12 articles for the paper. To be asked by one of the more intellectual, thinking newspapers in the country was a real honour. I remember the frustration my ex-husband Neil and I had felt when the only press interested in the radical ideas we lived by were 'women's' magazines. My 'chickens came home to roost' when I wrote for *The Australian*. And my self-image changed through writing.

The response to my articles has spurred me to write more. After publication of the first edition of *Tumble Turns*, I realised how much of a personal interest people took in me. I was often asked questions about my life since I made the wrenching decisions to leave the farm and my marriage and to re-engage with public life. This interest and the reception I have received since entering public life again — so overwhelmingly shown during the Sydney 2000 Games — has given me confidence to speak boldly and to share new insights and knowledge I have gained. I hope the following chapters interest and benefit anyone involved in sport and recreational swimming, and also go some way to answering those personal issues people have been so curious about.

CHAPTER 16

Sydney 2000 Olympic Games

. . . Oh, that's my mum!

~

Joel Innes to customers and fellow restaurant workers when Shane
Gould appeared on TV carrying the Olympic torch

BEING INVOLVED WITH THE LIGHTING OF the cauldron at the
Opening Ceremony of the Sydney 2000 Olympic Games was my
second most exciting public appearance (Munich in 1972 was of
course the most exciting!). I was so warmly welcomed back into
public life that the experience wasn't as stressful or frightening as I'd
anticipated. Australians love their sporting heroes, and I was
showered with respect and love. It was a surprise and comfort to be
greeted and congratulated in very personal ways by moist-eyed
women and firm-handshaking men. It made me realise how much a
part of these Australians' memories I was.

Coming back into the public arena again I wanted to be sure I was
properly prepared. I approached my new role in a familiar way, as an
athlete would: doing training and skill development for the tasks at

hand. As a former Olympian I was in demand to speak to schools, companies and community groups during the lead-up to the Games, so I enlisted in 'speaker' training, which the Australian Olympic Committee offered to current and former Olympians. I also found a good hair stylist and learned how to use make-up. Wardrobe managers from Channel 7 gave me clothing suggestions. Toastmasters, an international speaker training organisation, gave me the best training and practice in organising my ideas and presenting them to an audience. I still belong to the Margaret River Club, learning from and with my friends and local people in a non-judgemental supportive environment.

Feeling incompetent in situations outside of the pool was a major reason for my early retirement at 16. I wasn't trained or prepared for the intense public exposure or the demands placed on me to perform duties in public as a successful athlete. No one was trained then, at least not in Australia. Most swimmers were young like me and Australian schools didn't have classes for public speaking — unlike the Californian school I went to in 1973. US swimmers were different. They were more eloquent and confident, and able to arrange their ideas and speak intelligently.

Things have changed now and over the past ten years Australian swimming, under Ian Hansen, has been teaching swimmers on national teams how to do impromptu interviews after races and handle themselves in press conferences. I was a guest speaker at a junior development camp in 2000 when Ian gave a class for the campers. He had found some archived interviews I had given when I was 14 and showed them as examples of what not to do — I was so shy and incoherent. The kids laughed and I squirmed at my incompetence! No wonder I didn't enjoy the media and public responsibilities. Kieren Perkins was one of the first swimmers who gained from this, and he became a role model for the next generation.

Swimming fans have asked me how it is that swimmers today are so confident — even the very young swimmers appear relaxed and eloquent in front of a camera and microphone. Just a little bit of training and modelling by peers has made a big difference. Many football clubs and larger sporting organisations now give public speaking and presentation training to their athletes, and the change is remarkable, as these players, skilled on the field, carry their image of competency off the field. It can also make a significant difference to fans, sponsors and parents of the next generation of players, and their perception of the athletes and the sport they play. One parent told me they chose swimming as their child's sport because they believed swimming would help them to be self-assured and possess humble confidence.

~

In the lead-up to the Sydney Games I was involved in many events and had the opportunity to meet a range of interesting people who inspired me with new ideas and fed my inquisitive nature. Just before the Games I met former Prime Minister Gough Whitlam at a ceremony at Olympic Park to unveil a plaque attached to the 'Munich' lighting tower outside the main stadium. The plaque was a memorial to the Israeli athletes killed in the terrorist attack at the Munich Olympics in 1972. Former Prime Minister Bob Hawke was also there, as was a relative of one of the Israelis who had been killed in the attack, and representatives from the Jewish community in Sydney.

I delivered a speech describing the impact that the terrorism had had on me personally and how it affected my Olympic experience. It didn't affect my swimming, as I had completed all my events, but it did affect celebrations of the events. I think most Australians didn't know whether to mourn or to celebrate. The terrorism certainly put a wet blanket over the positive emotions. In my speech, I went as far as saying that the athletes were treated like anti-heroes, like the Vietnam veterans when they returned after that senseless war. Many of the 40 Australian Olympic representatives of 1972 gathered at Olympic Park agreed — for many of them this was their first public outing as an Olympian in 30 years.

However, in a private conversation I had later with Gough Whitlam he said he didn't agree with what I had said; he thought there was no comparison. We discussed it but his knowledge of history and politics of the time certainly surpassed my own. He did concede that as an exaggeration it was a provocative idea, but he suggested I don't write a thesis about it. I have taken his advice.

Another great experience was being involved with the 'What Makes a Champion!' conference a few days before the Opening Ceremony of the Sydney Games. It was hosted by the Centre for the Mind, a joint project with the Australian National University and Sydney University. The keynote speaker was Nelson Mandela, a champion of humanity. It was awesome to be in his presence. He had a powerful, regal countenance that radiated around the Great Hall of Sydney University. Champions from all walks of Australian life — politics, sport, arts, science, business — attended the conference. The proceedings were published in the book *What Makes a Champion!*, which I launched in 2002. I was a substitute at the book launch for Prime Minister John Howard, patron of the conference, who at short notice couldn't be there. I stood up at the launch and said, 'The PM asked to say "sorry"... [long pause]... that he couldn't be here to launch the book.' A polite silence was interrupted by some muffled laughs and shuffling of feet. (No, I don't want to go into politics but I do have opinions and am not afraid to express them!) So I do feel comfortable in public now, as I can be the 'whole' of me, not a shy little girl in an adults' world, but an integrated and mature woman with more to speak about than just my swimming performances.

~

The brilliantly choreographed torch relay and lighting of the cauldron at the Sydney 2000 Games was an intensely public experience, with over 100 000 people in the stadium and another three billion television viewers, yet at the same time very private, as one's thoughts and feelings must be. The relay was performed by seven great Australian women Olympians. Betty Cuthbert in her wheelchair, pushed by Raelene Boyle, handed the torch to Dawn Fraser, who passed it to Shirley de la Hunty (formerly Strickland), who passed it to me. From me the torch went to Debbie Flintoff-King, then to Cathy Freeman, who lit the cauldron in a truly suspenseful manner.

During my 15-second run with the torch a sense of deep joy came over me and I found I was doing spontaneous skips and cantering leaps. I was celebrating being Shane Gould, Olympic champion. I was once again a 'player', once again at the Olympics, and this time, compared with being 15 at Munich, a lot more in control and aware of what I was doing.

My relay leg finished at the opposite end of the stadium to the cauldron, so while Debbie Flintoff-King was running with the torch down the centre of the arena among the athletes, I jogged back down the running track of the arena, in the dark, past Australian athletes and officials who were calling out 'Good onya!'. That meant a lot to me. We torch-bearers then formed a guard of honour while the much-loved Cathy Freeman lit the spectacular spaceship cauldron that was intended to climb a ramp to its resting place at the top of the stadium.

I was really moved by the ingenuity of the spaceship-like device, water cascading over its curves as it rose eerily above Cathy. Standing with the other five great athletes I had the best view in the stadium; we were so close I could feel the spray of the water on my skin. Flickering shadows and reflections of the flame on the water added to the mystery and spectacle.

A temporary glitch occurred when the cauldron stalled at the bottom of the incline. The two-minute wait while engineers decided to manually override the computerised system to get the cauldron moving again was very disconcerting. We felt for Cathy who was waiting patiently, dripping wet in her lycra suit, getting colder by the second in the cool evening breeze. Cathy was eventually told to walk down the steps and was reassured she had done her job well. Dawn Fraser obtained a raincoat from a volunteer security guard and wrapped Cathy with motherly attention. Dawn quickly took control after that moment of crisis in an immense public event and looked after Cathy. I was impressed by her tenderness and leadership.

As we still waited tensely we discussed what to do if the cauldron didn't move and the gas for the flame ran out. There was a spare lantern and a torch at the foot of the steps which could be used to reignite the flame if needed. When the engineers finally restarted the cauldron on its ascent, we were very relieved. The rest of the effect was enthralling as the cauldron slid up the ramp, coming to rest in its position high above the stadium where it burned for the duration of the Games.

To my delight I had been involved in the secret of who and how the cauldron would be lit for about three months before the Games. I had received a phone call from John Coates, the Australian Olympic Committee President, to ask me if I would like to be one of seven athlete torch-bearers, one of whom would light the cauldron. 'Yes,' I replied, 'I would love to!'. We were sworn to secrecy and told we would be given more information when we attended a rehearsal close to the date. I shared the news only with my parents and a close friend.

To be sure I could carry the torch without tripping while jogging — not the physical activity I am most skilled at — I practised carrying a stick as a substitute torch while jogging on the bush tracks behind Gnarabup Beach. I may have looked silly doing it but the practice was helpful! Knowing the close-up cameras would be on me for five seconds of my allocated total 40 seconds with the torch in the arena, I couldn't resist using the occasion to 'say' something to the world. I decided to borrow a gesture from creative-thinking genius Edward de Bono: a 'Kings greeting' — a hand signal that indicates a flying dove of peace. Here is how to do it: Cross your arms at the wrist, with palms facing up, fingers extended. Next interlink the thumbs and wave the hands back and forward as though they are the wings of a dove. Keep flapping your wing-like hands and raise them up towards the sky.

I told Shirley de la Hunty, who was to pass the torch to me, that I may do some action before I took the torch from her. She kindly waited while I did the peace symbol before receiving the torch from her. I'm not sure that many people knew what I was doing. At least one person did — Edward de Bono was one of the spectators at the Opening Ceremony.

It was hard keeping my part in the event secret from my family. I could only tell my kids to watch the ceremony and that they might be surprised by what they saw. My daughter was out in the bush leading an outdoor adventure school camp so she didn't see the Opening Ceremony live. She was really pleased for me and said later, 'It looked like you were having a really good time, Mum.' Joel was on his first day at a new job at a golf club restaurant. When I came on TV with the torch he proudly and matter-of-factly said to his customers and fellow workers, 'Oh, that's my mum!'. Some didn't believe him! The two other boys watched the ceremony with their mates and were really happy for me. My sister Debbie was actually at the Opening Ceremony, having received a couple of free tickets from me which I didn't need because I was given a place in the Lord Mayor's box (to make it easier for organisers to find me!). Back in Margaret River after the Games, my friends welcomed me home with a terrific 'Onya!'. At the Toastmasters club, members were so keen to hear my first-hand account that they let me speak for 20 minutes — well beyond the usual allotted seven minutes!

~

My experience at the Sydney Games was unusual because of my four-way 'status': I was a media person, a VIP, a spectator, and a famous former Olympic swimmer. My media involvement was with Channel 7, the official Australian television broadcaster of the Games. I was one of the Network's seven 'Olympic Legends', helping with publicity in the lead-up to the Games and as a proposed swimming commentator during the Games. Working with my co-legends (Dawn Fraser, Murray Rose, Shirley de la Hunty, Ron Clarke, Marjorie Jackson and Herb Elliott), as well as swimmer Nicole Stevenson, was a thrill. They knew way more about Olympic sport and performances than I did, so I had history at my fingertips. We used to do pop quizzes about Olympic history. Reading cereal packs and newspaper accounts also increased my knowledge exponentially! I had a companion who acted as my guard, escort and secretary/scheduler to get me to my appointments on time.

As it happened, none of the swimming legends were used for special comments as had been planned. It seemed as if three years of 'training' had gone down the drain. I felt I had been used as an object to promote the Games, not for my skills and knowledge. Some of the other legends felt the same way, but having been to other Games before, they just sat back and enjoyed themselves knowing they didn't have to work. They all kept level heads: they viewed Olympic Games with respect but were not overawed, and had a life beyond these events. Getting to know the other six legends at the sponsors' tents or in corporate boxes was the most memorable thing about the work with Channel 7.

I also felt very disappointed when Tracey Holmes left the Channel 7 team. I had worked with Tracey on a series of biographical interviews for ABC Radio and had found her compassionate and understanding of my struggle, particularly in regard to my identity and retirement issues. Tracey was also a fellow surfer and understood the fringe culture of surfing.

Not having to commentate gave me time to write for *The Australian*, do other paid work with Ansett in the evenings and see more events. The sport was superb and the atmosphere terrific, such as when the roof was nearly cheered off at the swimming centre when an Australian was introduced at the start, or won a race — or when Cathy Freeman curled up on the track in a personal moment of triumph after her winning 400-metres run. I was in a media seat about 20 metres from the finish of Cathy's big race, so I could just about hear her breathing. She took that very public moment for herself before acknowledging the spectators.

Sometimes I chose to be part of the crowd, catching the train from the main stadium with 90,000 others. While the athletes were inspiring, what impressed me was how the Sydney Games really celebrated our Australian culture and good nature. There was gregariousness and showmanship without being crass. There was humour and colour. The Games were like a street theatre performance where *everyone* there was an actor. If you tend to agree with Peter Ueberroth (President and Chief Executive of the 1984 Los Angeles Games) that Olympics are a TV event and the spectators just extras to make the TV broadcast look better, I say you had to have been in Sydney to experience the show. It was such a dramatic and emotionally charged event. I also felt it at Munich — people in the global village coming together to peacefully play games and celebrate life. The television coverage could not convey the electric emotions, friendly people, and global village 'feel'.

Like every spectator, I did a lot of walking from venues to the train or bus that would transport us home. Even that was entertaining, with street performers, Olympic pin sellers and singing crowd controllers sitting on towers similar to a tennis umpire's perch or a beach lifeguard's lookout. Seeing a uniformed volunteer at every street corner in the city was like finding Grandma — someone wanting to help calm lost tempers and soothe sore feet.

I was fortunate also to have passes to the sponsors' areas at the venues, which provided cool, restful places with refreshing drinks and food. I was exhausted most nights after often starting the day with an appearance on morning TV, then travelling to Olympic Park to watch heats, then doing a stint as a guest in a sponsor's tent, meeting and greeting people, then attending swimming finals at night or a speaker's engagement somewhere else.

After the Closing Ceremony I waited with the patient crowds lining up to catch the train home. I felt a sense of disappointment with the flame having been extinguished but also a sense of awe at having been involved in a historic event. By the time I eventually arrived at Central station, transport across Sydney Harbour had virtually stopped because of the huge fireworks display that was taking place from the Harbour Bridge to mark the end of the Games. With the closing of the Games it was as if Sydney's 'smooth running switch' had been flicked off. The volunteers seemed to disappear, the crowds to get more unruly, and the well-organised transport system to shut down. It was after midnight when I walked through Darling Harbour with a friend who was staying at the same Milsons Point hotel as me; we were trying to find a bus or ferry going north. Darling Harbour was chaotic; it seemed as if every 18-year-old Sydneysider must have been there. We made our way through the throng only to discover there were no ferries running and resigned ourselves to walking over the bridge to our longed-for beds. Leaving the partying crowds behind we headed north, uncertain of how to reach the walkway over the bridge. My friend noticed a police launch moored nearby and we went to ask directions. The police were actually waiting for forensic staff to arrive following a stabbing there. Despite the gruesome situation, they were all pretty relaxed and we got into conversation. One of the men recognised me and told me his wife had gone to school with me. Then they kindly offered to take us across the Harbour on the launch — an offer we were very happy to accept, even if it did mean stepping over a pool of blood into the boat. It was the only blight I felt on an altogether amazing two weeks.

~

Olympic Games have become truly spectacular events, extending beyond sport to affect the arts, tourism and industry, bringing contact between citizens of nations across the globe in a spirit of hospitality and competition. One of the goals of the Olympic Movement is to build *'a peaceful and better world by educating youth through sport practised without discrimination of any kind and in the Olympic spirit which requires mutual understanding with a spirit of friendship solidarity and fair play'*. The Olympic Movement promotes this value outside the Games period and beyond *young* people. In 1995 the Movement created the World Olympians Association (WOA) to promote relations between Olympic athletes all over the world and spread the Olympic values.

As part of this overall mission, I travelled to Olympia in Greece in September 1998 — with 100 other international Olympic winners — for the first International Olympic Academy Conference of Olympic Winners. Prior to this I hadn't even been aware that there was an Olympic Academy. The buildings of the campus are set in beautiful tree-lined surrounds, and are located just down the road from the ancient Olympic stadium and archaeological museum. Congresses and educational programs are conducted there to educate people about Olympism. The students, who come from all over the world, are elected to be Olympic ambassadors to spread the word in their home country about the aims and ideals of Olympism.

I met some amazing, humble and dignified ex-Olympians during my visit, including: Ulrike Meyfarth, who won a gold medal in high jump in 1972, took a break from competition, had children, and came back in 1984 to win the high jump again; and Victor Saneev, who competed in four Olympic Games, winning gold three times and silver in his fourth Games. I felt like a rookie in comparison. Just small fry! Meeting petite Spanish marathon runner Rosa Mota was a treat and inspiration — she was so happy and she loved to run. Another great was Dick Fosbury, who changed the technique of high jumping with his Fosbury Flop, which won him a gold medal in 1968. He developed his jumping technique by trial and error; as the bar got higher in competition his body became flatter and he leaned more onto his back, so his leap over the bar looked like a flop. Dick Fosbury had a presence that commanded respect, not because of his height!

I also had a brief chat with Irish swimmer Michelle Smith, triple Olympic gold medal winner in 1996, who was in the process of appealing a four-year ban for tampering with a urine sample when I met her. She was generally shunned by the others — no one sat with her at meals or invited her to join the conversation. I believe the Irish Federation has since erased her name from all the Irish record books, but she has kept her medals as she did not test positive at the 1996 Games. She was pleasant to talk to and I was dying to ask her straight up: Did you use drugs to get your Atlanta medals? I was restrained by my companions and by my own good sense, knowing that one's own conscience is harsher than anyone else's judgement.

At the congress I had a taste of what I believe the Athens Olympics will be like. The congress was conducted with religious-like reverence for the ideology of the Olympic Movement and included a ceremony in the Grove of Coubertin, where the heart of the founder of the modern Olympics, Pierre de Coubertin, is enshrined in a marble column. I wasn't prepared for such solemnity, and was a little non-committal during the rituals of prayer, silence, and recitation of Olympic oaths. The Athens organisers want to revitalise the idea of the Olympiad — the period of four years culminating in the Olympic

Games sporting festival. They say that they want to be radically different and focus on cultural dimensions — on the Olympics of spirit and arts, not commercialisation. I look forward to being there to see if they achieve this aim and learning how they do it.

Each country that hosts the Olympic Games brings its own cultural essence to the celebrations and the Olympic organisation, which becomes part of Olympic heritage. I think Australia's contribution was our fresh, young (by comparison with Europe and Asia) society's enthusiasm and optimism for life, generated by our comparatively general safety from war and racial disputes, and through our mostly tolerant multicultural society. This optimism and enjoyment was displayed by the friendly helpful volunteers, and by Roy Slaven and H.G. Nelson's irreverent but favourite alternative mascot, Fatso the fat-arsed Wombat, who featured on the boys' hugely successful late-night television show during the Games. It was also displayed in the Opening Ceremony's parade of cultural icons, such as the corrugated iron shed, the Victa lawnmower, the Hills hoist and the Globite suitcase so many of us carried our books and lunches to school in. I think few viewers besides Australians really understood the significance of these symbols. It was like a private joke; taking the 'micky' out of the seriousness of the Olympics. On the other hand, there was a good deal of reverence and respect displayed by patient and polite Sydneysiders, bus drivers, train drivers and visitors in long queues, and by the deafening cheers for medal-winning or gallant performances regardless of an athlete's nationality. In short, the Sydney Games were darn good fun. Truly Games being played.

CHAPTER 17

Learning to Swim Again

I learn much from people in the way they meet the unknown in life and water is a great test. I am sure no adventurer nor discoverer ever lived who could not swim. Swimming cultivates imagination; the man with the most is he who can swim his solitary course night or day and forget a black earth full of people that push. This love of the unknown is the greatest of all the joys which swimming has for me. I am still looking for my chest of gold in a cool dripping sea cave — or a mermaid combing her long green hair.

~

Annette Kellerman, as quoted by Charles Sprawson in *Haunts of the Black Masseur: The Swimmer as Hero*

THE FREESTYLE SWIMMING STROKE THAT WON me those gold medals at Munich has been described as one of the best ever. But I am now in the process of dismantling it completely and starting all over again. Why? Because I have discovered a whole new approach to swimming — a way that is more natural, less prone to injury and much more 'in tune' with the water.

Recreational swimming has been around for centuries, but it is only in recent times that significant changes have been made in the way we swim. According to Charles Sprawson's *Haunts of the Black Masseur* (a great book about literature's depiction of the swimmer as hero) the Romans defined an ignorant man as 'someone who could neither read nor swim'! How effectively the Romans swam isn't recorded but that they valued the skills and enjoyed the water and moving through it says enough. The Greeks, the Romans, even Roman-occupied England and the Nordic countries enjoyed their many man-made baths and natural pools, and frolicking in lakes and fjords, usually naked, was very popular.

With the rise of Christianity (and its notions of the body's sinfulness) the status of the swimmer as hero declined in the Western world. After that time Nordic and Greek fables spoke about swimmers needing supernatural intervention or miracles to save themselves. The fate of the ungodly was compared with that of a swimmer adrift in the vastness of the sea, denied the means of reaching safety, and finally being overcome by despair. The writers probably just needed a few swimming lessons to understand the mysteries of buoyancy, flow and drag. With heavy wool clothing covering their nakedness, they didn't stand a chance of knowing those watery delights!

Swimming became popular again in the more liberal early 19th century among the upper middle classes. The English became infatuated with swimming and built many swimming 'baths', some of which are still in use today. The poet Byron might be considered one of the forefathers of modern swimming. He is remembered in a plinth on the shore of the Aegean Sea dedicated to: 'Lord Byron, noted swimmer and poet', who swam the swirling 1-kilometre strait of Hellespont in 1810, making him a 'celebrated aquatic genius'.

From Roman times to Byron's Hellespont crossing, the only stroke used was probably a primitive breaststroke, with the arms recovering below the water. One exception to this is depicted in an Assyrian relief I saw at the International Swimming Hall of Fame in Florida, USA. It shows a soldier with an arrow stuck in his shoulder swimming away from his enemies using a type of overarm stroke. This is apparently the earliest recorded depiction of swimming. However, it wasn't until the early 20th century here in Australia that 'overarm' or 'Australian crawl' was 'invented' and swimming races really became popular.

Backstroke, too, soon began to develop as a competitive stroke and in the 1950s butterfly evolved from breaststroke. Early butterfliers used a breaststroke kick rather than today's two-beat flutter kick. In fact, many of the older masters swimmers still use this rather ungainly combination of the two strokes.

Forbes Carlile, my old swimming coach, said in a fascinating lecture about the history of freestyle that there have been no major changes in technique since 1976. Interestingly, Edward de Bono provoked me with a question in 2000: 'Have there been any new ways of swimming developed recently?' I played around with different ways of moving through the water, but came up with nothing that was going to be any faster than the current four competitive strokes. What the question did, however, was prepare my mind to be opened and to welcome new ideas. I didn't know it at the time, but circumstances were going to force me to explore this much further. Meanwhile, I was preparing for the Sydney Games.

In expectation of making special comments for host television broadcaster Channel 7 during the Sydney 2000 Games (and with some sense of urgency) I had accelerated my learning about swimming by training in the pool four to six times a week. Often this was with age-group swim teams around Australia, but mostly I trained with the masters swim club: the Margaret River Breakers. At the club we coached ourselves, doing regular time trials in all strokes and encouraging one another. One of the members, Margrit Vlahos, persuaded me with persistent goading to attend the World Masters Swimming Championships in Munich in July 2000. I hadn't been back to Munich since 1972 and it seemed a good opportunity to make a pilgrimage and confront any demons that might have been subconsciously lurking within me.

I didn't find any demons, just childhood memories. The stadium and the village looked much smaller and closer together than I remembered. Diving into the Olympic pool and seeing the patterns and shapes of the tiles on the bottom gave me a sense of déjà vu and momentarily confused me. Even with pool renovations the tile patterns were the same as I remembered. It was as though I was in a time warp. A quick look around at some of the 6000 masters — swimmers of all ages and shapes — brought me back to the present. My Munich experience of 1972 receded into a dreamy memory.

Like all masters sports, masters swimming is popular around the world, and many competitors go to events as a part of their annual holiday. Some are very serious athletes competing for titles and records. It's great to see all needs and reasons for competing being catered for, and fit, agile oldies proving that youth does not have a monopoly on health and vitality!

I swam for times and did a creditable 1.01.6 for the 100 metres freestyle. I swam 59.04 at the Munich Olympics and my best was the world record time of 58.5. Not bad on five 3-kilometre training sessions a week, compared with the ten 7-kilometre ones I did in the 1970s.

After the Sydney 2000 Games, opportunities for sponsorships, endorsements and public speaking quietened down. Three years of constant Olympic advertisements and stories meant the public had heard enough from athletes and wanted to have a go at sport themselves. I understand that sporting club memberships and sporting goods sales increased after the Games.

For me it felt good to stay put in Margaret River for extended periods. I swam with the masters group, rode my mare, Lalinka, bought a young horse, a Waler called Oscar, and started training him. I spent time with my boys Kristin and Tom as they finished high school — the end of an era, with no more school lunches, reports and parent–teacher meetings. I wrote the occasional article for *The Australian* newspaper, but I realised pretty quickly that I'd have to create my own new income source.

I framed a Shane Gould Enterprises 'company policy' to do only activities and jobs that promoted 'Fitness for Life': physical, emotional, social and environmental health.

This was an excellent filter for appearance requests and job offers.

Using 'design thinking', which I was learning from Edward de Bono, I set about developing an online business based around the subject I knew best — swimming. I was already fairly confident using the Internet and email, and I regularly updated my own shanegould.com.au website. I knew I wasn't an expert but I had more knowledge than the average bear swimmer and was open to learning. I saw a lot of people swimming in pools and in the ocean around Australia who, I thought, could benefit from some simple swimming tips! And, from my observations while surfing the net, the swimming improvement market seemed to be largely unserviced.

My market research was more intuitive and subjective than quantitative, and with no business plan I went ahead and developed a website. The website operated with a program which collected a database of clients and a merchant account which took online orders. I then gave set lessons online to students from countries as disparate as India, Canada, Germany and Australia!

It was a great summer going into 2001. I went for early morning swims with friends and prepared for the Rottnest Channel swim. Organised ocean swimming — the ocean counterpart to fun runs — are increasingly popular events. Older swimmers (over 30) are realising that with a few swims a week, some gumption and positive peer pressure from friends, it is a realistic and achievable goal to finish such races as the 1.2-kilometre Pier to Pub Swim in Lorne (which attracted 3900 entrants in 2000), or the 4-kilometre Palm Beach to Whale Beach event traditionally swum on Australia Day, or even the longer 20-kilometre Rottnest Channel swim. I met four former swimming team-mates in that race in 2001 — some just venturing into open water for the first time as a part of a fitness program after coming out of nappy valley!

Open-water swimmers are also, to my mind, the new environmentalists. When we swim in rivers, lakes and oceans we want them to be safe and beautiful to be in, and to have their foreshores and beaches healthy as well. Four thousand or so witnesses of trashed sea bottoms, eroded beaches and riverbanks (some of whom may also suffer post-swim bouts of diarrhoea) make a formiddable lobby group! Recycling, reducing greenhouse gas emissions and using renewable energy are now a part of government policy and an accepted way of life (as well as influencing arhcitectural style in this country!); it is imperative that we are able to continue to sustainably utilise the valuable natural resources that we have long fought to protect. Being in the water is a form of environmental protection.

I swam the crossing from Cottesloe to Rottnest Island in a duo with Carol McCarthy, the woman who had encouraged me to swim laps again and participate in masters races. Our strategy was to swim for five minutes, then rest out of the water in the support boat for five minutes — basically doing 350 metres every 10 minutes over five to six hours. The 2001 event was pretty choppy, with a strong southwest wind creating white caps and wind waves. About halfway I got very tired and started trying to claw my way over the waves instead of gliding though them. My shoulders became sore, but I pushed through the pain to keep swimming my segments and reached the island in good time.

'To complete is to win' is the motto of horse endurance riding and it's the same for open-water races. Just to swim to Rottnest Island is an achievement in itself. Tired and sore, swimmers recovered with sleep under paperbark trees, or with cold beer and free massages from student therapists. The recounting of stories of close shaves with ships, stinger jellyfish, and of competitive races between teams of four along the way became louder and more embellished as the evening wore on!

Back in Margaret River my shoulder pain got worse. I figured a week's break from swimming would enable rest and healing but when I got back into the water to swim, I could do no more than four strokes without severe pain. This was a real concern, as I had never had shoulder problems or any other injury from swimming. I wrote to Forbes Carlile, my old swimming coach, and also to John Leonard at the American Swimming Coaches Association (whom I'd met during the 1998 World Swimming Championships), to ask why my shoulders were injured. The reply from both was: *poor technique*!

I was stunned at first, I didn't think that I was incompetent. I was so proud of my good technique and pleased by comments made by observers of how graceful I looked in the water. It was a big blow to my ego!

As the pain persisted I began to have grave concerns that I would never be able to swim again. Figuring that soft tissue healing would happen over time I resigned myself to about four months out of the water. This period proved incredibly productive and enlightening. I made changes to my diet and my exercise regime, doing more aerobic exercise and taking in fewer carbohydrates, and engaged an online health coach to supervise this transition. I surfed the Internet, spoke with swimmers, coaches, physiologists and doctors, and became aware of a near epidemic of shoulder injuries and strains among age-group, elite, masters and fitness swimmers.

There must be another way, I thought, to swim without risk of injury. Swimming is a non-contact individual sport; water is soft; so where does the impact come from to cause injury?

About April 2001 I made contact with Terry Laughlin, a US swimming coach and prominent contributor to swimming websites. He had formed the swimming improvement company Total Immersion Swimming to fill a gap in the swimming fitness and wellness market. Terry used information he learned from a US swim coach called Bill Boomer in the late 1980s as a base to develop his ideas. This virtual meeting with Terry was to catapult me to my next tumble turn and set me on my current course.

Terry sent me his book *Swimming Made Easy*, which explained how to rebuild my stroke, from the first step of relaxing in the water to lengthening the bodyline, rotating the body and using the chest to press into the water to gain stability. I still couldn't swim without severe pain so I cajoled some of the very good-natured Margaret River Breakers club members to let me teach them the series of drills outlined in the book so I could learn them and better understand what Terry was trying to convey. I was surprised at the effectiveness of the drills and how dramatically, quickly and easily they could be taught and learned. The systematic building of a stroke through its parts or component actions was very similar in methodology to the Parelli natural horsemanship I had learned and taught.

My imagination went into overdrive, envisaging how I could use this not only for my own benefit but also to the benefit of all swimmers wanting to improve. I sat at my computer with fingers poised at various times over a month-long period preparing to write to Terry to ask his permission to officially teach his methods. I had a serious intuition that asking this would change my life again. I wanted to be sure that I was prepared for it.

I ran through my commitments and responsibilities. My four children, now grown up, were engaged in their own studies and careers. All were financial, though not quite independent of my bank account. My contracts with Zoggs, Narellan Pools and Vitasoy didn't require a lot of time, and there had still been very little promotional work since the Olympics. Importantly, my online coaching site wasn't going to be successful with the content I had on it; I had found a product superior to my own basic swimming program. My delivery concept was great but the content was not the best available. This inventory of responsibilities revealed that I was free to follow my curiosity and take a career dive into the swimming industry.

What I have learned from this journey in the past two years, from May 2001 to April 2003, has totally transformed my outlook on life. I have been learning to swim all over again, challenging my premises, technique, water feel, teaching and training methodologies.

Many of my life's metaphors and benchmarks have been to do with my experience of swimming. I swam during my formative years, when my brain was developing the patterns and awareness of movement that were successful or unsuccessful. The pace clock in the pool at training commanded a lot of attention. And I was rewarded for my application. Fighting the pressure and drag of water produced speed and exhilaration. I swam fast, it felt good, and I won attention from parents, coaches, swimming mates, and ultimately the media and public.

I incorporated these habits into all areas of my life. Repetitive practice regimes (I go at things like a hungry dog with a bone), work and strain (four children, pioneer farming), using effort for extended periods of time and having stubborn, uncompromising determination became my foundation principles for living.

It was this whole way of existing I had to reject to embrace the new swimming style.

Inspired by what I had so far leaned from Total Immersion, in May 2002 I met the pioneers of this methodology, Bill Boomer and Milton Nelms, at the Australian Swimming Coaches and Teachers Association Conference on the Gold Coast, where they were keynote speakers. At the conference I got in the hotel pool and asked Bill and Milt if they could show me the practical application of what they were saying in their lectures. I was gobsmacked by the delightful sensations and dramatic freedom of movement I felt with just a small postural shift in my neck and back and the changed arm recovery that they suggested. That was just the beginning!

Professor Bill Boomer, now retired, was a college swim coach in the USA for most of his working life and had developed some very intriguing ideas about swimming technique which he shared on lecture tours and at clinics with interested coaches. Sometimes these clinics were sponsored by US Swimming. He had a unique position as technical consultant to the 2000 US Women's Olympic Swim Team.

Milton Nelms began working with Bill Boomer about eight years ago to help develop Bill's ideas and allow Bill to retire to his Pennsylvanian farm. Milt's swimming coaching experience is in age-group through to elite level swimming, as well as learn-to-swim for both children and adults. He is now a consultant to elite-level US swimming coaches and athletes, and to swimmers, coaches, and swimming federations around the world. He also consults with adult wellness (swimming for fitness, injury recovery, and recreation) age-group, masters and competition swimmers, and is collaborating on a children's learn-to-swim curriculum with Edie Flood at Wings Over Water swim school in Brewster, New York.

With Milt's help I have been learning to swim again. He suggested that I start by looking at the physics and psychological issues involved with simply being in the water before taking on the issues of moving through the water. So I began to re-examine my basic relationship with the water, both physically and emotionally. What I mean by 'relationship' is how my spine, muscles and breathing respond to the forces of the water with emotional survival instincts. For example, two responses we have to lying in the water are to press down on it with our hands as we try to keep our balance, and to lift our heads out of the head-spine line as we look for air — and for the horizon in search of balance. But, as I learned from Milt, these responses inhibit effective swimming. They are counterproductive.

Energy is wasted through unneeded muscle contractions. Drags are created through misalignment of the body. Propulsive pressures of the arms and legs are diverted into achieving stability. Most importantly, the sense of rhythm and flow that makes being in the water so pleasurable is compromised when our survival instincts kick in.

What is interesting to me is how Milt has been able to interpret my personality and character from the way I relate to the water when I swim. I asked him to describe how I used to swim and how I could swim.

> *Shane's stroke has been a somewhat confrontational relationship with the water, which is fairly typical. Her remarkable success has been a reflection of her will and physical genius. This physical genius should allow her to access the energy and forces available in the water if she simply 'lets' it happen. Her will and competitiveness, the desire to make things happen, actually compromise her relationship with the water by interfering with her natural talent. In a sense, she is getting in her own way. The art of being an elite athlete is to learn how to get out of your own way, in other words: reduce error. This is especially true in the water where the fluid amplifies error.*
>
> *Humans in the water tend to react to effort or exertion by shortening their body line. Shane is no different but her will amplifies this tendency — when she really wants to 'go' or she becomes fatigued, she gets shorter and fractured, somewhat linear and mechanical in her movements. In ranching country in the USA, where I come from, we call this 'hunkering down'.*
>
> *The water reacts adversely to this instinctive emotional response, creating more drag resistance. This makes swimming harder and slower, taking away the efficiency of rhythmic movement.*
>
> *Animal 'athletes', like hunting cats and horses, create body energy by lengthening or 'letting go' when they want to accelerate.*

This allows them to shift rhythm patterns quickly. Shane is
quickly learning to use her talent and intelligence to take cues
from the aquatic environment and from her own increasing body
awareness. She is using this developing awareness to 'let go' and
use rather than attack the water. Just as a plane can fly and a
fish can swim, we humans can use the water's own qualities to
move through it. Shane can use the water's 'potential energy' to
help her swim. It is simple physics.

It has been remarkable just how much the changes in my relationship
with the water have affected my swimming stroke. Part of my learning
has involved developing an internal sense of balance and overcoming
years of poor posture and movement which were the result of the type
of training I did as a teenager. Most swimmers end up with swimmers'
posture — rounded shoulders, collapsed upper chest, head and neck
sitting forward of the torso, tight hip flexors and poor core-muscle
tone, despite firm big-muscle-group tone. This is all made worse by
20th-century lifestyle slouching. To help regain my posture I went to
the Centre of Balance Studio in Mountain View near Stanford
University (a return, of sorts, as I had gone to Mountain View High
School in 1973!). Milt Nelms was doing consulting coaching there and
Tom McCook, also a consultant with the US Women's Olympic Swim
Team at the Sydney Games, was principal 'body art' therapist. I learned
a lot about correct body postures and movements to enhance my
swimming. Now I practise 'freestyle' — my new swimming postures
— when I ride my horse, drive the car or work at the computer!

Bill Boomer and Milt Nelms are at the cutting edge of the evolution
of swimming, and I'm privileged to now have unlimited access to
these innovative coaches. Bill and Milt used a whole new swimming
language which, to start with, was foreign to me. But after months of
intensive learning with them in Australia, New Zealand and the USA,
both in and out of the water, it has become part of my vocabulary.

To me my new style feels easier and more graceful, and the less I do the more energetic my movements are. 'Letting go' of muscle strain and tension is a mantra I repeat. It feels light and lively, harmonic and very powerful. It takes a lot of concentration to make the changes, as my childhood muscle memory and 20th-century lifestyle postures are deeply embedded. But my research and persistent study are being rewarded. In spite of residual trauma in my shoulders, my present understanding of alignment and movement allows me to swim pain- and injury-free. In addition, attending to diet, metabolism and hormone and nutrient levels has greatly boosted my energy and eliminated a nagging unexplained lethargy.

In undertaking my retraining, I feel I have realigned my swimming with my soul, basically working with Mother Nature's laws of physics rather than against them. Whereas before I had a confrontational relationship with the water, I now try to move *with* the water.

My new movement patterns in the pool will be tested at masters competitions during the coming year. Already I have had the opportunity to swim 'with the water' in the World Masters Games in Melbourne in October 2002. Preparing for this event not only tested my new techniques but also my new training. When I became frustrated by the lack of familiar work focusing on time and effort which I was used to, Milt suggested I try 'Rain Man' sets. He was referring to the Dustin Hoffman character in the Barry Levinson film *Rain Man* ('Uh oh, I should be training, oh no, it's not good, uh oh, not training, not training, uh oh') and meant I should put my focus on neural rewiring and managing my relationship with the water. I followed his advice and did only 2-kilometre swims per session, and highly demanding physical management about six times per week. I walked for half an hour three times a week and experimented with Pilates and the Alexander technique to hasten, through awareness, the inhibiting of my instinctive responses and improve my water movement patterns. This type of 'not-training' worked! I won three events in good time: 1.02.8 for the 100 metres freestyle; 30.88 for the 50 metres butterfly; and 2.19 for the 200 metres freestyle.

I also put myself to the test in ocean conditions during the 2003 Rottnest Channel swim. The actual swim and the conditions weren't very enjoyable. The seas were very rough, with 20-knot winds, a 1.8-metre swell, cross wind chop, and sea sickness, to add spice and texture to the challenge! Only about 30 per cent of entries made the 20-kilometre crossing, in the worst conditions in the 13-year history of the event. It was a real mental challenge to endure the unpleasantness of the rough open ocean between the mainland and the island, but ultimately another soul-filling experience.

Our team of four, the Winettes of Margaret River, had prepared for three months with morning swims in the pool and ocean swims on Sunday (and coffee at the Gnarabup café afterwards). Enduring cold sea-weedy water some days, stinging jelly fish on others, or blissing out on still, crystal-clear turquoise water and swimming like fish in an aquarium, was all part of the channel experience. Despite the dreadful conditions I found the race easier than in previous years and finished with no sore muscles. What was even more remarkable was that I didn't have the tiredness that usually dogged me for days after a race of this kind.

~

To speak just about the results of a swimming race is to take the soul out of the sport. Might as well not do it! With a few more years of reflection since I wrote my book, I see even more clearly the reasons why I quit swimming when I was 16. With so much emphasis on results and records there was no soul to the activity I was doing. I was too young and impressionable to have my own opinions. In a way my opinion was in the action of leaving it to others to do.

So how can soul-swimming be nurtured within the current culture and structures of swimming?

Firstly, the way swimming is taught and coached needs to change. Swimming with soul involves a relationship with water. It's so important that swimming teachers, coaches and swimmers *know* the water. That is, they need to know some essential physics or the nature of the human–water relationship to be able to teach or do holistic swimming. Again, this is a concept similar to the one I learned in Parelli natural horsemanship. The horse is an animal of prey; the human a predator. In order to relate to the horse and use it we need to recognise where it places us in its world and what its responses to our actions instinctively are. Similarly, we need to understand what effect we have on water and what it will do to us when we enter it. This is universal for swimmers and non-swimmers of all ages, abilities and ambitions.

Secondly, we need to understand swimming as a process so it can feed into other areas of our lives. I know we like results and I am still competitive — we were the fastest women's team in the Rottnest Channel race, and I don't hesitate, where appropriate, to speak of my five Olympic medals — but it's what I gained from the process of doing the race, not what I gained from the race result that is more important. The process of a race encompasses the friendships formed, the rhythmic routines, the skill challenges, the personal discipline, the body awareness, the self-care over months of dieting, sleeping and fitness, the self-confidence gained, the wellbeing established and taken into life. I think this is the biggest lesson I have had reinforced by my involvement in masters and fitness swimming. For me today, swimming is an art, like dance or golf. Very technical and beautiful when executed well.

I do some unusual things in the water now to train my brain into an awareness of aquatic physics, such as buoyancy in water. I also take great delight in sharing my pleasure of the water — by teaching or by swimming in wild places with others. In the outdoor pool at Coffs Harbour last January, I was curled up in a ball in the shallow end, with my knees hugged into my chest, bobbing around and breathing through a front-mounted snorkel. A little girl about 11 and her younger brother and cousin were playing nearby. The girl tapped me on the shoulder and asked bluntly, 'What are you doing?'

I explained, with a little irritation at being interrupted from my experiments and meditation, that I was feeling the water support me, and then what it felt like when I shifted my weight forward and back while I was in a ball. Seeing her interest I suggested she try it too. In three goes she had mastered the rudiments of the skill and knew for sure that the water was holding her up without her having to do anything with her arms or legs. We bounced her 'body-ball' so she could further feel buoyancy, then sank our 'body-balls' to experience the opposite of floating — sinking — and understood that it required a gusty exhalation of air to get to the bottom.

We played for about an hour at all sorts of explorations and water skills. My new friend had a private swimming lesson and I had the incredible experience of spending time with a curious, receptive little girl. It was a simple and treasured time for me, a real highlight of my life, because she captured the essence of soul swimming. She experienced the joy of the environment and developed a harmonious relationship with the water.

Given the right conditions, kids can learn to love the water and know it's a great place to be — to respect it and use it, and not to be frightened by it. So many kids just don't 'get the water', more often than not because of fear and ignorance, poor instruction or transference of parental anxiety. I spent some time recently with Edie Flood at her swim school in New York, contributing to the development of her curriculum with Milt Nelms. Children at her swim school are learning non-traditional ways of moving in the water that address, among other things, our survival instincts as land-based creatures in an aquatic environment. To see kids moving through the water, comfortable, quiet, and calm, without using one of the four competition strokes, is beautiful and a challenge to the imagination.

~

It is intriguing to me how popular swimming is. Nearly anywhere that it is possible to safely swim on a swimmable day will see at least a couple of people rhythmically stroking from A to B. For many it is a meditation, a daily ritual. There is something about swimming — perhaps to do with its sensuous nature and weightless environment, or that it is a bit wild — that attracts people to it. Public and private pools have tamed it somewhat but there are still swimmers who use the ocean, rivers and lakes to feed their wildish natures and get some exercise in the process. I think this partly explains the popularity of open-water events. There are more people who swim for the enjoyment of doing it than those who do it for speed in competition. This is swimming for wellness and it constantly surprises me just how many people do it.

Swimming has been very good to me. I made a contribution to the culture and history of swimming when I was young and I hope to make another contribution to the evolution of swimming methods in my more mature years. I have already filmed a fundamental 'swimming for fun and fitness' video with Zoggs that introduces some of the basic concepts I have learned. More instructional videos are being planned.

My new challenge is to continue to experiment, learn and teach via all sorts of media (electronic, face-to-face lessons and clinics, and through print), to provide pathways to this new way of swimming which has captured me, body and soul.

CHAPTER 18

New Life and New Love

Life is a process. No one can own the process, there's no end to it, there's always something more to discover.

~

Bill Boomer

I'M A PASSENGER IN A YANK TANK — a suburban station wagon filled with a friend's possessions, driving from San Francisco to Portland in Oregon. We are driving through a heavily wooded valley with hills covered in Douglas fir, cedar and the occasional redwood. It's northern California and I'm taking time to learn, observe and explore. I'm on an adventure; it's organic, going in the directions that nature leads: when the sun sets or hunger and tiredness compel us we stop and get a hotel room.

Driving further north we come to stands of old majestic redwoods, making the road so dark with their canopy that we have to turn on the car headlights. Being in a forest is familiar, as I lived in the jarrah, marri and karri forests in the southwest of Western Australia. But these forests have different smells, colours, shapes and textures. Driving on the right-hand side of the road rather than the left gives me another perspective too. This is all symbolic of things being familiar but different.

I am in the process of reformation — tumble turning yet again. I am a citizen of the world travelling most weeks, home in Margaret River less than 40 per cent of the year. Each time I return from an overseas trip home never looks the same; that's the thing about travelling. It changes your perspective on life. I enjoy travelling very much. I think I might have been an explorer if I lived in the 1800s. Australian outback-pioneer women are some of my greatest heroes. I'm also drawn to innovative, original thinkers — cultural explorers.

Throughout my life I have sought out cultural explorers — people who could give me answers I needed at particular points. I met Neil Innes who helped me to answer the questions: 'Is there life after sport?', 'Is there more to life than winning gold medals?'. We lived a dynamic, adventurous life together, seeking and finding answers. In the early 1990s I sought out pastor Brian Arthur to answer questions about suffering and grace. Through this experience and other insights I gained the confidence to be free to chose my own destiny, to leave my marriage and stop feeling sorry for myself for winning five Olympic medals. In 1997 I went to a Tony Robbins seminar in the USA seeking answers about my destiny, my value and about the guilt I felt after leaving Neil and disrupting the family unit. I also spent time with Robert Kiyosaki, author of *Rich Dad Poor Dad*, learning to understand money — its value, as well as how to use it, make it and keep it. I chose voluntary poverty early in my life with Neil but ultimately found it did not serve my goals and needs. Another cultural explorer, Edward de Bono, also opened doors to me, teaching me to think my way through situations without judging or condemning. He helped me to see thinking as play and creativity. Bill Boomer, master swimming coach, has enlightened me about my current passion — swimming improvement for personal transformation.

There has been another powerful force more recently. I've met a man who has given my personal life a warm workout, and a new challenge has been set: can I love again? After my divorce it was hard to feel worthy of being loved and to trust enough to open myself to love again. I was practically a child bride when I first married at 18 years of age. Time is a great healer and maturer. My new friendship at this stage shows all the signs that it will be a long-term relationship. We have a strong mutual attraction that has surprised and delighted us both. Our keen curiosity about process, whether in sport, culture, literature, or horsemanship, is great for conversation and sharing books. He also has a great sense of humour.

Milton Nelms' profession involves a busy international schedule, so we have spent much of the past twelve months apart. We both know the best phone cards to use! We had Christmas 2002 together in Pennsylvania where it snowed 13 inches on Christmas Day. I was like a kid playing in the snow, skiing and skating. We are like teenage sweethearts without the teenage drama. While there is the excitement of romance, now at an older age it is the qualities of companionship and respect that are most important. We were able to enjoy simple pleasures such as watching cable TV movies, eating homemade popcorn, and discussing story line and character development, while outside, snowflakes drifted onto the iced-over pond we had been hitting golf balls and skating on the day before. Snowshoeing on Christmas Day, in the silent snowy landscape of the evergreen woods, noticing the blue shadows in the clumsy icy footprints we made next to delicate deer prints, was another special moment that enriched and unified our friendship.

Like Milt I have been travelling all over the world giving swimming workshops and lessons, exchanging information, learning about how the brain operates and how the body moves. Most of this work has been directed at people interested in their own wellbeing. I am also working on improving my own swimming to satisfy my enquiring mind and so I can become a better teacher. By understanding swimming's complexities I am becoming better at being able to simplify it.

I have had some success here. In Bangkok in September 2002, with the help of an interpreter, I taught entry-level age-group coaches, who were very receptive to the new techniques. They made some great changes in their own swimming which they were excited to share with their students. In Portugal, again through an interpreter, I taught a school swim team, and was shown wonderful abundant hospitality. I have also taught in the UK, the USA, New Zealand and all over Australia. My sister Jenny Gould and my daughter, Kim, have become swimming instructors also — accompanying me and also teaching overseas. It was brilliant to share those experiences with them. But the most satisfying thing to me in all of this is to make swimming enjoyable, understandable and do-able by anyone of any age and ability.

I have also updated my website (www.shanegould.com.au) to reflect my new knowledge. It is now a swimming resource for learn-to-swim and swimming improvement, incorporating all the new concepts I have learned. My aim is to eventually provide an online learning program backed up by camps and workshops.

Milt has been keen about this work as well as his own research for a number of years. His teaching and diligent study of unusual areas such as dance in relation to posture and breathing, and his remarkable perception of physical activity combined with his artistic eye means that he has come up with some great insights. Physics, engineering and harmonic movement are other sources from which Milt learns and develops his knowledge and skill as a swimming stroke technician.

For both of us our curiosity is rewarded handsomely by seeing people swimming with grace and ease, because they are working with the physics of Mother Nature. We enjoy working with coaches too, sharing their excitement about the innovative approach we teach, which explains some of the mysteries of swimming. Every time we work with a swimmer or a coach we learn something. It's exciting to be part of the evolution of swimming.

But the brain work can be tiring. I unwind by spending time in the garden, swimming in the ocean, reading with a cuppa, surfing, and through my horsemanship. Milt unwinds by hiking, playing golf, going to the movies or reading the newspaper with a latte in hand. He has just discovered horses, which is very pleasing to me!

While swimming is what brought us together — and is often the occasion for us being together — it is our interest in observing and learning about life processes that aligns us. Whether it is family nurturing, farm management, creating wooden signs, horsemanship, coaching young people, or being at the cutting edge of the evolution of swimming — as Bill Boomer says of swimming: 'It is all process. No one can own the process, there's no end to it, there's always something more to discover. Go through the process and learn from it, extend it.' Even though I am 46 I can still learn both with my brain and with my body. This is challenging and stimulating and gives me a bounce in my step!

~

There are some things from my old life that I miss — the farm and the life lived around the seasonal changes. I also miss the horses in my backyard: their herd games and their frolicking 'yippee' gallops around the paddocks. The bird sounds of the forest, including the farmyard guinea fowl squawks, are noticeably absent where I live on the coast. I also miss my wood stove for cooking. Despite its messy soot, sawdust and smoke, it added a great atmosphere to our farmhouse. (It was also a great bum warmer.) I still have two horses, which are agisted on a farm I often visit, so I still get dusty, muddy, sweaty and horse-smelly. I relish that earthiness after dressing up for a public function. I definitely *don't* miss the financial struggle or living with rundown equipment and the rustic timber house that was hard to keep clean and neat. I am financially comfortable now, living in a low-maintenance house which is a welcome relief from a never-ending domestic treadmill. It frees me up to develop my talents and skills and be creative in using them.

My relationship with my children is close and dynamic. They are now young adults who can competently live independently. Isn't that one of the functions of parenthood? This in itself is a huge change in identity for me! It is another life transition with issues similar to retirement from sports or work.

I am really proud of my children and their choices in life. Like all children going through separation and divorce they were loyal to both parents, and rightly so. At times they felt compassion for Neil and his public exposure — and his anger with me for exposing the incident of domestic violence. It seems trite to say time heals, but it has. Love consistently expressed by both Neil and me towards our children has seen them through this trauma. Fortunately they all had good friends their own age as well as adult friends they could speak to and confide in. There is a saying, 'It takes a village to raise a child'. I'm fortunate that we lived in the 'village' of Margaret River.

Two of my sons live with me in Margaret River (when I'm there), another lives close by, and my daughter has made her life in Sydney. Like their parents, my children are learning in the university of life, studying courses while on the job. Joel (now 24) has chosen study and work as a computer technician (I now have a live-in computer expert). He also works as a farmhand to supplement his income. He continues to successfully hunt and gather crayfish and other seafood while freediving, and when he is not playing underwater hockey at the pool, he surfs. Twenty-three-year-old Kim has found a niche in white-water rafting and kayaking. She works, trains and plays at the white-water course in Penrith, Sydney. She also leads swimming improvement workshops with me and regularly organises and leads outdoor adventure camps. She is an excellent teacher and has great understanding of and skill in guiding learners.

Tom, at 20, is on course to becoming a professional surfer. He works at whatever seasonal work he can get in between surf competitions, has a contract with the Salomon Company which uses him as a surfboard tester for its innovative blue hollow 'S-core' surfboards. He is excellent at documenting and giving technical feedback to the surfboard engineers. Tom's best competition result in 2002 was winning the open division of the Margaret River Masters in November. He is also becoming very good at speaking to the media after his wins and about Salomon surf boards.

'Bobcat' — or Kristin — is now 19 and in his second year as an apprentice carpenter. He has a great group of friends who he surfs and plays golf with. He's also a popular cook in the household he lives in. I miss his stir fries and flavoursome casseroles.

When I travel, I keep in touch with my family by phone and email. Neil lives in the district, so is available to them and for the sporadic emergency when I'm not in town. Our children are great young people to be with — to share experiences with: eating, watching movies, videoing, surfing, or just hanging out.

~

One of the reasons for expanding *Tumble Turns* is to affirm my life as an integrated person, celebrating the incorporation of Shane Gould, wife, mother and citizen with the powerful identity/persona of Shane Gould Olympic Champion, and now teacher and lifelong learner. When I began *Tumble Turns* in 1999, I recounted the experiences and challenges that had formed and influenced me, and had brought me to that point. Yet somehow they seemed disconnected. I felt that I was pushing off into another pool — that each change was a point of departure. My recent travelling experiences and the insights gained from writing have led me to believe that I am, and always have been, in the same pool, but just didn't know it. Life is a process. Such is the wisdom of reflection and hindsight.

my
favourite recipes

Anzac Biscuits

If you came to my place for a cuppa at the kitchen table, we'd be snacking on Anzac biscuits, or snacks from some of these recipes. We'd be yarning about the life issues I've raised in this book, common to all of us.

1 cup plain flour
1 cup rolled oats
1 cup sugar
1 cup coconut
250 g margarine
2 tablespoons golden syrup
1 teaspoon bicarbonate of soda
¼ cup hot (near-boiling) water

Preheat the oven to 180°C.
Combine the flour, rolled oats, sugar and coconut in a bowl and mix well.
In a saucepan, melt the margarine and golden syrup over a medium heat. Add the bicarbonate of soda and hot water. (The mixture will foam.)
Add the margarine mixture to the dry ingredients in the bowl and mix well. If it seems a little too dry, add a touch more water.
Place teaspoonfuls of the mixture on a well-greased baking tray, leaving enough space to allow for them spreading.
Bake for 15–20 minutes or until golden brown.

Makes 24

Pumpkin Muffins

These muffins make a filling and nutritious snack. They're also a tasty way of using up homegrown pumpkins.

1½ cups self-raising flour
a pinch of salt
¼ teaspoon nutmeg
¼ teaspoon mixed spice
½ cup dark brown sugar
½ cup sultanas
1 egg
¼ cup vegetable oil
½ cup cooked mashed pumpkin
½ cup milk

Preheat the oven to 200°C.
Combine the flour, salt, nutmeg, mixed spice, sugar and sultanas.
Combine the remaining ingredients separately and then add the mixture to the dry ingredients. Stir until mixed well.
Fill the cups of a well-greased muffin tin with the mixture.
Bake for 18-20 minutes.

Makes 12

Carob Cake

This cake was made for our afternoon tea party wedding reception. It's my favourite cake recipe.

1 cup water
1½ cups raw sugar,
2 tablespoons carob powder
4 oz margarine
2 eggs
1½ cups wholemeal plain flour
2 teaspoons baking powder
½ teaspoon bicarbonate of soda

Preheat the oven to 180°C.
In a saucepan, combine the water, raw sugar, carob powder and margarine. Bring to the boil, set aside and allow to cool.
Add the eggs to the cooled mixture.
Combine the remaining ingredients, then pour the mixture in the saucepan on top. Stir well.
Grease a 20 cm round tin well and sprinkle lightly with flour. Pour in the cake mixture.
Bake at 180°C for 60-75 minutes.

Cornmeal Cake

A Canadian man who helped nail weatherboards while we were building our house in Margaret River left this recipe with me. He often added a dash of rum and substituted buckwheat flour for the wholemeal flour, too. It's nearly a meal — and a good, hearty morning tea!

1 cup cornmeal (polenta)
1 cup wholemeal flour
1 cup raw sugar
3 teaspoons baking powder
2 tablespoons margarine or butter
3 eggs
1 cup milk
1 teaspoon vanilla essence

Preheat the oven to 180°C.
Combine the cornmeal, wholemeal flour, raw sugar and baking powder.
Melt the butter and combine with the eggs, milk and vanilla essence.
Stir in the dry ingredients and mix to a pouring consistency.
Pour into a greased 20 cm round tin and bake for an hour at 180°C, or until cooked.
If the cake is too dry and crumbly when cooked, add more milk to the mixture next time. It may take another 10 minutes to cook, too.

Tomato Relish

*This is great as a tasty spread for toasted sandwiches, a spread for pizza
bases or the perfect condiment for cold meats.*

1½ kg ripe tomatoes, finely chopped
500 g onions, finely chopped
1 tablespoon salt
500 g sugar
600 ml white vinegar
2 tablespoons plain flour
1½ tablespoons mustard
1 heaped tablespoon curry powder

Combine the tomatoes and onions in a large bowl.
Sprinkle with salt and leave overnight.
The next day, drain the mixture and discard the liquid. Place
the onion and tomato mixture in a saucepan and add the sugar.
Almost cover the mixture with the white vinegar, leaving about
half a cup of vinegar for the next step. Bring to the boil and
continue boiling for 5 minutes.
Combine the flour, mustard and curry powder to make a paste
with the remaining vinegar. Add this paste to the onion and
tomato mixture in the saucepan. Simmer for 1 hour with the lid off.
Place in hot sterilised glass jars with screw-top lids while the mixture
is hot.

Pumpkin Soup

Adding half a cup of coconut milk to this recipe gives a lovely flavour.
A dash of cummin and coriander complements the coconut, too.

½ a large pumpkin (or a whole small pumpkin), peeled and
   roughly chopped
1 litre water
2 onions, chopped
3 chicken stock cubes
pepper to taste
1 tablespoon grated orange rind
1 teaspoon nutmeg
sour cream or yoghurt, to taste

Boil the pumpkin pieces in a litre of water until they are soft. Set
aside to cool in the cooking liquid.

Place the pumpkin and liquid in a blender with the chicken stock
cubes, pepper, orange rind and nutmeg, and purée until the mixture
is smooth.

Heat the puréed mixture gently. Add extra water if desired.

To serve, pour the soup into bowls and stir in a teaspoon of sour
cream or yoghurt.

Serves 6 plus plenty of leftovers for lunch

Fried Rice Racing Food

This is an excellent pre-race meal to have two hours before competition, or as a meal during a day of races. It can be stored in a wide-mouthed thermos. Sometimes I like soy or tomato sauce on top!

1 rasher bacon, fat trimmed off
1 egg, beaten
1 cup cooked rice, brown or white

Cut the bacon into small pieces and fry it in a non-stick frying pan.
Add the egg and scramble it with the bacon.
Add the cooked rice. Mix well and serve.

Serves 1

Swimming Records

13 Australian Titles

	1971	1972	1973
100m freestyle	1.00.3	1.00.10	59.60
200m freestyle	2.07.80		2.09.30
400m freestyle	4.22.80		4.31.30
800m freestyle		9.01.8	
1500m freestyle			16.56.90
100m butterfly			1.04.40
200m individual medley	2.29.20		2.28.50
400m individual medley			5.08.80

11 World Records

100m freestyle London 30 April 1971 equalled the world record 58.9
200m freestyle London 1 May 1971 2.06.5
400m freestyle Santa Clara California 9 July 1971 4.21.2
200m freestyle Drummoyne Sydney 26 November 1971 2.05.8
800m freestyle Drummoyne Sydney 3 December 1971 8.58.1
1500m freestyle Birrong Sydney 12 December 1971 17.00.6
100m freestyle North Sydney pool 8 January* 1972 58.5
200m individual medley Munich Germany 28 August 1972 2.23.07
200m freestyle Munich Germany 30 August 2.03.56
400m freestyle Munich Germany 1 September 4.19.04
1500m freestyle Adelaide February 1973 16.56.9

* At this time I held all freestyle world records 100m to 1500m

Olympic Games Results, Munich 1972

Gold 200m individual medley 2.23.07 (world record)
Bronze 100m freestyle 59.06
Gold 200m freestyle 2.03.56 (world record)
Gold 400m freestyle 4.19.04 (world record)
Silver 800m freestyle 8.56.39 (personal best)

Progressive Record

100m Freestyle times in a 50m pool

January 1967 (aged 10) 1.18.3 Sydney
January 1968 (aged 11) 1.08.3 Sydney
January 1969 (aged 12) 1.05.7 Rockhampton Queensland
March 1970 (aged 13) 1.01.9 Brisbane
January1971 (aged 14) 1.00.3 Hobart
February 1971 (aged 14) 59.7 Sydney
April 1971 (aged 14) 58.9 London
January 1972 (aged 15) 58.5 Sydney
April 1999 (aged 42) 1.04.80 Perth
July 2000 (aged 43) 1.01.6 Munich
October 2002 (aged 45) 1.02.8 Melbourne

Awards

Australian of the Year, 1972
ABC-TV Sportsman of the Year Award 1971,1972
Caltex Sportsman of the Year, 1971
Pravda Sportsman of the Year, 1971
Australian Sports Hall of Fame, 1977
MBE, 1981
Olympic Order, 1994
Legend of Australian Sport, 1995
National Living Treasure, 1998

Other Skills and Awards

Parelli Natural Horsemanship Level 2, 1996

WA State Ploughing Champion
(with a pair of horses and single furrow plough), 1994 and 1995

Blackwood marathon relay completion
2 times swimming and 2 times horse-riding leg

Golden Oldies One-day events — Margaret River participant, 1988 to 1995

South West Games women campdraft finalist 1992